Website Design
and Development

100 QUESTIONS TO ASK BEFORE BUILDING A WEBSITE

George Plumley

WILEY

Wiley Publishing, Inc.

Website Design & Development: 100 Questions to Ask before Building a Website

Published by
Wiley Publishing, Inc.
10475 Crosspoint Boulevard
Indianapolis, IN 46256
www.wiley.com

Copyright © 2011 by George Plumley

Published by Wiley Publishing, Inc., Indianapolis, Indiana

Published simultaneously in Canada

ISBN: 978-0-470-88952-7

ISBN: 978-1-118-01319-9 (ebk)

ISBN: 978-1-118-01391-5 (ebk)

ISBN: 978-1-118-01392-2 (ebk)

Manufactured in the United States of America

10 9 8 7 6 5 4 3 2 1

For general information on our other products and services please contact our Customer Care Department within the United States at (877) 762-2974, outside the United States at (317) 572-3993 or fax (317) 572-4002.

Wiley also publishes its books in a variety of electronic formats. Some content that appears in print may not be available in electronic books.

Library of Congress Control Number: 2010933472

This book is dedicated to my family: to my wife, Kim, and our daughters, Grace and Ella (you're all so patient with me while I'm in writing mode), and to my parents, Adelaide and Stan, and my sister, Patricia.

It's also dedicated to anyone who has ever felt lost while trying to build a website.

Credits

EXECUTIVE EDITOR
Carol Long

PROJECT EDITORS
Ed Connor
Deadline Driven Publishing

TECHNICAL EDITOR
Warren E. Wyrostek

SENIOR PRODUCTION EDITOR
Debra Banninger

COPY EDITOR
Nancy Sixsmith

EDITORIAL DIRECTOR
Robyn B. Siesky

EDITORIAL MANAGER
Mary Beth Wakefield

FREELANCER EDITORIAL MANAGER
Rosemarie Graham

MARKETING MANAGER
Ashley Zurcher

PRODUCTION MANAGER
Tim Tate

VICE PRESIDENT AND
EXECUTIVE GROUP PUBLISHER
Richard Swadley

VICE PRESIDENT AND
EXECUTIVE PUBLISHER
Barry Pruett

ASSOCIATE PUBLISHER
Jim Minatel

PROJECT COORDINATOR, COVER
Lynsey Stanford

COMPOSITOR
Chris Gillespie,
Happenstance-Type-O-Rama

PROOFREADER
Nancy Carrasco

INDEXER
Robert Swanson

COVER IMAGE
Aaltazar / iStockPhoto

COVER DESIGNER
Ryan Sneed

About the Author

George Plumley is a web developer living on Vancouver Island, Canada. After a career in broadcasting and completing graduate work in Philosophy at York University, Washington University in St. Louis, and Rutgers, he went on to web development in 1993. He specializes in building small business websites and conducting workshops on website makeovers and WordPress. He is the author of *WordPress 24-Hour Trainer* (Wiley, 2009) and runs the free WordPress video training site www.seehowtwo.com.

About the Technical Editor

Warren E. Wyrostek is the owner of Warren E. Wyrostek, M.Ed. and 3WsCertification.com (a portal dedicated to Technical Training and Support). He holds a Master's degree in Vocational-Technical Education from Valdosta State College, a Master's in Divinity from New York's Union Theological Seminary, and is currently a Doctoral student in Curriculum and Instruction at Valdosta State University.

Warren is devoted to technical education as reflected by his list of over 50 certifications. Warren has been teaching for over 25 years and has taught on the University and Secondary School levels. He is the creator of the Master of Integrated Networking credential. He has been the Technical Editor for over 30 certification titles in the last few years. He is also the author of the *Novell NetWare 6.5 CNA Exam Cram2* (Que Publishing, 2005), and "A Career Changer's Checklist."

He currently is employed by McKesson Corp, as the Lead Certification Specialist and Operations Manager for Assessments for a corporate-wide certification and assessment program. Vocationally, Warren's main interest is the care and counseling of Geriatrics and Terminally Ill adults.

You can reach Warren at wyrostekw@msn.com or through 3WsCertification.com.

Acknowledgments

The entire team at Wiley has been so supportive of the idea for this book. I can never thank them enough. Carol Long got the ball rolling and was very patient while it gathered momentum. Ed Connor kept things rolling along very smoothly, every once and a while reminding me which direction the ball was headed. Ginny Munroe stepped in very capably for Ed when vacation time came around. Nancy Sixsmith was there to catch the lack of clarity in sentences and to be my "which-that" coach. Warren Wyrostek helped keep the technical issues clear and correct and was responsible for there being as many illustrations as there are. The staff in the media department made the whole process of creating the DVD seem so easy (I just record videos and they show up in the book…).

For the content of the book, I need to thank all of my clients over the years and the people who have asked me questions in various capacities. You helped me better understand how to communicate concepts (often on the second or third try). It's extremely satisfying to see the light go on in another person's mind after you've explained something to them—even more satisfying to see them make use of it and do well.

Thanks too, to the Internet. It's like having that friend who knows everything about a subject, except this friend knows everything about everything. There are so many countless articles, blogs, comments, and websites that have been useful in the research for this book that I can't begin to acknowledge all of the people behind them. Some are acknowledged in the Resource section of this book, and still more with links on the book's website.

And to all the friends and family who helped look after the kids when work or writing called during the summer of 2010, Kim and I are eternally grateful. In the future, I'll try to write during another season.

Contents

Introduction

About a year ago, I was talking to the marketing manager of a large organization. He was very excited about a major redesign they had recently made to their website, but he had a question about updating some information at the bottom of each page on the site. I asked what content manager they were using. "Oh we got rid of that," he said.

I listened in horror as he described how a web developer advised them to take all their content out of a database and create hundreds of individual HTML pages. According to the developer, search engines don't like websites that are run by databases. Several thousands of dollars later, here the marketing manager was asking me the best way to change a phone number in all those pages. I'll never forget the look on his face when I explained that the search engine advice was nonsense and that changing the phone number with a content manager would have taken about two seconds.

I've heard far too many stories like this in my years as a web developer—time and money wasted on doing things the wrong way or a less efficient way—when all it would have taken is for someone to ask the right questions at the right time.

This book is for that marketing manager and everyone else who could use a coach to ask those questions at every stage of building a website.

In the best-case scenario, reading this book will confirm that everything's going well with your site. In the worst-case scenario, it might lead you to start again from scratch. Somewhere in between it will help you save time and money, and create a better website.

If you already have a website, use this book as a checklist. Again, it would be great to come away simply satisfied that the job had been done right the first time. But if there's something that needs fixing, this book will help you identify it and provide some guidance on how to correct it.

There's more and more pressure these days to have a presence on the Web. If you're feeling that pressure but feel equally lost about what it takes to create a website, I hope this book will ease the pressure and give you confidence about creating the best site possible.

How to Use This Book

The book is written as a series of questions that a coach or consultant might ask of web designers and developers on behalf of a website owner. The questions take the form of "Have you thought about?" or "Will you be doing such and such?"; the answers in the book are intended to help you understand what good responses to those questions would be.

I tried to make the writing and the structure of this book as user-friendly as possible. The writing aims to be clear and simple about complex topics without being simplistic, while the layout and design aim to present information clearly and make it simple to find what you need.

Here's a list of features to help you use the book:

◆ **Numbered questions**—These not only make it easier to remember where in the book a question is located but on the accompanying website you also can easily enter the number of any question and be taken to the part of the site that contains updates, further information, and reader comments.

◆ **Prioritized questions**—Each question is given a priority level from 1 to 4. This can be helpful when time and resources are limited, and you want to know where best to utilize them.

◆ **Organized by topic**—Questions are grouped by topic to make it easier to find all information about, say, search engine optimization.

◆ **Alternative organizations**—Special lists on the DVD provide some additional ways of ordering and grouping the questions.

◆ **Sidebars**—Tips, notes, warnings, and video references can be found in the side margins. Within the text you'll also find the Rule of Thumb sidebars to help you remember key points.

◆ **Search terms are highlighted**—Throughout the text you'll find suggestions for search phrases to find more information, designated with this symbol: 🔍.

◆ **Cross-referencing**—Each question also suggests additional questions within the book, and Appendix A contains additional reading material, on- and offline.

◆ **Action items**—Each question finishes with action items to get you started.

◆ **Glossary**—There's a comprehensive glossary in Appendix B, which is supplemented on the book's website along with useful links.

The 101st Question

It was once popular to name books 1001 this or 101 that, but I always found that a bit gimmicky, so I deliberately stayed away from using 101 in the title. However, late in the writing process I realized that there was an all-encompassing question I hadn't addressed in the book: *Why do you want to build a website?*

I'd taken it for granted that this is a book about building websites. But because the goal is to raise questions and avoid wasted time, energy, and money, it's crucial to ask why you're building a site in the first place. So that's the 101st question of the book: Why?

In this increasingly web-oriented world, it's easy to shrug off the question by saying everyone needs a website and leave it at that. The answers to the question are important for you, the website owner, because they'll help shape the nature and growth of the site, as well as provide a way of judging the success of the site.

I say *answers* because you can and probably should have several reasons for building a website, and they fall roughly into two camps:

+ Outcomes you expect from your site
+ Tasks you expect your site to perform

THE PURPOSES OF YOUR SITE

Maybe you expect your site to make you more money, convince people of your point of view, get you more fans, provide support for existing customers, unite people who share your interests, or accomplish any other number of purposes. You might expect your site to achieve several of these goals, but whatever the case, it's crucial that you have these purposes clearly in mind as you plan, execute, and grow your site.

The best way to have your purposes clearly in mind is to write them down. Six months down the road, let alone six hours, you might alter those purposes, however slightly, to suit the circumstances of the moment and then convince yourself that these had been the purposes all along. The written word can help keep our minds honest.

As you compile a list of purposes, some will be immediately obvious, but it's important not to stop there. Keep thinking and writing. Don't question or second-guess what you come up with; write it down. And get specific. In a sense, wanting to get more new customers is the same as wanting to make more money, but by being more specific, it's a goal that's easier to measure and one that gets you closer to deciding what tasks your website must perform. Which brings me to the second type of answer to the question: Why do you want to build a website?

THE TASKS YOUR SITE MUST PERFORM

A website is a communications tool you're building to help achieve the goals you've set. But, it's a communications tool unique in the history of the world because it can perform a variety of tasks that no tool before it could have hoped to perform on its own. In fact, a website can be virtually every communication tool that ever existed, and then some.

A website can be a diary, brochure, book, television, telephone, radio, slide-show, billboard, business card, and on and on. Not only that, but it can be all of them at the same time, or it can be some now and others later. And a year from now it could be something no one has thought of yet.

However, all this power and flexibility can be a bit daunting. Even when the purposes of your site are clear, you face a myriad of choices for accomplishing those goals. Of course, time and money will limit everyone, but that still doesn't resolve the question of exactly which tasks your site should perform; what kind of communications tools it should be. You'll need to look at which tools are best for reaching your audience.

Then there's the problem of peer pressure. Everyone will have their opinion of what your website should do—you've got to have a blog; video is an absolute must; you're going to have a feed from your TwitLinkedBook account; a live chat button is so cool. It's like having a whole lot of relatives telling you what you ought to be when you grow up. When you're dealing with something new, that kind of pressure can be real.

Let me take off some of the pressure. It's just fine if your website is a static one-page "business card" as long as it's professional-looking, gives a good description of your business, has your contact information, and so on. In other words, make it a good online business card. Of course you can't expect such a website to do a lot for you, but at least you've started a web presence.

After reading this book, I think you'll understand why you shouldn't leave your website as a business card for very long. But it's important that you make decisions like that for good reasons rather than because everyone says so.

STARTING TO PLAN

Once you've got your purposes in mind and the tasks your site will need to perform, you can begin the process of planning the site.

Don't worry at this stage about organizing anything. Just write down messages you want to convey on the site: Describe your window cleaning services; explain how your sand-blasting process is revolutionary; how you can help homeowners to sell their house.

Some messages might be a single page on your site; others might involve several pages describing different aspects of the message. Or you might find that the message is too general and there are actually several messages behind them.

The rest of this book will help you develop and refine this plan, but getting the basic ideas down on paper as soon as possible is extremely valuable. You'll get more out of this book the more you've given some thought already to what you want your website to do.

Accompanying Videos on DVD

The Web is dynamic, and printed pages have limited space, so video is a great way of showing dynamic content as well as providing additional ideas and comments. Most questions have an accompanying video, for which a brief description is provided in the book as well as on the DVD menu.

Errata

We make every effort to ensure that there are no errors in the text or in the code. However, no one is perfect, and mistakes do occur. If you find an error in one of our books, such as a spelling mistake or faulty piece of code, we would be very grateful for your feedback. By sending in errata you might save another reader hours of frustration, and at the same time you will be helping us provide even higher quality information.

To find the errata page for this book, go to www.wiley.com and locate the title using the Search box or one of the title lists. Then, on the Book Search Results page, click the Errata link. On this page you can view all errata that has been submitted for this book and posted by Wiley editors.

Chapter 1

Domain Names

In this chapter:

- ➜ 1. Have you thought of a good domain name for your website?
- ➜ 2. Do you need multiple domain names?
- ➜ 3. How much should you pay for a domain?
- ➜ 4. Do you know what makes a good domain registrar?
- ➜ 5. Who will register your domain and in whose name?

Importance

On Video

Watch how to use an online domain search tool to brainstorm al-ternative versions of a domain name.

!

There's a lot to con-sider when choosing a domain name, but don't take too long deciding. People have checked a domain's availability in the evening only to find that it's been taken by morning.

1. Have You Thought of a Good Domain Name for Your Website?

Choosing a domain name is a key step in developing your website. Aside from being part of your branding, a domain name is one of the most common ways people will find you on the Internet. That's why a domain name needs to be memorable—by matching or relating to an existing name or by simply being catchy and unique.

If You Have an Existing Offline Name

If you already have an established name, you'll want your domain name to be the same (or very close to it). If your company name is Healthwise Fitness Equipment, the top of your list will be healthwisefitnessequipment.com. Even if you're commonly known as Healthwise Fitness, it would be better to have the word *equipment* in the domain because it will help the search engines distinguish you from fitness clubs or other businesses that use the name Healthwise Fitness.

In case you can't get the full name you want, have some variations prepared. For Healthwise Fitness Equipment, healthwiseequipment.com would be a good alternative. It retains the key part of your brand name as well as the search engine-friendly term *equipment*. The word *health* should be enough to keep you from being confused with a construction equipment company.

Another alternative is to place dashes between each word: healthwise-fitness-equipment.com. Keep in mind, however, that communicating those dashes can be tricky, and people will often forget to put them in. Other alternatives include short forms or acronyms—hfe.com—or if your business is confined to a region or a country, find a domain name using your country's extension, such as healthwiseequipment.us. Quite often a name that's taken for .com will be available for a particular country.

Some people say it's better to keep your domain name as short as possible. Aside from the fact that many shorter names have already been snapped up, the length of the domain is not as important as its memorability. If your company name is four words long, it will be easy to remember a domain name that matches those four words exactly. You can also help visitors remember a longer name by capitalizing words in print (`HealthWiseFitnessEquipment.com`) or using different colors for the parts of the name.

If You Don't Have an Offline Name

For some businesses, deciding on a company name is one and the same with choosing a domain name. In most situations it's best to find a name that describes what you do. If your business is fitness equipment, try to get those terms in the domain name.

It's also possible to choose an unrelated but catchy or distinctive name. Take the thousands of social media startup companies on the Internet, for example, with names such as Squidoo, Ning, and Reddit. They're trying to follow in the footsteps of online giants such as Amazon and Google, which have shown that an unusual domain name can be turned into a household word (with a lot of hard work and heavy marketing)

Before finishing your list, you need to consider whether it would be good to have multiple domain names for your website—the topic of the next question.

> ### Registering vs. Owning
>
> You often see domains written as **www**`.mydomain.com`, but the *www* is not actually part of the domain name. Increasingly you'll see URL's without the www but check with your host to see if your account is configured to accept either version. If it's not and you leave off the www, your site won't come up.

Related Questions

→ 2. Do you need multiple domain names? **Page 4**

→ 3. How much should you pay for a domain? **Page 6**

Action Item

→ Draw up a list of as many good primary domain names as you can think of and rank them in order of desirability. You want to be sure to have plenty of alternatives if the ones you really want aren't available.

Importance

You need to make sure that you correctly point additional domain names at your website. There can be negative consequences when dealing with search engines unless you do it right, which involves creating what's called a *301 redirect*. What this redirect tells search engines is that the website has permanently moved from one domain name to another. For detailed instructions try the search phrase 🔍 **redirect multiple domains 301.**

The part of the domain that comes after the very last dot (mydomain.**com**, mydomain.co.**uk**) is called the root or top level domain (TLD) extension. There are two common types: generic (gTLDs) such as .com, .org, and .biz; and country-code (ccTLDs) such as .uk, .ca, .au, .tv, and .co.

2. Do You Need Multiple Domain Names?

Every website should have only one domain name by which it's known, but there are all sorts of reasons to have additional domain names pointing to that site. Here are a few:

➜ **Common misspellings**—Suppose that your name is Healthwize; it would make sense to get an additional domain name with the spelling Healthwise because most people will enter it that way out of habit.

➜ **Common variations**—If you use a number in your primary domain (health2you), you should register an additional domain name with the literal spelling (healthtoyou).

➜ **Doing business in multiple countries**—A British company might have a domain name with the country top level domain .uk, but also have the domain name with .com. Keep in mind that most country domain regulators require a legal presence to register their domains.

➜ **Block competing domains**—Someone else might register the same domain with a different extension. You can prevent this by registering the .com, .net, and .org versions of your domain name, for example.

➜ **Special promotional domain names**—Suppose that you develop a fitness calculator on your Healthwise fitness website. It might be worth registering a domain such as takethefitnesschallenge.com and point it at that page on your site.

Although most new domain names are not expensive, having a lot of domain names can add up, so you'll need to weigh how important some of these variations are: how likely misspellings might be, how much competition there is, and whether people in a certain country care if they're going to a domain with their country's extension.

As more top-level domain (TLD) extensions are added or country codes are opened to general use, there can be a lot of hype about the need to register your domain name with a particular extension to prevent competitors from snapping it up. Sometimes, that's all it is—hype. But if a TLD extension does take off and come close to .com in popularity, you'd hate to miss out.

The best bet is to keep an eye out for which TLD extensions are actually being used (how many .info domains you see, for example, after being available for several years now). Or if the price isn't much more than a regular domain, it might be worth registering on a year-by-year basis to see where the extension goes.

Related Questions

➡ 1. Have you thought of a good domain name for your website? **Page 2**

➡ 3. How much should you pay for a domain? **Page 6**

Action Item

➡ The most important type of additional domain name is the kind that visitors might easily mistype. So brainstorm some possible ways they can get it wrong. You can also do some testing by telling friends the proper domain name over the phone and asking them to write it out.

Importance

3. How Much Should You Pay for a Domain?

The price of a domain name is determined by two variables: the base price set by the agencies that control the various domain name extensions (.com, .us, .tv, and so on) and the markup charged by domain name registrars.

That's why you see such a variation in the prices charged by a single registrar for different domain extensions, as shown in Figure 1-1.

FIGURE 1-1

On top of that, different registrars might offer radically different prices for the same domain extension by creating special offers; for instance, if you transfer over from another registrar or host your website through the registrar. Figure 1-2 shows different prices for a .com domain.

FIGURE 1-2

You can also get an existing domain name by agreeing to pay the current registrant to transfer the registration to you. Many registrars offer domain name brokering services to facilitate these kinds of transactions, or some will run domain name auctions. The cost of registering a domain name this way is completely a matter of what you're willing to pay the current registrant—it can be a couple of hundred dollars or a couple of thousand (or more). Figure 1-3 shows an example of a domains-for-sale page.

FitnessSet.net	Health	$388	Add to Cart
FitnessWork.net	Health	$888	Add to Cart
FitnessWay.net	Health	$888	Add to Cart
FitnessRunning.com	Health	$3,188	Add to Cart
FitnessPart.com	Health	$1,895	Add to Cart
FitnessPosition.com	Health	$595	Add to Cart
FitnessHeads.com	Health	$1,295	Add to Cart
FitnessPoint.net	Health	$2,970	Add to Cart
FitnessPoints.com	Health	$992	Add to Cart
fitnesscall.com	Health	$1,488	Add to Cart
FitnessFirst.net	Health	$1,188	Add to Cart

FIGURE 1-3

> Sometimes you'll see offers of a *free* domain, but remember that you're paying for the domain somehow—usually by committing to a hosting contract for a period of time. Always read the fine print to understand the terms. For example, the domain might be free for only one year of registration, or you have to pay a high yearly rate for the domain name if you stop hosting with the registrar. The same can be true even for low-priced domains, so check to see what's involved with any special deal.

These are some of the reasons why it's impossible to say what you should pay for any particular domain name, but here are a couple of rules of thumb for you to follow:

Rule of Thumb   Do not pay more than $12 per year for a new .com domain (subject to fee changes from ICANN, the governing body).

You can get .com names for less, but usually because you have to buy some other product or buy in bulk or transfer from another registrar, and so on. The point is, you don't have pay more than $12 to get a .com with no strings attached from good quality registrars.

Rule of Thumb   Expect to pay more for specialty TLDs such as .tv, .co, .pro.

> **On Video**
>
> Watch the video on DVD showing an example of a domain registration scam letter and what it says in the fine print.

A popular scam is when a domain registrar sends out a notice saying that your domain is expiring soon, so you should make sure that it's safe by renewing now. Except that when you sign the form, you're actually agreeing to transfer the domain from your existing registrar to this other company, and usually at crazy high rates (upward of $70 per year). *Do not respond to these notices!* Instead, use them as a reminder to log in to your true registrar and renew your domain at your regular rate.

Some top-level domains such as .tv are actually country codes which have been licensed by the country to be sold to anyone in the world. You're paying for the privilege of having this exclusive extension. In the case of other extensions, such as .pro, you're paying for an accreditation process among other things. Some specialty domains such as .me have come down considerably in price after initial sales were slow, so sometimes it can pay to wait.

Many domain extensions allow you to register a name for up to 10 years, whereas the minimum registration period is generally 1 year, but can sometimes be 2 years.

Although registering for several years in advance eliminates the worry of missing a renewal, make sure that you don't forget about your domain. In particular, it's easy for your contact e-mail to have changed in a few years, so you end up not getting the renewal notice. As long as you keep your information up to date, lengthy registration times can be helpful.

If you've registered a domain for a fairly new extension, it might be worth doing a yearly registration. The price for those domains can well go down over time (the .com names were $35 per year not that long ago), and it would be a shame to lock it in at the higher price.

The final point to keep in mind about domain pricing is that domain registrars have nothing to offer except price and service. Having an amazing price with poor service is no deal at all. But what counts as good service from a registrar? That's the topic of the next question.

Related Question

→   2. Do you need multiple domain names? **Page 4**

Action Item

→   Survey the sites of several registrars to get a sense of what they're all charging for a particular domain extension.

4. Do You Know What Makes a Good Domain Registrar?

Importance

There really isn't much for a domain registrar to do except record who registered which domain name, so the only way to tell registrars apart is by the other services they offer. These services break down into two broad categories:

➔ **Domain management**—How easy is it for you to manage your domains, update information, organize multiple domains, and so on?

➔ **Add-on functions**—Does the registrar offer services such as auto renewal or free e-mail accounts?

If you have only one domain, the quality of a registrar's domain management interface might not be all that important. But if you have more than one, you'll appreciate being able to easily tell the status of all your domains, organize them into groups, sort them in various ways, quickly manage where the domains are pointing, and so on. Figure 1-4 shows an example of a good domain manager layout.

The other important part of a domain management system is the help function. You deal with domain names once and then maybe not again for another year or more. Without a good help system, it can be difficult to remember what you should be doing. Contextual popup help screens are good, but video tutorials are even better.

Registrars vs. Hosts

It's easy to think these two are one and the same because so many registrars offer web hosting and so many web hosting providers offer domain names. But there is absolutely no requirement that you have your domain names registered through the company that hosts your website, or vice versa. Registering domains and hosting websites are two distinct functions.

If you discover a domain registrar with better pricing or services, you can transfer your domain to that other registrar at any time. Your existing registrar should not charge any fee for this, but the new registrar will charge you for an additional year of registration (which you would have spent anyway).

Home » Domains » My Domains							View our help video library

my domains names of interest sub-account domains

| registered | dns hosted | expiring | expired | redemption | folders | search |

Quick Search: starting with ▾ registered ▾ [   ] search 1 - 50 of 107 « Back | Next »

☐ Domain Name / TLD	Our DNS	Exp Date	Folder	Auto Renew	ID Protect	Business Listing
☐	✕	8/24/2010		auto	🔒	📇
☐	✕	6/4/2011		auto	🔒	📇
☐	✕	5/27/2011		auto	🔒	📇
☐	✕	2/10/2011	📁	auto	🔒	📇
☐	✕	5/10/2011		auto	🔒	📇
☐	✕	8/11/2010		auto	🔒	📇
☐	✕	10/6/2010		auto	N/A	📇

FIGURE 1-4

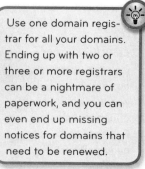

On Video

For a detailed view of a domain management interface, I've created a short tour on the DVD.

Use one domain registrar for all your domains. Ending up with two or three or more registrars can be a nightmare of paperwork, and you can even end up missing notices for domains that need to be renewed.

When you're checking out domain registrars, look for a demo of the domain management interface on their websites: a live demo that you can try out or at the very least a video demo. If there's nothing there, you can always call their sales department and request a tour. Remember, you can get good quality management tools *and* very low domain prices, so don't just settle for low prices.

It's also useful for domain registrars to offer add-on functions that make your life easier. Here's a checklist in order of what I think is most important:

- **Frequent renewal notices**—Receive at least 60, 30, 15, and 7 days before a domain expires (e-mail gets lost, or you're away, and so on).

- **Auto renewal**—You can turn this on if you don't want to worry about renewal notices at all. Just make sure your credit card is up to date.

- **Auto lock**—This requires a special code if you want to transfer to another registrar, but it also means that someone can't easily transfer the domain without your authorization.

- **Free e-mail**—If you don't have a website yet, you can still have e-mail service using the domain name.

- **301 redirects**—If you want to use the domain name to point to an existing website, this is the proper way to do it.

Related Question

- 3. How much should you pay for a domain? **Page 6**

Action Item

- To get you started on finding registrars, search for the phrase 🔍 **top 10 domain registrars**.

5. Who Will Register Your Domain and in Whose Name?

Importance

Although registering a domain name is straightforward, some people are not comfortable doing it themselves or they're too busy, so it's not uncommon for a web designer or a company to register a domain on behalf of their client. If that's how you're having your domain name registered, there are several steps you'll want to take to make sure that the domain remains under your control.

At the very least, you should be listed as the registrant: Use your mailing information, your e-mail address, and so on. The registrant is the one who controls the domain name. There are three other contacts for a domain name: administrative, technical, and billing. Usually all four contacts are the same, but it can be useful to have the person or company helping you listed as the technical contact. That way they have authority to talk to the registrar if there are technical issues to be resolved. The key is that you be listed as the registrant.

Of all the information listed for you as registrant, the most important is your e-mail address. It's used for a number of crucial tasks:

> **On Video**
>
> Watch how you can register a domain name yourself.

- Notifying you of the domain's expiration date
- Sending approval requests should you want to transfer to another domain registrar
- Sending password information should you ever lose your password

Once the domain name has been configured so that it's pointing to your server and your website is functional, you should change the password for the domain manager. You can always supply the designer or company with this new information should they later need to help you with the domain name. What you don't want is to discover a year later that some former employee still has access to your domain and goes in and changes the registrant e-mail and password, thereby taking control of the domain.

If you've had a domain name registered, but you don't have any of the login information for the domain, do what's called a *whois search* at

> It's a good idea for your contact e-mail not to be the same as your domain name. If your domain name expired, any communication from the domain registrar would no longer work. Be careful about using an e-mail address from your ISP—if you change ISPs or move, be sure to update your contact e-mail address for your domain name.

Your domain management login is completely separate from your hosting control panel login. Remember that your domain name is not the same as your website—the domain tells the world which server has your website files. Make sure the login data for your domain and your hosting control panel are different.

a site like domaintools.com. You can find out the registrar and whether you're listed as the domain registrant. If your e-mail is listed properly, you can use the registrar's lost password function to gain access.

If you're not listed as the registrant, contact the company or person who registered on your behalf and get the login information from them; then go in and change the registrant information to your own. If the domain is one of many in the other party's domain manager, simply sign up with the same registrar and initiate a domain transfer (or if you already have a domain manager, start the transfer).

If you're not listed as the registrant and the existing registrant won't give you the login information or do a transfer, start by contacting the registrar with proof that you hired that company or person to register the domain name on your behalf. After that there are varying types of dispute resolution depending on the agency overseeing the TLD.

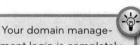

Related Questions

➤ 4. Do you know what makes a good domain registrar? **Page 9**

➤ 96. Will you routinely check your contact information? **Page 282**

➤ 98. Will your site administration be securely accessed? **Page 288**

Action Items

➤ If you don't have a domain name yet, registration is very easy to do yourself. You can get someone to help you later with correctly pointing the domain at the server, and then change the password when they're done.

➤ If someone else is going to register your domain for you, clarify in whose name it's being registered. Make sure it's yours. Also, make sure they're paying a good price.

➤ If you already have a domain name registered, but didn't do it yourself, check who is listed as the registrant.

Web Hosting

Importance

6. Do You Need to Find a Web Hosting Provider for Your Site?

For most people, the answer is yes, but not if you're planning to use the growing number of what I'll refer to as *turnkey website services*.

These are sites that you can have up and running within a very short time and then start entering your own content. With these sites, which fall into two general categories, the web hosting is included as part of the service:

Make sure that you have a strong user-name and password for accessing a turnkey solution. Anyone who accesses it has com-plete control over your website.

➔ **Free turnkey solutions**—There are many types of websites that can be set up for free, and part of the "free" includes the hosting of the site. If you want a blog, for example, you can easily sign up with services such as WordPress.com or Blogger. Or if you want a community website, you can sign up with social media sites such as Ning or Spruz. Figure 2-1 shows the control panel for Blogger.

With any turnkey web-site solution, check to see what the legal sta-tus is of your content. It should always remain yours; if not, find another solution.

➔ **Paid turnkey solutions**—These range from basic site builder programs to shopping carts to specialized platforms for real estate sites or travel agencies, for example. The idea is that all websites need certain basic functions, as do sites in specific industries, so the service provider includes them, along with design templates and a content management system for a monthly fee. Because the services are all on the provider's servers, you don't need to think about hosting.

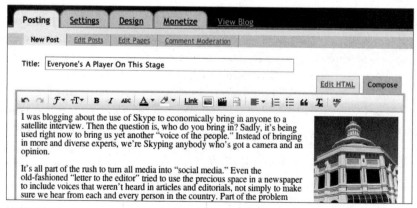

FIGURE 2-1

No doubt you're wondering at this point why everyone isn't using a turnkey solution for websites. On the face of it, the idea is very attractive: easy to set up, focused on your needs, no technical headaches, and one monthly fee (or no fee!).

There are two situations for which turnkey websites can be well suited:

➔ Simple sites which require no branding, such as personal blogs, hobby sites, or small organizations like clubs.

➔ Complex sites with common technical requirements, such as real estate sites or online stores. Building a database and administrative interface from scratch would be cost-prohibitive, and even the setup and maintenance of self-hosted programs might not be worth the time and energy. Figure 2-2 shows the control panel for a turnkey real estate system:

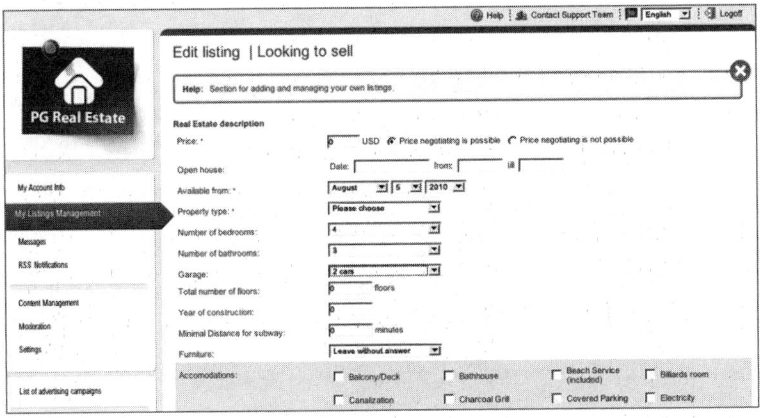

FIGURE 2-2

Whatever the situation, if you're considering a turnkey solution there are some questions you need to ask:

➔ How much control do you have over design and layout? Switching the look of a site is no trick at all because of the use of templates, but within a particular template, how much can you switch things around?

➔ Can you have different page structures for different areas of your site (different sidebars or a special home page structure for example)?

On Video

Watch some examples of turnkey websites and how they work.

- ▶ Are you able to use your own domain name?

- ▶ Are you able to install your own scripts to create new functionality on your site?

- ▶ Are there limits on the files you can upload: limits on type, size, and so on?

- ▶ What exactly can you take with you if you leave? Not the software that runs the site, but what about designs, and so on? Again, it's likely they belong to the provider.

 Related Questions

- ▶ 7. What is the difference between a web hosting provider and an ISP? **Page 17**

- ▶ 48. Will your site be built with a content management system (CMS)? **Page 124**

Action Item

- ▶ If you're considering a turnkey solution, make a list of features you know you need now and then try to imagine what other features you might want down the road. Use the list to assess various turnkey solutions.

7. What Is the Difference between a Web Hosting Provider and an ISP?

Importance

An *Internet service provider* (*ISP*) is the company that enables you to get on the Internet (via DSL, cable, satellite, and so on); a *web hosting provider* manages space on the Internet for storing and accessing websites and other files.

This distinction often gets blurred in people's minds because ISPs also offer varying levels of hosting services. In particular, ISPs provide e-mail hosting, and for many people the e-mail account they get from their ISP is the only one they have. It's very common for an ISP to also provide free or low cost web hosting when you sign up, although this isn't always well publicized.

ISP Hosting

Web hosting accounts from ISPs generally are meant for personal web space. They have web addresses (URLs) such as `http://members.your provider.com/yourname` and typically don't have features that a business website needs: databases, large amounts of storage space, handling large numbers of visitors, or the ability to use your own domain name. In fact ISP hosting accounts can be very restrictive, as the excerpt in Figure 2-3 demonstrates.

Even when an ISP does offer useful business features, you need to assess its support for hosting services, online hosting interface, and all the other questions about hosting being raised in this chapter. There's a lot to being an ISP and supporting that side of the business: Do they have the resources to adequately support hosting as well?

The other important consideration is search engine visibility. If you host your site with your ISP and use its domain name, and then a year down the road you want more features, get your own domain, and move to a web hosting provider, links to your site will no longer work and any search engine ranking you've built up will be lost because your web address will have changed.

> You can always use your ISP's free web space for a hobby or family website or as a place for the kids to create their own website.

> If you decide to sign up with a web hosting provider, don't cancel services with your ISP. You still need them to connect to the Internet.

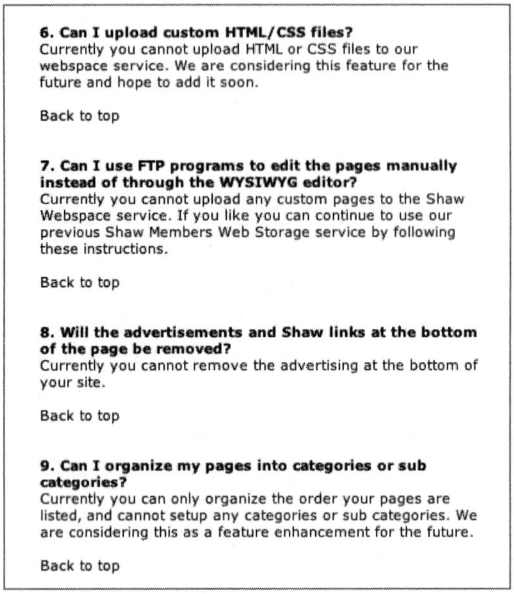

6. Can I upload custom HTML/CSS files?
Currently you cannot upload HTML or CSS files to our webspace service. We are considering this feature for the future and hope to add it soon.

Back to top

7. Can I use FTP programs to edit the pages manually instead of through the WYSIWYG editor?
Currently you cannot upload any custom pages to the Shaw Webspace service. If you like you can continue to use our previous Shaw Members Web Storage service by following these instructions.

Back to top

8. Will the advertisements and Shaw links at the bottom of the page be removed?
Currently you cannot remove the advertising at the bottom of your site.

Back to top

9. Can I organize my pages into categories or sub categories?
Currently you can only organize the order your pages are listed, and cannot setup any categories or sub categories. We are considering this as a feature enhancement for the future.

Back to top

FIGURE 2-3

Related Questions

➡ 6. Do you need to find a web hosting provider? **Page 14**

➡ 9. What kind of support does the web hosting provider offer? **Page 21**

➡ 13. How much storage space and bandwidth do you need for your site? **Page 30**

➡ 17. Does your e-mail address use your domain name? **Page 40**

Action Item

➡ Be sure to check what your ISP is offering at the moment. Account features are always changing (and usually improving) and might be adequate for your needs. Use the questions in the rest of this chapter to help decide whether your needs will be met.

8. How Reliable Is the Web Hosting Provider?

Importance

A great website is useless if no one can get to it, so the reliability of your web hosting provider is vital. Having said that, you need to understand that absolutely no provider can promise that your site will be available 24 hours per day, 365 days per year. There is no such thing as 100 percent uptime.

It's just a fact of operating web servers that they need to be maintained, and doing so might require going offline (downtime). Of course, providers try to keep this planned downtime to a minimum, and they try to schedule it for overnight or during other low-traffic times. What you want to know is that the web hosting provider is working to minimize unplanned downtime as well as drastic slowdowns in the loading time of your site.

These accidental outages or drops in speed will happen to any host at some point, so the real questions are these: How frequently do outages happen, how long do they last, and when do they happen?

If your site is down accidentally for a couple of minutes, two or three times a year, even if it's during prime traffic periods, that probably won't affect you much. However, if the site is unavailable for 10 minutes once a week during peak visiting hours or very slow to load for a few hours each week in the same time frame, you'll develop a bad reputation, not to mention lose revenue.

Are uptime guarantees of any value? Check the fine print to understand what kind or amount of downtime qualifies for the guarantee—most don't include planned downtime. Then there's the question of compensation if the guarantee is broken. If you're paying $9.95 per month for hosting, will a free month of service make up for your loss?

All other things being equal, if one host has an uptime guarantee and the other doesn't, you might as well have the guarantee to give you at least something to point at during a dispute.

?

It's common for web hosting providers to tout the fact that they have a 99.9 percent uptime record. Even with that impressive number, if you apply the percentages to a single month, that's still 43 minutes of downtime. And this figure usually doesn't include planned downtime.

If you're particularly concerned with reliability, there are monitoring services that will give you uptime reports on your site. Consider using one of them for the first month or two that you are with a hosting provider to give you a more accurate picture of reliability. Search for the phrase 🔍 **website monitoring** or see the resource appendix for this chapter.

Unplanned Downtime or Slowdowns

You can find out roughly how many websites are hosted on your shared server by entering your domain name into a reverse ip lookup tool.

One of the most common causes of unplanned downtime or server slowdowns is poor security. Most sites are hosted on a shared server (multiple accounts on a single server), and if one of the other sites is using an unsecure piece of software, it can let in hackers who use up the server's resources. If the hosting company isn't on top of things or has a poor security system between hosting accounts, your site can be slowed down or knocked out.

Another common cause of server disruptions on shared servers is the attempt to squeeze too many sites onto one server without leaving some breathing room for unexpected bursts of traffic. Ask the hosting provider what its policy is for limiting sites on any one server.

Related Questions

→ 13. How much storage space and bandwidth do you need for your site? **Page 30**

→ 100. How will your protect your site from attacks? **Page 295**

Action Items

→ Ask friends or business associates who have had a website for a long time what hosting provider they use and how reliable they've been. Then do a search on those firms and see what others say about them. If you don't want to spend much time researching, start by looking at web hosting providers that have a lot of clients: **largest hosting providers**. Big isn't always better, of course, but usually they get there by offering good service and not just because of heavy marketing.

→ When you've decided on a host, sign up only for a month-to-month contract. If it proves unreliable, you won't be trying to get out of something long term.

9. What Kind of Support Does the Web Hosting Provider Offer?

Importance

Whether your website is down or you can't figure out how to add a new e-mail account, how easily can you get support from a web hosting provider? There are five key types of support to look for:

➜ **Direct support**—Whether by phone, live chat, or even e-mail (as long as they get back to you within minutes), this is your ultimate form of tech support because it allows you to pinpoint your exact problem and hopefully reach a resolution quickly. At the very least, you'll want direct support from 9 a.m.–5 p.m. in your time zone, but 24/7 is always best.

➜ **Video tutorials**—Being able to see how to do something is the next best thing to being walked through the process in person, but these do tend to cover general topics only.

➜ **Contextual help screens**—Instead of reaching a general help page, clicking these help buttons gives you information based on where you are or what you're doing. Look for good detailed information, though, not a two-line description that's thoroughly useless. Figure 2-4 shows an example of a contextual help screen.

On Video

I walk you through some support areas from a couple of web hosting providers, and tour a knowledge base to get a feel for how they operate.

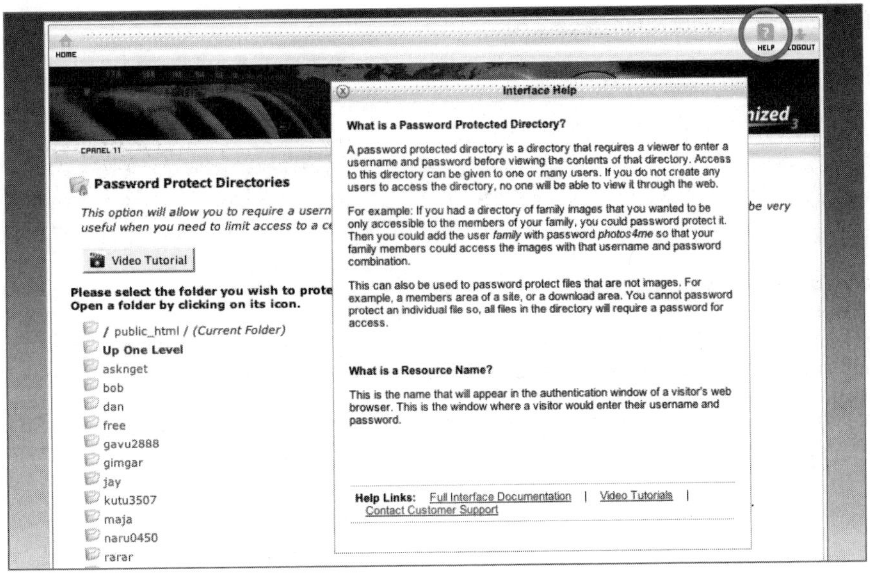

FIGURE 2-4

➜ **Knowledge base**—A comprehensive, well-written set of articles covering all aspects of the server's features is important, especially one that includes troubleshooting articles. Some knowledge bases will ask you if the problem was solved by the articles you just read; if not, it will offer other suggested articles.

> Keep in mind that many postings to user forums are the result of the user not understanding something, not a problem with the host. That's why you need to look through a large number of posts to get a more accurate picture of the host's reliability.

➜ **User forum**—In a sense this is an extension of the knowledge base because it features real-world troubleshooting and often contains information that hasn't made it into the general knowledge base because it's very specific. User forums can be particularly helpful for keeping up with very immediate issues and for spotting recurring issues. But a user forum is highly dependent on the quality of the users. There's nothing worse than someone reporting the exact problem you have, posting "it's been solved," and not telling anyone how it was solved. Often there's a forum section in which the hosting company posts the latest information about its servers; how proactive are they in letting users know of potential issues?

Related Questions

➜ 8. How reliable is the web hosting provider? **Page 19**

➜ 10. Does the web hosting provider have a good hosting control panel? **Page 23**

➜ 93. How will you back up your site? **Page 270**

Action Items

➜ Try calling a web hosting provider's help line and asking some questions.

➜ How large is the provider's knowledge base? If there are only five articles on e-mail, it's unlikely that you'll find the answers you need when troubleshooting specific problems.

➜ Most user forums include a presales forum in which you can search for questions about support or even post your own.

10. Does the Web Hosting Provider Have a Good Hosting Control Panel?

Importance

A hosting control panel is an interface that makes it easy for the average user to perform tasks that, in the past, had to be performed by the web hosting provider's staff. For example, anyone can easily create a new e-mail account with just a few clicks using one of these panels.

If a hosting provider does not have a hosting control panel, that's a good sign to move on. If it does, you'll want to try it out or at least get detailed information about it, including screenshots like the one in Figure 2-5, which shows part of the home page for the popular hosting control panel cPanel.

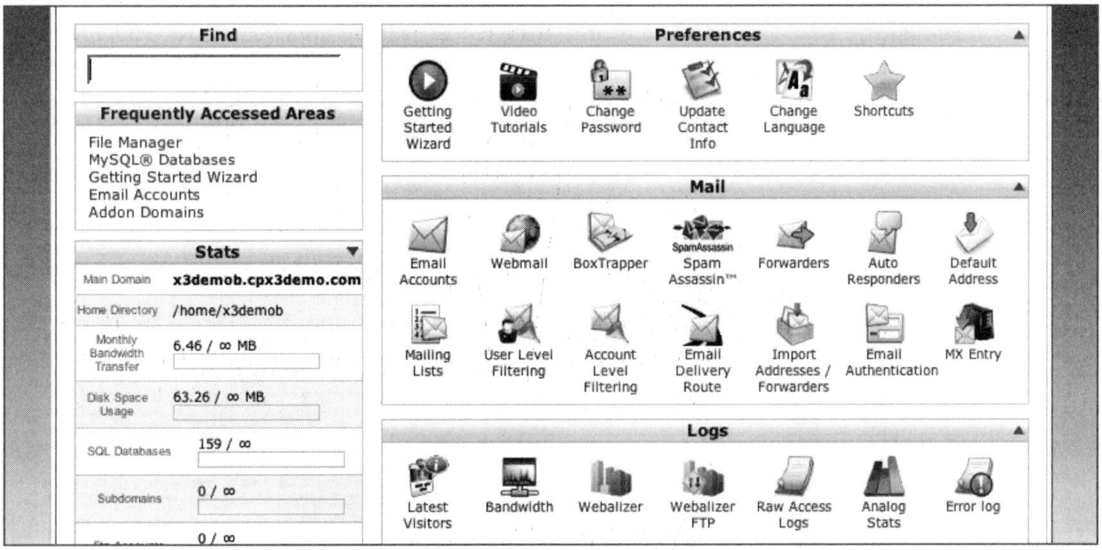

FIGURE 2-5

The left column shows the current status of your account, such as how much space you're using, the number of e-mail accounts, databases, and other features you're using. The main section contains links to all the features of the control panel.

There are two qualities to look for in a hosting control panel:

◆ **Comprehensiveness** —The panel should allow you to control much more than just e-mail accounts and file uploading. Even if you're planning on having someone else do some of the tasks for you, you want to have control over as many aspects of your hosting account as possible.

◆ **Ease of use** —Are the various areas of the panel easy to navigate? Does the panel provide good instructions, and are the inputting and report screens clearly laid out? Is there good help available right there in the panel (text or video help)?

Hosting control panels generally are third-party software, although some web hosting providers have created their own systems that are as good or sometimes better. The two most popular third-party packages used by providers are cPanel and Parallels/Plesk.

The most common tasks you'll probably perform through a hosting control panel are :

◆ E-mail management (creating accounts, autoresponders, and so on)

◆ File uploading

◆ Viewing your site's statistics

◆ Accessing your web mail.

A screen for creating e-mail filters is shown in Figure 2-6.

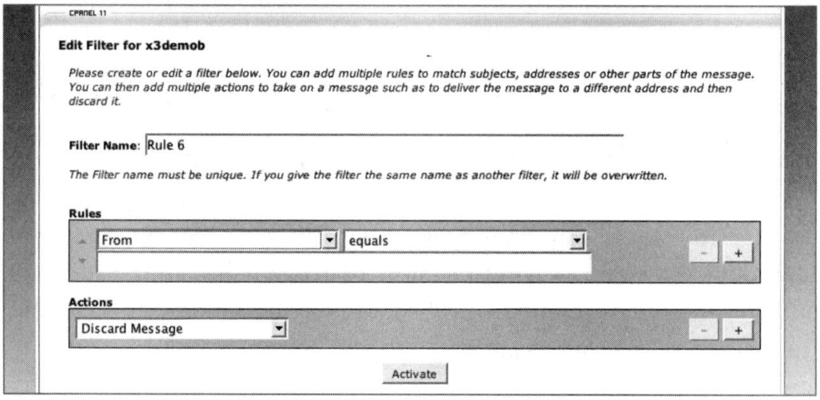

> One advantage of going with a web hosting provider that uses a popular third-party hosting control panel is that if you switch providers, you can easily find another that uses the same control panel.

> The more features a control panel offers, the more chance you can do some serious damage if you don't know what you're doing. For example, many hosting control panels allow you to modify your domain name records—the information that tells browsers where to find your website files, e-mail, and so on—but you'd better have the technical knowledge or you can mess up your site.

FIGURE 2-6

These functions generally are very straightforward and there's not much you can mess up. Tasks that you might want to have handled by someone who knows what they're doing include setting up or modifying databases, creating subdomains, or setting up redirects.

Whether or not you're the one who's going to be using it, a good hosting control panel is a must. It will save you a lot of time, money, and frustration.

On Video

Take a tour of key features on a hosting control panel.

Related Questions

➧ 18. Can you easily manage e-mail through your web hosting provider? **Page 42**

➧ 19. Can you access your domain e-mail through a web browser? **Page 44**

Action Item

➧ Try out various hosting control panels, especially to test common functions such as creating e-mail accounts or uploading files. You can find online demos of the most common control panels by searching for 🔍 hosting control panel demo.

Importance

11. What Type of Server and Which Operating System Do You Require?

Web hosting providers offer a wide range of server types and operating systems, but for most users the choices are pretty simple.

Types of Servers

Web servers fall into two broad categories:

- ➴ Shared servers
- ➴ Dedicated servers

In a shared hosting environment, your website is on a server with hundreds or even thousands of other websites. Dedicated servers host your content exclusively (there are a number of different types of dedicated servers, but those aren't important in this context). Hosting a website on a shared server costs a lot less and offers all the features most websites will need, so choosing a shared server makes sense for the vast majority of sites.

> **Rule of Thumb**   A shared server hosting account is all that's needed for most websites.

However, there are two factors in particular that can affect the performance of your website on a shared server:

- ➴ Overcrowding
- ➴ Lax security

It's important to check what policies a web hosting provider has to deal with each.

How many sites a server can support depends on the size and power of the machine, and in each case web hosting providers have to balance service with profitability. They need enough sites to make their money, but too many sites will slow down the server and leave less room to cope with spikes in traffic. Poor-quality providers will sacrifice service for profitability.

> **?** Would you benefit from a dedicated server? You might if you expect extremely heavy traffic to your site, require very specialized software that shared hosts don't have or won't install, or need high-level security.

The other issue is how good the provider's security measures are. If another website on the shared server gets hit with a virus, you don't want it to infect your site or bring down the entire server. With adequate security in place, these issues can be avoided—that's what separates good web hosting providers from the poor ones.

Operating Systems

Just like your computer at home or at work, web server hardware runs on an operating system. The two most common systems offered by web hosting providers are:

- Linux/UNIX
- Windows

Both will run HTML files just fine, so the key in deciding which one to choose is whether your website requires software such as a content management system.

Generally speaking, if software uses a language called PHP, you're better off on a Linux operating system; if the software runs on a language called ASP or ASP.net, your site belongs on a Windows machine. If your website needs to interact with Microsoft products such as Sharepoint or Access, a Windows system is required.

Related Questions

- 12. Does your website have specific software requirements? **Page 28**
- 48. Will your site be built with a content management system (CMS)? **Page 124**
- 55. Which languages other than HTML will you use to build your site? **Page 143**

> **?**
> The operating system you use at home or at work is entirely separate from the operating system you need for your website. For example, if you use Windows at home you don't have to have a Windows server for your site.

> If you get set up with Linux and discover that you really need a Windows server, or vice versa, your web hosting provider can switch things over. This is very easy if your site doesn't run special software at the moment. If it does, it's simply a matter of making sure that the software can run on the other operating system or being aware of potential issues.

Action Items

- Check the shared hosting forums on a web hosting provider's site to see whether there are constant complaints of slow servers or security breaches affecting entire servers.

- If you're working with a web designer or developer, they can help you decide whether you need a Linux or Windows server; if you're creating the site yourself, check the requirements list of any software you're running and ask your web hosting provider for advice.

12. Does Your Website Have Specific Software Requirements?

Knowing which operating system you'll need for your hosting account is a start, but you'll probably need to be more specific to ensure that your website will function properly. For example, I mentioned that if you have software that runs on PHP (the most widely used scripting language on the Internet), you're best off with a Linux server. But does the software require PHP5 or PHP4; even more specifically, does it require a minimum of, say, PHP4.3? These are the kinds of details you'll want to get.

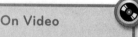

On Video

See more examples of the kinds of software requirements you might have and examples of hosting companies listing their software capabilities.

You don't need to know what any of this means; you simply need a list of the requirements that you can show to potential web hosting providers or give to the person who's arranging hosting for you. Figure 2-7 shows an example of a requirements list from the site of WordPress, an open source content management system.

Requirements

Intro

Requirements

Features

Testimonials

Books

Logos and Graphics

To run WordPress your host just needs a couple of things:
- PHP version 4.3 or greater
- MySQL version 4.1.2 or greater

That's really it. We recommend Apache or Nginx as the most robust and featureful server for running WordPress, but any server that supports PHP and MySQL will do. That said, we can't test every possible environment and each of the hosts on our hosting page supports the above and more with no problems.

FIGURE 2-7

Many software companies not only have a list of server requirements, but they'll also tell you the names of recommended hosts, which can save you a lot of time looking around for a provider.

To use another example from this list: You know that WordPress requires a database. In particular, it needs a type of database called MySQL, and furthermore it needs a version of MySQL newer than version 4.3.

Here are some examples of other types of software hosting requirements:

- ◆ Special graphics capabilities for scripting languages such as PHP or ASP.net

- ◆ Nonstandard modules for the server software (Apache, IIS, and so on)

- ◆ Running special services such as Ruby on Rails, Front Page extensions, JavaServer Pages, and so on

Again, you're not expected to know what any of these requirements mean, but I just want to make you aware of asking these questions of web designers, developers, and anyone assisting you with your website. If someone's suggesting that you use certain software for your website, they should be taking care of ensuring that requirements are met—but now you know to ask the question as a double-check.

Often, web hosting providers will provide a list of commonly used web features that they support for a particular account, as in the example shown in Figure 2-8.

> If your web developer or designer is taking care of everything, be sure to get a list of software requirements so you have it on file. Later, if you need to move servers or you're using someone else to help you, you have these details on hand.

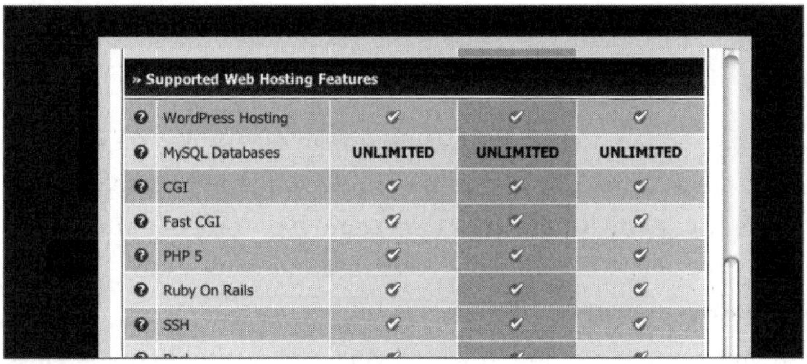

» Supported Web Hosting Features			
❷ WordPress Hosting	✓	✓	✓
❷ MySQL Databases	UNLIMITED	UNLIMITED	UNLIMITED
❷ CGI	✓	✓	✓
❷ Fast CGI	✓	✓	✓
❷ PHP 5	✓	✓	✓
❷ Ruby On Rails	✓	✓	✓
❷ SSH	✓	✓	✓

FIGURE 2-8

You might need more specifics, but at least you'll know you're on the right track if you see a feature listed that your web designer says you need.

Related Questions

✦ 47. Will your site be static or dynamic? **Page 122**

✦ 48. Will your site be built with a content management system (CMS)? **Page 124**

✦ 55. Which languages other than HTML will you use to build your site? **Page 143**

Action Item

✦ Make a list of any software you're expecting to run on your website or that you can anticipate running in the future. For instance, do you think you might need a shopping cart at some point? Even if you're not sure which shopping cart software you'll use, find out the requirements of a couple of possible carts and use that information. Find the requirements of each piece of software or ask for the list from your web designer.

Importance

13. How Much Storage Space and Bandwidth Do You Need for Your Site?

Ironically, two of the most prominent features you see in ads for web hosting are disk storage space and bandwidth, when in fact the drop in price for both of them has almost made them irrelevant in choosing a provider. Still, it pays to know you're getting enough of both.

Storage

Websites are made up of files: HTML files, image files, video files, document files, and so on. How much storage you need on the web server depends on the types and amounts of files you'll have on your site. You want to make sure you think ahead—you might not have many files now, but they can add up quickly.

Suppose that you have a blog in which you're planning to upload lots of photos and some videos. Let's do the math for one year's activities:

> Blogging software and database = 20MB
> 5 × 1.5MB photos per week = 390MB
> 1 × 5MB video every two weeks = 130MB
> Total after 1 year = 540MB (about half a gigabyte)

From this rough calculation, you'd want a web hosting account with at least 1GB of storage space. Fortunately, these days that's a fairly basic starting point for storage limits, even for low-priced hosting. Often you'll get much more for the money.

> **Rule of Thumb**   Look for a hosting account that offers a minimum of 1GB of storage space.

If you're running e-mail through your hosting account, remember to include mailbox quotas in your space calculations—they're part of your site's storage limits. We're sending larger and larger files by e-mail these days, and if you need several e-mail accounts, their storage requirements might put you over your limit.

Bandwidth

Whenever people visit your site, they're downloading files (such as HTML files, images, and so on) so their browser can display the site. Web hosting providers track all this downloading based on the number of bytes of data, and the monthly total of all this traffic is referred to as your *bandwidth*.

In the blogging example, with all the photos and videos, each visitor would use a good deal of bandwidth when viewing the site. You want more visitors coming to your site, but keep in mind that this means you're using more bandwidth. So you want to make sure that your hosting account has sufficient bandwidth to meet your needs or projected needs.

As with storage, bandwidth costs have dropped dramatically in recent years, so you can get plenty of bandwidth for very little money. For a basic business website without a lot of images or documents such as PDFs, and several thousand visitors per month, you might get away with 1GB or so of bandwidth. But of course, the more you can get for your money, the better —you never know when your promotional efforts will pay off and you're swamped with visitors.

Having lots of bandwidth doesn't mean your site can't get overloaded with traffic. That's because the bandwidth everyone talks about is actually a total data transfer limit over a one-month period. Technically, bandwidth is the rate at which data can be transferred at any given moment.

If you think of data flowing through a pipe, bandwidth is the diameter (the bigger the pipe, the more that can flow through in any given moment). But any pipe has a limit. So if your website is featured in a national media outlet, and tens of thousands of people flood your site all at once, it won't matter how much monthly data transfer you've got; you can overload the bandwidth (pipe) and slow down your site or crash the server.

What about all those advertisements that say "unlimited disk space" and "unlimited bandwidth"? The truth is that every server has limits. What the ads really mean is that average users won't need to pay for additional disk space if they go from 2GB of usage to 3GB, or if they have a similar jump in bandwidth. That's definitely a bonus.

You can save storage space (and, more importantly, bandwidth) by hosting large files such as videos or even photos on services such as YouTube or Flickr.

Related Questions

➡ 8. How reliable is the web hosting provider? **Page 19**

➡ 36. Is your site going to load quickly? **Page 93**

➡ 54. Will your nontext files use the proper file types? **Page 140**

➡ 62. Will you be using video or audio in your content? **Page 164**

Action Item

➡ Read the fine print for hosting accounts on shared servers (where your site is stored along with hundreds of others), and in particular ones that promise unlimited storage and bandwidth. You'll find the actual limits set out there —not necessarily in terms of numbers, but in terms of what you can and cannot do on your site (for example, no file sharing or auctions).

14. How Much Should You Be Paying for Web Hosting?

Importance

Like storage and bandwidth, the price of hosting has dropped so much that it's almost irrelevant these days. However, if you're paying more than you need to, it's quite relevant, so this question is designed to make sure that you don't pay too much.

Because most readers of this book will be going the route of shared hosting (your site is on a server with hundreds of others), that's what I'll be talking about here. The bottom line? For an average website, you shouldn't need to pay more than $10.95 per month for quality shared hosting.

> **Rule of Thumb**   Don't pay more than $10.95 per month for shared hosting.

Still, be sure that you're not comparing apples and oranges. For example, a web designer who has set up hosting for a client might be charging $19.99 per month, but they personally handle tech support, set up client e-mail, and do things such as back ups. In other words, the client isn't just paying for hosting, but for services as well. You might do everything yourself and pay only $5.99 per month on a multiyear contract, but you can't compare the two rates.

Here are pricing basics for some other types of shared hosting:

- **E-commerce hosting**—If you're hosting your own shopping cart system, you'll want a package that offers things such as added security. So you might be paying $14.99 per month and upward, depending on all the features you want.

- **Video hosting**—There are lots of free video hosting sites (the most popular is YouTube). They generally work very well, and the price is right, but you might want to consider how long smaller startups are going to be around. There are paid services, such as Amazon's S3 hosting, which typically charge by the amount stored and the amount of traffic.

What about providers who offer free hosting? I admit that there's always something alluring about that word "free," even in this day of inexpensive hosting. But think about it: They're giving you the hosting for free so they can put ads on your site. I can't imagine any business website in which someone else's ads would be welcome. (Let's face it, you're saving only a couple of coffees a month —is it worth it?). Even for personal sites, there are lots of free platforms these days (Blogger, Facebook, and so on) that have no ads or far less intrusive ones.

> Why jump right in? If you sign up with a host on a month-to-month basis, it will give you a chance to make sure the host is as reliable and supportive as it claims to be. After the trial period, you can sign up for the heavily discounted multiyear contract with confidence.

+ **Specialty software hosting** —If your site needs to run JavaServer Pages (JSP)—files with a .jsp extension—or some other special software, you might find that prices are a bit higher for those types of hosting accounts, say in the $12.95 range and upward.

+ **Turnkey websites or hosted applications**—If you're getting a special website system, such as for realtors or travel agents, the cost of hosting will be part of the monthly system fee. Expect to pay a bare minimum of $29.99 for these types of site management programs, more likely $39.99 and up.

When you see advertisements for web hosting that's only $4.95 a month or even less, they're likely based on signing a multiyear hosting contract. Assuming that you'll get all the features and services offered by a company that charges $9.95 on a month-to-month basis, make sure the contract terms are reasonable.

What are the penalties for leaving early? Multiyear contracts usually have penalties if you terminate early. Find out what the host's policy is. Can you terminate if it violates uptime or other guarantees? If you choose to leave, will you get back some portion of the money you paid up front, and on what is that portion based?

Related Questions

+ 3. How much should you pay for a domain? **Page 6**

+ 11. What type of server and which operating system do you require? **Page 26**

+ 93. How will you back up your site? **Page 270**

Action Items

+ Instead of getting caught up in all the hype of web hosting ads, use your site requirements worksheet on the DVD because those are the features you're concerned with. Find several hosts who meet those requirements; then compare their prices on a month-to-month basis.

+ Remember to give much more weight to things such as reliability, support, friends' recommendations, and software vendor recommendations; then make your choice. Price should be one of the smallest factors in your decision.

15. Do You Have a Strong Hosting Username and Password?

Importance

One of the crucial yet simple ways to protect your website from getting hacked is to have a strong password for your hosting account. A strong password has:

➜ more than eight characters

➜ no dictionary words

➜ a mix of upper- and lowercase letters, numbers, and symbols

Here's the difference between strong and week passwords:

➜ **Good Password**—t1U9r6K3e#Y

➜ **Bad Password**—sparky

Hosting account passwords are often assigned to you automatically and if it doesn't meet the criteria just listed, you should change it. You can do that through your hosting control panel.

Rule of Thumb   Change a password only if it's as strong or stronger than the original.

Don't change a strong password to something simple because it's easier for you to remember. Simpler also means simpler for hackers to break in. If you're not sure how to make a password strong, most control panels have a password strength indicator to guide you along.

Don't be tempted to use the same password for both your domain management and for your hosting account. Both provide access to key components of your online presence, so why make it easy for hackers to access both?

On Video

Watch how to create strong passwords and how to use a hosting control panel's change password function and password generator feature.

If you need people to work on your website temporarily, don't give them your username and password. Instead, create an FTP account for them through your hosting control panel. When the work is finished, you simply delete the account.

You might be asked by someone working on your website for the File Transfer Protocol (FTP) information. In most cases, the login information for FTP programs will be the same as the login for your hosting control panel, but your host should make it clear if they're different.

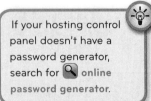

If your hosting control panel doesn't have a password generator, search for online password generator.

If you no longer are working with a web designer, or if an employee who had access to the company website leaves, be sure to change any passwords to which the employee had access.

Something that's often overlooked is the username for the hosting account. In many cases, the username is automatically generated and cannot be changed later; just as often, it's far too simple, like your domain name without the extension.

If you start an online signup process and you don't have the option to choose your username, call the hosting provider and check if you can choose your own nonobvious username.

Related Questions

➡ 96. Will you routinely check your contact information? **Page 282**

➡ 98. Will your site administration be securely accessed? **Page 288**

Action Item

➡ These days, we all have lots of usernames and passwords for all sorts of purposes. It's worth getting a program for your computer that will securely store all of them in one place. There are lots of paid and free programs out there if you search for : **password manager**.

Chapter 3
E-mail

Importance

16. Should Your E-mail Be on a Separate Server from Your Website?

For most people, the answer to this question is no. Hosting accounts for websites includes e-mail hosting, which can easily handle the typical needs of most users. However, there are certain situations in which it makes sense to host your domain's e-mail on a different server:

→ **You prefer using a web mail service**—If you already use an online service such as Gmail or Yahoo! Mail, you can also have your domain's e-mail handled through its servers instead of your web hosting provider.

→ **You have your own internal mail server**—Hosting your own e-mail on a server in an office is becoming more common, and you can easily keep that server while setting up a website with a web hosting provider.

> **Rule of Thumb**   The e-mail that comes with web hosting is adequate for the needs of most site owners, so there's no need to have a separate e-mail server.

→ **Your company is using special e-mail software**—Tools such as Microsoft Exchange, which integrate e-mail, voicemail, messaging, and other communications tools into a single package, require a special server for e-mail.

→ **You need high security**—If keeping e-mail secure is a top priority, you'll probably need a specialized e-mail hosting service.

→ **You need added reliability**—Having your website and e-mail go down together might be too risky, so having e-mail on a separate server is a way to solve this.

If you have an e-mail server in your office, why not just host your website there, too? The answer is that hosting websites is an entirely different process requiring an additional level of maintenance, not to mention issues of bandwidth (amount of traffic to the site), ISP restrictions, and more. Plus web hosting providers are so inexpensive.

What It Takes to Have Your E-mail on Another Server

It's beyond the scope of this book to go into the details of setting up the connection between a web server and a separate mail server, but the idea is that instructions on your web hosting provider's server redirect all incoming mail to a different address. This is done through the domain name server (DNS) records. To set up those instructions, you'll require the IP address (a numbered address such as 11.111.11.111) of the server that will handle the mail.

If you give them this IP address, most web hosting providers will make the necessary changes for you, either for free or for a very small fee. Or if you know IT people or have friends who have done this kind of redirection before, you can give them access to your hosting control panel. It is possible to make the changes yourself through your hosting control panel, but I don't recommend it.

> If you're determined to redirect mail to another server yourself, look for detailed help on your hosting control panel and follow the instructions exactly, or enter the search phrase 🔍 point mx record at another server.

Related Questions

➡ 7. What is the difference between a web hosting provider and an ISP? **Page 17**

➡ 18. Can you easily manage e-mail through your web hosting provider? **Page 46**

Action Items

➡ Be sure to weigh the costs of having e-mail on a separate server (especially an in-house server) vs. doing it through your hosting account. Legal requirements or increased productivity, for example, might well justify the expense of a separate mail server.

➡ If you already have an e-mail server, the people who set it up for you can also help with getting your domain name pointing properly to both it and your web hosting provider (or the mail server people might have a good hosting control panel and reliable hosting at a good price).

Importance

> Just because you set up an e-mail account with your domain name, don't get rid of the e-mail account with your ISP. If your website is for a business, you'll want to keep the old e-mail as your personal address, for example.

> Avoid using common e-mail usernames such as info@mydomain.com or sales@, service@ and so on, as spammers automatically include these on their lists on the off chance they've been set up..

> Remember that all e-mail you send from your computer is sent through your ISP. If you're having trouble **sending** e-mail, call your ISP, not your host. If you have trouble **receiving** e-mails, talk to the company in charge of the account (your ISP for e-mail accounts using its domain name or your web hosting provider for domain e-mails).

17. Does Your E-mail Address Use Your Domain Name?

If you're connected to the Web, you probably have an e-mail address that uses the name of your Internet service provider (ISP): myname@myisp.com. When you register a domain name for your website, it means you can also set up e-mail addresses that use that name myname@mydomain.com.

> **Rule of Thumb**   Set up at least one e-mail address using your domain name and use it for communication that involves your website.

Here are a few good reasons for having what I'll refer to as a domain e-mail:

➤ **A domain e-mail promotes your website**—If all people know about you is your e-mail address (sarah@mydomain.com), they can still find your website. If you continue to use the e-mail address you get from your ISP, you're promoting the provider instead.

➤ **A domain e-mail lends credibility**—If you're running a business and your e-mail address has the name of an ISP or a free e-mail service, it doesn't look very professional. Either you're not willing to put out the little bit of money it costs to get a domain name, you haven't thought of branding yourself with a domain name, or you have a domain name and couldn't be bothered setting up an e-mail account using that name. None of those is an impression you want to leave with clients or customers.

➤ **A domain e-mail never changes as long as you register that domain**—If you just use an ISP's e-mail address and then have to switch ISPs, the old e-mail address no longer works. Not only that, you can't even forward old e-mail to your new address. An e-mail from your domain will always be available as long as you keep that domain registered. Even if you decide to change your e-mail from sarah.miller@mydomain.com to sarah@mydomain.com, you can forward the old e-mail to the new.

You don't need a website to start using e-mail that has your domain name. If you've registered a name but aren't planning on building your website for some time, your domain registrar likely offers e-mail accounts for free or for a nominal fee. You could also temporarily point (redirect) your domain name from the registrar to a hosted e-mail service such as Gmail. Your registrar will have instructions for redirecting e-mail.

If your domain name has been pointed at a web hosting provider, and you're in the middle of building your website, you can use your hosting control panel to set up e-mail accounts with your domain name.

> Check that an e-mail address is set up and functioning before putting it on business cards or other printed materials.

Related Questions

➡ 4. Do you know what makes a good domain registrar? **Page 9**

➡ 18. Can you easily manage e-mail through your web hosting provider? **Page 46**

➡ 20. Do you need an e-mail account or an e-mail alias? **Page 51**

Action Items

➡ As soon as you have a domain name and are ready to start using it, set up at least one e-mail account for that domain, even if you haven't finished your website.

➡ Use this e-mail address to start promoting your site (if your site's not ready yet, make sure you have a promotional page that clearly describes what the site is about, how to contact you, your logo, and so on).

Importance

18. Can You Easily Manage E-mail through Your Web Hosting Provider?

If you've ever lost the password for your e-mail, you'll appreciate an easy-to-use e-mail management function on your hosting control panel. There is no need to call tech support; just log in to the control panel, create a new password, and put that in your e-mail program on your computer. Sometimes the e-mail manager might be separate from the hosting control panel, but the key is to make sure it's user-friendly. Figure 3-1 shows an example of the home section of e-mail management in a hosting control panel.

FIGURE 3-1

If someone else is setting up your hosting and your e-mail, at the very least, learn how to manage your e-mail accounts and the passwords in particular.

As you can see in Figure 3-1, there are a lot of e-mail functions available, some of which you'll never need to use. The basic tasks you should be able to perform from any e-mail interface are:

- Add and delete e-mail accounts.
- Change e-mail account passwords.
- Change the capacity (quota) of mail accounts.
- Forward an e-mail address to another.
- Add and delete autoresponders (out-of-office messages, and so on).
- Set up mailing lists.
- Control spam filtering.

With hosting control panels, setting up an e-mail account should be as simple as filling in a form with an e-mail address and a password, as shown in the top area of Figure 3-2.

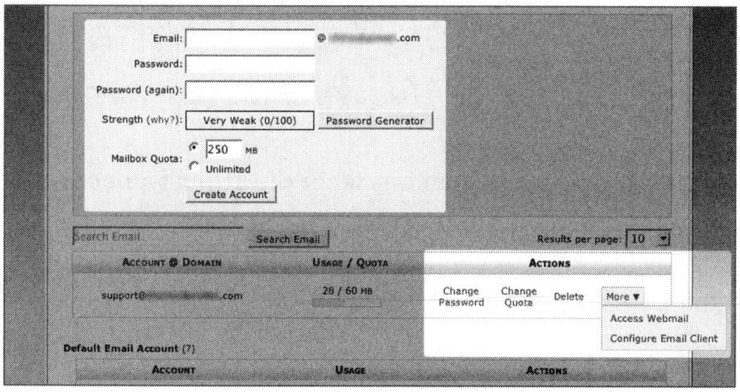

FIGURE 3-2

At the bottom of Figure 3-2 is an example of a link to instructions for configuring a new account in e-mail clients such as Outlook or Thunderbird. You might set up an e-mail account only once, so having good instructions is an important feature to look for in an e-mail interface.

There are two common approaches to managing e-mail accounts. The first is to group all functions under an individual account: forwarding, autoresponders, mailing lists, and so on. The other approach groups all accounts under individual functions. Forwarding for all accounts is handled on one screen with autoresponders on another, and so on.

If you have only a few e-mail accounts and aliases to deal with, this might not be much of an issue, but if you're constantly working with dozens of e-mail accounts, you might prefer one or the other. For example, if you had to make 20 autoresponder changes at one time, it can be a lot faster to manage on one screen than having to go in and out of 20 accounts.

On Video

Compare what it takes to create several e-mail aliases using two different hosting control panels.

Related Questions

→ 10. Does the web hosting provider have a good hosting control panel? **Page 23**

→ 20. Do you need an e-mail account or an e-mail alias? **Page 51**

Action Item

→ When you're testing the hosting control panels of potential web hosting providers, pay close attention to the e-mail functions.

Importance

19. Can You Access Your Domain E-mail through a Web Browser?

Being able to access your e-mail from anywhere is almost a necessity today. If you don't have a mobile device such as a smartphone, or you haven't got your laptop, can you still access the e-mail for your domain through any computer using a web browser? There are two ways to do this:

→ Use the web mail program that comes with your hosting account.

→ Have the e-mail for your domain handled by an online e-mail service such as Gmail or Yahoo! Mail.

The second option is discussed in Question 16 at the beginning of this chapter, so the focus here is on using the web mail programs offered by web hosting providers.

Rule of Thumb   Be sure your web hosting provider offers a web mail program. Even if you think you'd never use it, imagine if the computer with your e-mail program goes down...

You can access web mail through the control panel that comes with your hosting account, but often there's also a direct URL for your web mail interface. These addresses are typically in the form of webmail .mydomain.com or mydomain.com/webmail. Details on where to access web mail should be clearly laid out in your host's help section. Be sure to bookmark the login page.

To log in to your host's web mail program, you'll need your username (usually your full e-mail address or at least the first part up to the @ symbol), your e-mail account password (this is separate from your hosting control panel password), and an Internet connection.

As with your hosting control panel, you'll want to try out a web hosting provider's web mail program to ensure that you find it easy to use and that it has enough features you need. The most popular web mail programs these days are as powerful as the e-mail clients you use on your computer, allowing you to, for example, do the following:

- Compose and send messages.
- Organize messages into various folders.
- Perform filtering operations on incoming e-mails.
- Mark e-mail as read.
- Do e-mail encryption.

A typical web mail interface is familiar to users of offline e-mail programs, as you can see in Figure 3-3.

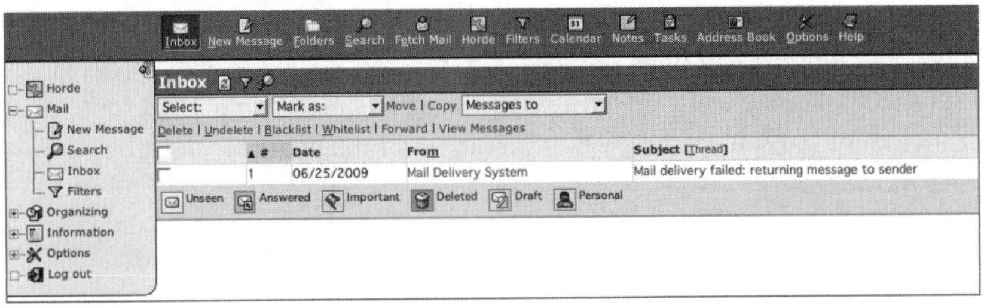

FIGURE 3-3

Some hosting providers offer multiple programs for web mail, as shown in Figure 3-4. Try out the different choices and see which one you're most comfortable with.

FIGURE 3-4

On Video

See more details of operating a web mail program that comes with a hosting control panel.

Remember, if you delete mail from your web mail program, it won't be available to download to your computer the next time you hit send/receive on your e-mail client.

When accessing your web mail from public terminals, remember to log out. See question 98 later in the book for some tips on protecting your login information when using a computer in a public place.

Related Questions

➤ 16. Should your e-mail be on a separate server from your website? **Page 42**

➤ 98. Will your site administration be securely accessed? **Page 48**

Action Item

➤ If the web hosting provider you're checking out does not have a demo or at least detailed screenshots or a video of its web mail program(s), try searching for 🔍 **webmail demo**. Look for names such as Horde, Squirrel Mail, and Roundcube, which are some of the most common programs offered by hosting providers.

20. Do You Need an E-mail Account or an E-mail Alias?

Importance

Most e-mail addresses are connected to an e-mail account (sometimes called a mailbox), which is space on a server where e-mail is stored and then retrieved by e-mail programs such as Outlook Express, Thunderbird, or your mobile device. Then there are e-mail addresses that don't have their own account and simply get redirected to an existing e-mail account; and they are known as aliases.

> **? Rule of Thumb**   You'll want at least one e-mail account for your website's domain name. If nothing else, it helps keep personal e-mail separated.

For example, if you have an e-mail account with the address myname@mydomain.com, you can set up an e-mail alias specialoffer@mydomain.com, which simply forwards mail to it. You don't have to set up anything in your e-mail program because there's no account for specialoffer@mydomain.com. You can create as many of these aliases as you like and point them at one e-mail account or a variety of accounts, as shown in Figure 3-5.

> **?** Sometimes e-mail aliases are referred to as forwarders, but actually any e-mail address can be forwarded. For example, you can forward the address of your business e-mail account to your home account and you would end up with a copy of an e-mail on each. An alias is an e-mail address that does nothing but forward.

Forwarders allow you to send a copy of all mail from one email address to another. For example, if you have two different email accounts joe@domain.com and joseph@domain.com, you could forward joe@domain.com to joseph@domain.com so you do not need to check both accounts. Note that the mail for a forwarded email address will still be delivered to that address as well.

Address		Forward To	Functions	
billing@ahundredquestionstoask.com	to	george@bravenewniche.com	Trace	Delete
eventslistings@ahundredquestionstoask.com	to	george@ahundredquestionstoask.com	Trace	Delete
george.plumley@ahundredquestionstoask.com	to	george@ahundredquestionstoask.com	Trace	Delete
questionbox@ahundredquestionstoask.com	to	george@ahundredquestionstoask.com	Trace	Delete

Add Forwarder

FIGURE 3-5

Here are a few reasons to use e-mail aliases:

♦ **Easily sort your mail**—Even if you're a one-person operation, you might have several areas on your website from which people contact you about different issues. The most common example would be Sales vs. Support. You can create an e-mail alias for each, and have them go to your main e-mail account. Not only will you know the e-mail is meant for a particular "department," but you can also create filters in your e-mail program, to place the e-mails in their own mail folders.

Designating your e-mail account as the catch-all or default address for your domain can fill some of the roles described for aliases, but there are good reasons not to take that approach. A catch-all address means that any e-mail address can get through, whether it's misspelled or whether there's no such account or alias. The problem is, unless you set up strong filtering, you can get a lot of spam because one tactic is to send out dozens or hundreds of e-mails with common names, such as info@ or sales@. If you have a catch-all account, these will all get passed through.

On Video

Watch how easy it can be to create e-mail accounts and aliases using a hosting control panel.

→ **Common misspellings**—If people regularly misspell the portion of your e-mail address before the @ symbol, you can set up an alias with the wrong spelling. That way the server won't reject the address. For example, if your address is `kimberly@mydomain.com` and people often type it with an "ley," just set up an alias called `kimberley@mydomain.com` and have it point to your e-mail account.

→ **Throwaway addresses**—It's fun to sign up for things on the Internet (newsletters, offers, contests, and so on), but you don't always want to give out your personal or primary e-mail address. Simply use an e-mail alias and then you can just turn off the address if you're getting lots of spam. Or if you're running a contest, it might be useful to have an e-mail address that you can delete when the contest is over.

However, e-mail aliases might not always be the best way to go. For example, many e-mail programs require your reply address to match the address of the e-mail account. For instance, if you have an e-mail alias `myname@mydomain.com` pointing to an account on your ISP's server—`myname@isp.com`—your reply address would have to be `myname@isp.com`. That could get confusing, so you'd want to set up the address as an e-mail account rather than an alias.

Related Questions

→ 17. Does your e-mail address use your domain name? **Page 44**

→ 18. Can you easily manage e-mail through your web hosting provider? **Page 46**

Action Items

→ In your hosting control panel, familiarize yourself with how e-mail aliases are created. Look for mail forwarders, forward e-mail, or similar phrases in your menu. Try creating one and test that it works.

→ Keep a list of the e-mail aliases you create, listing where they're directed and the purpose of the alias.

Design and Layout

Importance

21. Who Will Design Your Site?

To help answer this question, it's important to understand that web design is about a lot more than making a site look good. This common misconception confuses one of the tools of site design—visual appeal—with the actual goal, which is to effectively communicate whatever the website is required to do: entertain, sell, convince, inform, and so on.

Web design requires expertise in designing graphics and text, laying out pages, and translating it all into HTML and CSS. Keep that in mind when considering who will design your site, some alternatives for which are summarized in Table 4-1.

TABLE 4-1: Alternative Methods for Designing Your Site

METHOD	ADVANTAGES	DISADVANTAGES
Hire a web designer.	Your site is customized exactly the way you want it; not just in design, but in layout and function. All elements of design can be covered. You can get advice on alternatives.	Can be costly. If the designer is not good with web implementation, you'll need extra help.
Get a site template.	Low cost. A well-built template gives you the experience of a good designer. Coding is already done. Customization is possible.	Customization requires design and HTML knowledge. Even if a template includes several layouts, they probably aren't exactly what you need. No one to help you make decisions. Can't always check the HTML before you buy.
Get a templated site.	Low to no cost. Last to implement.	Little to no flexibility in design or layout. If you leave the host, you can take content but not design. No one to help you make decisions.
Do it yourself.	No labor costs.	Very steep learning curve. High time costs. Unless you have the programs, you might need to buy software. No one to help you.

Whichever route you take, you're the one who will be making the final decision on design, so it's important to know what to look for and what questions to ask. This includes the process of evaluating sites you see on the Web—what you like and don't like. The questions in this chapter will help you with that evaluation as well as the process of evaluating your own design at every stage.

Rule of Thumb   Use a web designer. Even if you begin with a template, you'll probably need at least some customization and someone to make sure the design is properly implemented in HTML.

Be honest about the real costs of each of the possible ways to do your site design. For example unless you're handy with design programs, the learning curve just to generate a site mockup might be very costly in time, or the cost of your site looking like just another template might outweigh the cost of hiring a designer.

Related Questions

➡ 22. Will the design of your site support your content or distract from it? **Page 52**

➡ 23. Will your site layout make your content clear? **Page 55**

➡ 31. Will your site design display well in different browsers? **Page 76**

➡ 47. Will your site be static or dynamic? **Page 122**

➡ 49. Will you use tables or style sheets to lay out your site? **Page 126**

Action Items

➡ Start a list of sites whose designs you like. Begin with sites in your field, but also look for great designs in radically different fields. Even if there's only one element about the site that strikes you, bookmark it and make a note. These sites will be helpful no matter which route you take for designing your site.

➡ When adding to your list, look at sites with different glasses on. One time, give yourself just 6 seconds to decide whether you like each site's design. Another time, choose designs based on how easily you can find information such as a phone number, or compare sites based on how easily you can read text.

➡ Ask friends and colleagues how they got their site designed. What was it like working with the designer? How did it work out using a template? How flexible was the site-building system they used?

Importance

22. Will the Design of Your Site Support Your Content or Distract from It?

When visitors first open a web page, statistics show they decide whether to stay within the first 6 to 8 seconds. Given that short time, you can understand the importance of design. Two of its tasks are to convey the feel and purpose of the site and to focus your attention by drawing your eye to what's important. If visitors get the wrong feel or focus on the wrong material, the greater the chance they're going to hit the back button.

Take a look at the sample home pages in Figure 4-1.

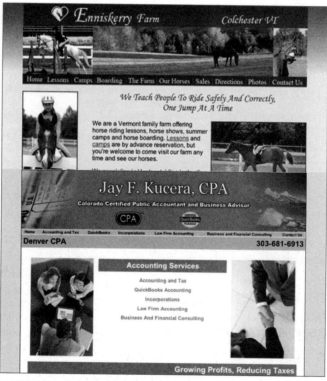

FIGURE 4-1

Because neither site has what can be called a beautiful design, some people think they are examples of what not to do. But if design is about clear communication, not about creating works of art, these sites actually do a pretty good job. In each case, you know immediately what business they're in, where they're located, and what general services they offer. It's not that their designs cannot be improved, but they give you good focus and don't distract.

When you're finding examples of sites you like, don't like them for their own sakes. Look for designs that speak to your purposes and style. Imagine that the site you're looking at is your own and ask how clearly it would communicate.

From the moment you have samples of sites you like, you need to start asking yourself this question about each element of the design: Does it further a visitor's understanding or use of the content? This will give a good starting point when you're talking to web designers, looking at potential templates, or sketching your own design. And then keep asking that question at every stage of your design development.

Once visitors have taken in the feel of the overall site, they want to find what they're looking for, and this is when the design must give focus to the important elements on the page. The first focus would typically be the name of the site, whether this is a logo or just a title, followed by the navigation, which helps visitors orient themselves. After that it's on to the content of the page.

Look at this sample site in Figure 4-2 and think about where your eye is being drawn.

> Many small businesses haven't thought enough about their brand or their style, and they rely on a web designer to come up with it for them. You need to have these concepts in your mind before starting a web design.

> **On Video**
>
> See some examples of sites whose designs do and do not communicate the purpose or feel, or focus you on the content.

FIGURE 4-2

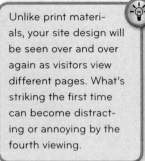

Unlike print materials, your site design will be seen over and over again as visitors view different pages. What's striking the first time can become distracting or annoying by the fourth viewing.

Here the eye is distracted by too much content and too many design elements, but your attention can also be misdirected by designs that are too intriguing or too garish, or elements within a design that are annoying (such as repetitive movements).

The rest of the questions in this chapter deal with specific issues of how design can help or hinder the communication of content, but the point to keep in mind through the entire design process is this: Can I remove a design element and still clearly understand what's happening and get the right feel?

Rule of Thumb   Less is always better in design. Keep taking away, stop when it doesn't look right, and add back that last element.

Related Questions

→ 28. How will your site design use color? **Page 68**

→ 23. Will your site layout make your content clear? **Page 55**

→ 25. How will the design of the text make your content clear? **Page 60**

→ 33. Will the design of your site navigation complement or clutter your site? **Page 82**

Action Items

→ Go back over the list of site designs you like and be honest about whether you just find the look appealing or whether it helps you understand what the site is about.

→ Show a variety of people a mockup of your site for just 6 seconds and ask them what the site is about.

23. Will Your Site Layout Make Your Content Clear?

Importance

The layout of a website serves as a kind of map for visitors. Once they understand the layout, they'll know where to look for different kinds of content. Creating a site layout can be divided into two tasks: laying out the general content areas and laying out specific content within those areas. Examples of these two tasks might include the following: deciding whether a sidebar will be on the left or right of the main content; and deciding what content belongs on the sidebar, how the content will be ordered, how it's spaced, and so on.

The job of a designer is to make sure that both aspects of a site's layout keep the visitor focused on what's important. In most cases, that means using conventional site layouts such as the ones shown in Figure 4-3.

> A great designer can probably focus visitors on the content using almost any sort of layout, but you would need a very good reason to spend the kind of money it would take to accomplish that.

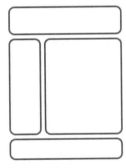 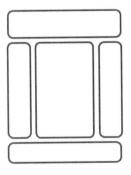 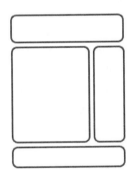

FIGURE 4-3

No surprises here—and that's a good thing. You want people to concentrate on your message, not on understanding radically new structures. In a famous study of the eye movements of users looking at different types of websites, usability guru Jakob Nielsen found a rough, common pattern in the shape of an F, as shown in Figure 4-4.

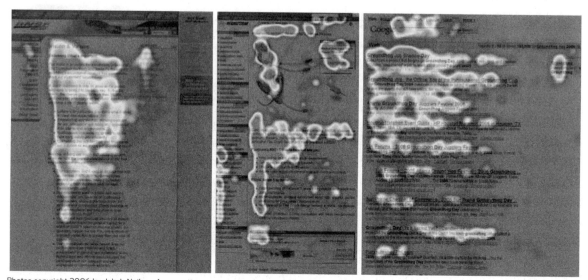

Photos copyright 2006 by Jakob Neilson, from useit.com

FIGURE 4-4

On Video

See a variety of layouts demonstrated and discussed.

It's true that studies like these focused on text-oriented pages and that eye patterns can differ on graphics-heavy pages. It's also been pointed out that subjects were led to these eye patterns by the layout of the page, so a different layout can lead them in other directions.

However, when you have only a few seconds to capture visitors' attention and make them feel at home, or if you don't have the money to design an alternative that works, why mess with what they've come to expect? Better to spend your design efforts on colors that complement the purpose and topic of the site, navigation that's easy to use, or images that stir relevant emotions instead of playing around with basic layout.

Experience and studies such as Nielsen's give you a guide for deciding how to place content within the areas of the general layout:

Rule of Thumb   Keep the most important content on the left and high.

This applies whether you're deciding where to put the most important content on the page as a whole or deciding the order of content within one part of the layout. For example, a callout (small box of additional content) is better placed as high as possible within an article to increase its chances of being read.

Just as your overall site layout needs to remain the same throughout the site, the placement of elements within that layout should remain consistent. For example, you cannot move the main navigation from one page to the next. That's just cruel. Even moving the main navigation for a section of your site is not very respectful of your visitors. There are ways to show section-specific navigation, but don't mess with the main navigation.

If you keep thinking of your site's layout as a map, it will help you decide whether you're leading visitors where they need to go. The questions in this chapter and the next are about making different elements of that map work together to achieve that goal.

> The one place where layout can vary to some extent without causing problems (in fact it can be very powerful) is on the home page of a site.

Related Questions

➜ 49. Will you use tables or style sheets to lay out your site? **Page 126**

➜ 57. Will your content be easily accessible? **Page 148**

Action Item

➜ Test your layout by asking people to point to some element as quickly as they can or asking them what the message is of a particular page. You want to do these kinds of tests as early in the design stage as possible, so even if you only have mockups to show people, that's fine.

Importance

24. What Will Be the Width and Height of Your Website?

When you're creating your site's layout, you'll need to decide how wide it will be when viewed in a web browser and to ensure that your design does not take up too much of the first screen's worth of real estate.

The first decision you'll need to make about width is whether to have a fixed or a fluid width. As the name suggests, a fixed width is set once and never changes, whereas a fluid width means the site automatically adjusts its width to match the size of the visitor's browser. A sample of a fluid width (left) and a fixed width (right) are shown in Figure 4-5.

The advantage of a fixed width layout is that you have more control over the structure of the site. The disadvantage is that you're at the mercy of different monitor sizes and people resizing their browser windows. Some people will see wide margins around your site, whereas others might have to scroll left and right to see all your content.

FIGURE 4-5

You can keep up with the average settings of computer monitors by using this search phrase: 🔍 **screen resolution statistics** and refine the search results to the last year.

The key is to minimize how many people might need to scroll horizontally by keeping your site width a bit less than the width of the current average screen resolution. At the time of printing, that resolution is 1024 pixels. That means if you set your site width at 960 pixels, there will be a bit of breathing room on either side of the average screen (always center your fixed width site).

Rule of Thumb   A fixed width site should be at least 60 pixels narrower than the width of the current average screen resolution.

A fluid width avoids the too-narrow or too-wide problem because the website is always exactly the same width as the visitor's browser. The disadvantage is that your text and image elements, in particular, move around and can affect the readability and look of the site. Don't assume fluid sites are immune from horizontal scroll; fixed elements such as images can keep the site from fully resizing with the browser window.

Even though web pages are infinite in length, height plays a role in design because people pay special attention to what they see when they first open a web page. Following the tradition of the most important headlines of a newspaper being visible when it's folded, this very important region of your site is referred to as "above the fold." With today's monitors, that height is roughly the first 700 pixels only—what people will see without scrolling.

From a design standpoint, what you want to ensure is that the header area of the website does not take up too much of this valuable real estate. The header, of course, carries your branding and your navigation, and although you don't want this to be too small, you also don't want it to distract from the page title and the first few paragraphs of text.

The biggest culprit of wasted height is images. You might feel very strongly about an effective photo being displayed in the header area, but if that image is too tall, it's taking away from content, and in most cases that's not a good thing.

Home pages are one of the exceptions to this rule. Because there's usually a small amount of content, there's room to play with white space, images, and so on.

Related Questions

→ 23. Will your site layout make your content clear? **Page 55**

→ 29. Will the background of your site help focus the content or distract from it? **Page 70**

→ 49. Will you use tables or style sheets to lay out your site? **Page 126**

→ 64. What content will be on your home page? **Page 170**

At some point, simply increasing width to match monitor trends will require an actual re-design because there's a limit to the width of text that the human eye can easily take in, and you'll need to break up content into more columns.

Some designers have addressed the question of height by creating fixed height layouts in which the content scrolls within the design frame. There are a number of disadvantages to this. Scrolling content is often done with what are called iframes and these pose issues for search engines. Another disadvantage is that you lose a lot of real estate on the side because it's limited to the screen height.

Having a top margin in the design of the site—not being flush to the top of the browser window—uses up valuable real estate, so it's worth considering if that margin is necessary, even if it's only a small margin.

Action Item

→ Whether to use a fixed or fluid structure needs to be decided early in the design process.

Importance

25. How Will the Design of the Text Make Your Content Clear?

When you talk about text and design, most people think of choosing fonts, but that's only a part of what's referred to as *typography*. They forget that most of the text on a page is in the body of the content, and if it's not presented clearly and in an organized, consistent way, the visitor has to work harder.

Of course, the font you choose for your body text does play an important role in its readability. There are not a lot of fonts you can count on all users having, but in Figure 4-6 you can see a comparison between two common fonts.

Lorem ipsum dolor sit amet, convallis tincidunt non varius magna voluptatibus, lacus rutrum iaculis laoreet sem, posuere nullam pellentesque eu vulputate dapibus fringilla, mi mattis risus libero condimentum sed. Sed natoque tellus, est senectus condimentum in, elementum rhoncus mauris sapien. A consectetuer pede feugiat ipsum mollis cursus, in semper nunc, non in proin fringilla proin enim. Tellus habitant ornare, sodales massa nunc metus amet, cursus leo quis eros sagittis quam, cursus orci feugiat lacinia ligula, felis odio quis etiam euismod.

Lorem ipsum dolor sit amet, convallis tincidunt non varius magna voluptatibus, lacus rutrum iaculis laoreet sem, posuere nullam pellentesque eu vulputate dapibus fringilla, mi mattis risus libero condimentum sed. Sed natoque tellus, est senectus condimentum in, elementum rhoncus mauris sapien. A consectetuer pede feugiat ipsum mollis cursus, in semper nunc, non in proin fringilla proin enim. Tellus habitant ornare, sodales massa nunc metus amet, cursus leo quis eros sagittis quam, cursus orci feugiat lacinia ligula, felis odio quis etiam euismod.

Veranda   **Times Roman**

All text is set at 12px with no line or letter spacing added

FIGURE 4-6

You can see how differently each font reads. On the Web, sans-serif fonts are more commonly used for body text, in part because the tiny edges on serif fonts don't display well on low-resolution monitors.

Rule of Thumb   Don't mix more than two fonts within the content area of your site (if the body font is sans-serif, use a serif heading and vice versa).

Font size is another important factor in the readability of text. Avoid making your body text too small. Although users can change text size in their browsers, why make it likely they'll need to by choosing a small font size?

Another role of text size in typography is the proportion between different levels of headings. Good design involves making clear the relative importance of sections of text by setting them off with the properly sized headings. Headings also help to break up the text into manageable pieces.

Two other elements of typography are particularly important for reading online, but are often neglected in design: the measure or width of a body of text and the leading or height between lines of text.

The example in Figure 4-7 shows how a poor choice of width makes the reading of text difficult.

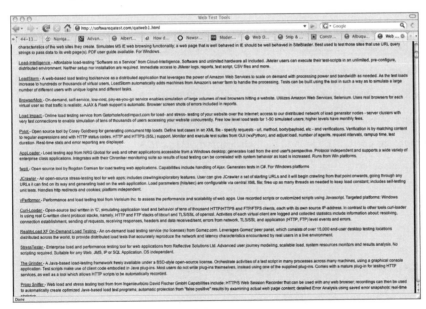

FIGURE 4-7

The standard range of readability on the Web is between 50 and 70 characters per line, which is far less than the overall width of most websites. This means that breaking up the page into columns or using sidebars is crucial for maintaining readability.

Even if you have a good readable size for your body text, consider putting buttons on your site that make it easy for visitors to change font size. Many people aren't aware that they can change font size in their browsers, so they'll welcome the buttons on your site.

Designers can organize only text that's been written with a clear organization to begin with.

If you use a fluid layout for your site (it matches the width of the user's browser), be aware that the wider a person's monitor, the more chance your body text will be too wide.

Line height or leading is the amount of space between lines of text and, as Figure 4-8 illustrates, it can have a dramatic effect on body text:

Lorem ipsum dolor sit amet, convallis tincidunt non varius magna voluptatibus, lacus rutrum iaculis laoreet sem, posuere nullam pellentesque eu vulputate dapibus fringilla, mi mattis risus libero condimentum sed. Sed natoque tellus, est senectus condimentum in, elementum rhoncus mauris sapien. A consectetuer pede feugiat ipsum mollis cursus, in semper nunc, non in proin fringilla proin enim. Tellus habitant ornare, sodales massa nunc metus amet, cursus leo quis eros sagittis quam, cursus orci feugiat lacinia ligula, felis odio quis etiam euismod.

Lorem ipsum dolor sit amet, convallis tincidunt non varius magna voluptatibus, lacus rutrum iaculis laoreet sem, posuere nullam pellentesque eu vulputate dapibus fringilla, mi mattis risus libero condimentum sed. Sed natoque tellus, est senectus condimentum in, elementum rhoncus mauris sapien. A consectetuer pede feugiat ipsum mollis cursus, in semper nunc, non in proin fringilla proin enim. Tellus habitant ornare, sodales massa nunc metus amet, cursus leo quis eros sagittis quam, cursus orci feugiat lacinia ligula, felis odio quis etiam euismod.

FIGURE 4-8

Not only does the text on the right look more inviting to read but it's easier to find the next line as your eye moves down the paragraph, which is particularly important if you have a wide width for the column.

Related Questions

→ 27. Will your design make good use of white space? **Page 65**

→ 30. How will elements within content be set off from the body text? **Page 73**

→ 50. How effectively will style sheets be used on your website? **Page 129**

→ 59. Will your written content be correct, clear, and well structured? **Page 153**

Action Items

→ When you're studying other sites, think about how the typography is affecting the readability of the content. Choose long pieces of text and see which font is easiest to read.

→ During testing, experiment by using different fonts, line heights, and line widths to see if you get different reactions from users, especially with longer text areas.

26. Will Images Be Used Effectively in Your Design?

Importance

Images are a powerful part of a website's design, but that power should be used for good and not evil. Images in a design should complement the content of the site, not distract from it.

For the purposes of this question, I want to divide design images into three groups:

→ Graphics

→ Photos

→ Elements (icons, divider lines, and so on)

> Images that appear within content will be discussed in the chapter on content, and background images for the site as a whole are left to a separate question in this chapter.

In all cases, one of the assumptions will be that the images add to the purpose and enhance the content by being relevant. The concern in this question is whether the images do that in a way that helps rather than hinders focus.

Keep both the quantity and the complexity of graphics in your design to a level that does not distract. For example, if you're an organization that promotes better housing, it might be true that you deal with all kinds of shelter, from houses to apartments to townhouses, but to have images of each type in your header can be visual overkill. If each image is also very detailed, you further increase the distraction factor. A simple outline of a roof might be enough to make your point, look good, and not draw your eye away from content.

How do you know when to stop taking away? One important criterion is your purpose and your content. In the housing example, if people aren't aware that you deal with apartments, keep a drawing of an apartment in the design that is as simple as the roof outline.

But there's more to the principle of taking away than simply removing images. It can include taking away color (a monotone is less distracting than full color), lowering opacity (an image at 40 percent is less distracting than 80 percent), or showing only a portion of a graphic, as the examples in Figure 4-9 demonstrate.

Incorporating photos into your design is very important, in particular for quickly making clear your purpose and conveying the feel of the site. Except for the home page, keep photos in the design as small as possible. If photos are too small, of course, visitors will be distracted by trying to make out what's in the photo.

FIGURE 4-9

Try to use people in the photos for your design, in particular on the home page. Studies show that human beings are drawn more to photos of people, especially their faces.

Finally, there are the smaller images in a design, such as divider lines, icons, or heading elements. Obviously, they need to match the overall design both in color and in style. A flourish within a design of straight edges would be out of place, as would gel-style buttons on a form when the gel look is not used anywhere else in the site's design.

When it comes to icons, be sure that they're clear. Having to stop to decipher an icon makes visitors work too hard. Sometimes the lack of clarity is caused by making the icons too small, but you also don't want them so large as to draw the eye unnecessarily.

Small elements in a design are particularly good candidates for the "Can it be removed?" test. Even if you don't think they're vital, it's easy to suppose they're small enough not to distract you. Try taking them out—often the resulting white space is better.

Related Questions

➜ 29. Will the background of your site help focus the content or distract from it? **Page 70**

➜ 34. Will you be using animation in your design? **Page 84**

➜ 61. Will you effectively use images in your content? **Page 160**

➜ 63. Will your site use a splash page? **Page 167**

Action Items

➜ Check your list of sites whose designs you like and remind yourself how they use images in all areas of their designs.

➜ Using your site map, list how many images you think you might use on each page's content to get a sense of whether your overall content will be image-heavy. This will influence how image-intensive your design can be.

27. Will Your Design Make Good Use of White Space?

Importance

White space, or negative space, is what designers refer to as areas that contain little or no content. When you visit a website that feels crowded, you're experiencing a lack of white space, and this crowding makes it difficult to find what you need or to know what's most important. One of the great advantages of the Internet over print media is that space is virtually unlimited, so there isn't the same imperative to fit in as much as one can, and white space can flourish.

Look at how the site in Figure 4-10 gives mental breathing room to take in the message.

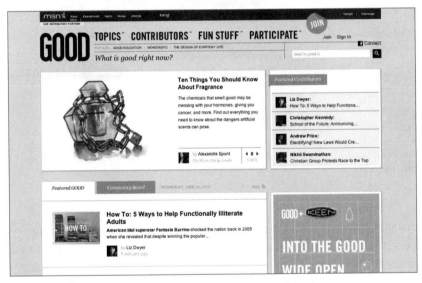

FIGURE 4-10

There are plenty of visual elements here, but they're given the space to stand out rather than overpowering you. In other words, good use of white space does not mean boring or being devoid of colors and graphical elements.

White space is any area separating content on a page, even the amount of spacing between lines of text (the details of working with white space in text are dealt with in a separate question).

The margins between sections of text or other content are often neglected when thinking about white space. Jamming elements together not only makes the page hard to digest but the value of each is also greatly reduced. Look at these three examples of the same sidebar content in Figure 4-11.

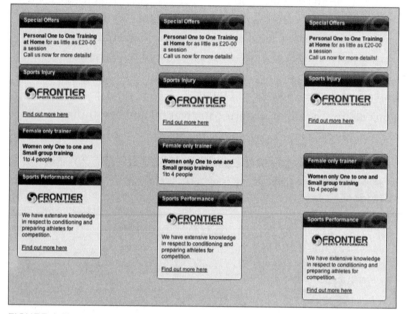

FIGURE 4-11

Without any margins at all the sidebar on the left makes you feel claustrophobic. The example in the middle uses very small margins, yet greatly reduces the visual clutter. Margins are also used in the third example, but rather than being cluttered, it looks disorganized because the margins are not consistent.

Margins, or any type of white space such as the spacing between lines of text, must always be consistent within a given context. You can have different margin widths in different areas of a site (the content versus the sidebar), but within those areas, keep the margins the same.

Even apparently small elements on a page can distract you and can be better left as complete white space. Take these two examples of dividing sections of a web page shown in Figure 4-12.

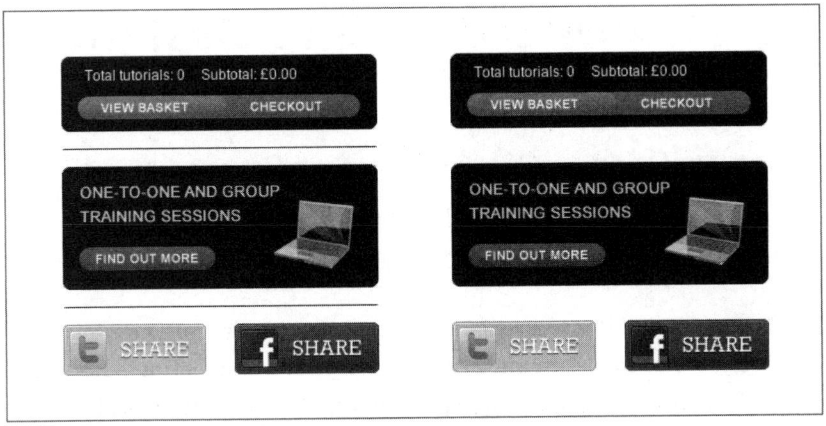

FIGURE 4-12

The dividing line on the left is thin, yet it's one more element for your eye to take in. Simply leaving this dividing space empty accomplishes the same task.

On Video

See more examples of how white space can be used effectively in layouts.

Related Questions

➡ 29. Will the background of your site help focus the content or distract from it? **Page 70**

➡ 30. How will elements within content be set off from the body text? **Page 73**

➡ 44. Could you hide some content or options to reduce visual clutter? **Page 113**

Action Items

➡ From a distance, look at your mockup on a screen. Is there enough white space between key areas of the page that you can easily distinguish between them?

➡ Focus on divider lines in your design and ask if they're even necessary or would plain white space accomplish the same task?

Importance

28. How Will Your Site Design Use Color?

There are two basic considerations for using color on your website:

➜ Does the central color fit the purpose and mood of the site?

➜ Does the color scheme based on that color work well?

Although it might not be exact science, you know from your own experience that color can affect your perceptions and feelings. Red, for example, can be associated with passion and energy, whereas blue can be associated with order and authority. Of course, some people will see these associations as positive, and others as negative.

How people perceive colors is the result of many influences: culture, gender, age, socioeconomic factors, and so much more. That means thinking about color must take into account your audience as well as your goals. For example, a company that once used blue might start using green and other earthy tones because their customers have become more concerned about the environment. To get an overview of opinions on the use of color in marketing, search for the term 🔍 color psychology marketing.

Having settled on a color for your site, you need to find a color scheme based on it. A color scheme is a set of colors that go together in some way, and some principal types include: analogous, triadic, and complementary. Starting from the same base color, each scheme will contain some very different colors, as illustrated in Figure 4-13 (even in black and white you can see the differences).

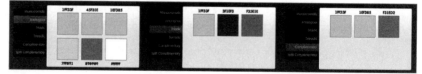

FIGURE 4-13

This is not the place to go into color theory, but you can quickly see how these schemes work by using one of the many great online color pickers; search for the term 🔍 **color chooser**.

Making sure that color variations and additional colors go with your base color is very important because it keeps your design professional, easy on the eye, and more focused. A hot pink button will jump out if the rest of the site has a green color scheme. But even if you want the button to stand out, using hot pink is probably not the best way to go about it. Find a contrasting color that goes with your color scheme. There's a difference between standing out and being jarring.

Don't forget about contrast when placing one color next to or on top of another, particularly with text. If there isn't enough contrast, the two colors will blend into one another. This is particularly important with body text if you want a colored background. Too low a contrast will make the text difficult to read and equally hard to print.

> **On Video**
>
> Watch how colorschemedesigner.com and other online tools can help you find exactly the right colors. Also see how color contrast can affect the readability of text.

> In your design program, try to turn off color to spot contrast problems. As you're testing your site online, there are tools for catching contrast problems. Search for 🔍 **color contrast checker**.

Related Questions

➤ 29. Will the background of your site help focus the content or distract from it? **Page 70**

➤ 33. Will the design of your site navigation complement or clutter your site? **Page 82**

➤ 42. How user-friendly will your links be? **Page 109**

Action Items

➤ Make a note of the colors used by your competitors (both online and off). Is there a common color?

➤ Try the same design with two or three base colors and test a mockup on several people of different genders, ages, and so on to see how they feel when they first look at it.

Importance

29. Will the Background of Your Site Help Focus the Content or Distract from It?

If you use a fixed width design for your site, part of the browser window will display a background. The styling of this background can either help set off the rest of your design or really distract from it.

You have two basic choices for the background of your site: a solid color or images, which can be used in several ways.

When deciding on a solid color, it is simplest to consult your color scheme. Designers often choose a very light color or a light grey, which will set off almost any site. Others use very dark colors or black as a background to offset the site, but particularly if you have a lot of background area, very dark colors can be overwhelming after a while because the contrast is so great.

Backgrounds can also be created with images. Unless otherwise specified, background images are automatically repeated over and over again by the browser. This effect, known as tiling, creates apparently solid backgrounds using tiny images. The background in Figure 4-14 consists of a single image (shown on the right) repeated over and over again.

> If you go with the same background color as the background of the site content areas, you'll probably still want to frame the site in some way (a light line around the outside, for example).

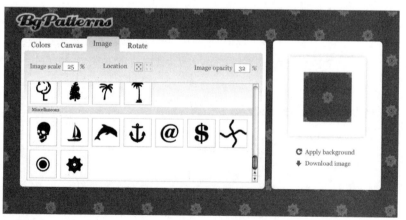

FIGURE 4-14

> If you have a background color or image, make sure that you hide it when you're formatting pages for printing.

If you want to use a complex image or photo for your site background, think about the potential visual clutter it can create. If you do choose to go that route, at least have a solid background behind your content (preferably white or close to it) to avoid the hard-to-read examples in Figure 4-15:

FIGURE 4-15

 Rule of Thumb   Avoid using photographs in website backgrounds.

Gradients are a popular way of creating website backgrounds, a couple of examples of which are shown in Figure 4-16.

FIGURE 4-16

If you want to use a single image as your site background, remember that tiling still applies. The image might fill your browser window, but on a larger screen, the image starts to repeat unless you give specific instructions in your style sheet. I show an example of this on the video. For more about backgrounds, search on this phrase: **how to create website backgrounds**.

Patterns in the background can also work well if they're subtle—heavily faded and using only one or two tones (nothing full color)—as you can see in Figure 4-17.

The background of a website is sometimes used to create space between the top edge of the browser window and the site content, as shown in the first frame of Figure 4-18. However, this just adds complexity for the eye (particularly if the background has any pattern), so keep the content flush to the top as illustrated in the second frame of Figure 4-18.

On Video

Watch some samples of good and bad back-grounds, including potential problems with tiling backgrounds.

FIGURE 4-17

If you need more breathing room at the top edge, add the space to your content background, as shown in the third frame of Figure 4-18.

FIGURE 4-18

Related Questions

➧ 24. What will be the width and height of your website? **Page 58**

➧ 28. How will your site design use color? **Page 68**

➧ 41. How easily will your pages print? **Page 106**

Action Items

➧ Make sure the background of the site is part of the design process from day one.

➧ Try replacing the background of your design with a light grey and then with white. Did it help create more of a focus for your design?

30. How Will Elements within Content Be Set Off from the Body Text?

Importance

It's common within the actual content of web pages to see boxes of additional information, option menus, or images. Sometimes referred to as "callouts" or "sidebars," these elements are meant to supplement the main body of the text with added resources (this book uses callouts for Tips, Added Info, Warnings, and so on). The design of these callouts needs to draw attention to them, but without distracting from the main body of the text. Remember, elements such as callouts are meant to supplement the content of the page, not supplant it.

Several different approaches to text boxes are shown in Figure 4-19.

Lorem ipsum dolor sit amet, convallis tincidunt non varius magna voluptatibus, lacus rutrum iaculis laoreet sem, posuere nullam pellentesque eu vulputate dapibus fringilla, mi mattis risus libero condimentum sed. Sed natoque tellus, est senectus condimentum in, elementum rhoncus mauris sapien. A consectetuer pede feugiat ipsum mollis cursus, in semper nunc, non in proin fringilla proin enim. Tellus habitant ornare, sodales massa nunc metus amet, cursus leo quis eros sagittis quam, cursus orci feugiat lacinia ligula, felis odio quis etiam euismod.

SED NATOQUE

Ut quis ligula luctus odio placerat mattis sed at nibh. Vestibulum tempus imperdiet tempor. Vivamus auctor pellentesque ligula.

Lorem ipsum dolor sit amet, convallis tincidunt non varius magna voluptatibus, lacus rutrum iaculis laoreet sem, posuere nullam pellentesque eu vulputate dapibus fringilla, mi mattis risus libero condimentum sed. Sed natoque tellus, est senectus condimentum in, elementum rhoncus mauris sapien. A consectetuer pede feugiat ipsum mollis cursus, in semper nunc, non in proin fringilla proin enim. Tellus habitant ornare, sodales massa nunc metus amet, cursus leo quis eros sagittis quam, cursus orci feugiat lacinia ligula, felis odio quis etiam euismod.

SED NATOQUE

Ut quis ligula luctus odio placerat mattis sed at nibh. Vestibulum tempus imperdiet tempor. Vivamus auctor pellentesque ligula.

Lorem ipsum dolor sit amet, convallis tincidunt non varius magna voluptatibus, lacus rutrum iaculis laoreet sem, posuere nullam pellentesque eu vulputate dapibus fringilla, mi mattis risus libero condimentum sed. Sed natoque tellus, est senectus condimentum in, elementum rhoncus mauris sapien. A consectetuer pede feugiat ipsum mollis cursus, in semper nunc, non in proin fringilla proin enim. Tellus habitant ornare, sodales massa nunc metus amet, cursus leo quis eros sagittis quam, cursus orci feugiat lacinia ligula, felis odio quis etiam euismod.

SED NATOQUE

Ut quis ligula luctus odio placerat mattis sed at nibh. Vestibulum tempus imperdiet tempor. Vivamus auctor pellentesque ligula.

FIGURE 4-19

Notice the difference between boxes that simply use a line and those that use a colored background to define the border around them. The third example shows a combination of these approaches by setting off only the header with color. Notice that the inner and outer margins of the boxes have been kept the same for comparison purposes. Whatever the style of your callouts, it's important that they all follow the same margin spacing.

You'll want to style different types of boxes in different ways. For example, a box that contains functions, such as printing the page or sharing on social media, needs to be distinguished from a box that adds information to the content, as shown in Figure 4-20.

> Whenever text flows around an element, make sure that the element is not so wide that it makes the text too narrow.

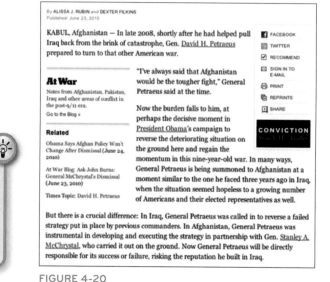

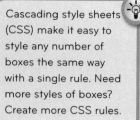

Cascading style sheets (CSS) make it easy to style any number of boxes the same way with a single rule. Need more styles of boxes? Create more CSS rules.

FIGURE 4-20

Figure 4-21 shows two examples of highlighting social media links within a content area.

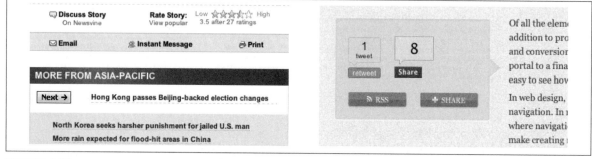

FIGURE 4-21

When displaying these boxes or images within body text, it's important to have adequate margins so they're not pressing up against the text. Figure 4-22 shows three different examples of a photo set within a body of text.

Clearly the lack of margins on the left does not work at all. The example on the right has added a border around the image. Typically, these borders are fairly light, so they don't add too much visual complexity. Part of the idea of putting borders on images is that some-times the image will have white or nearly white edges on one or more sides, and the border helps to define the image in these white areas.

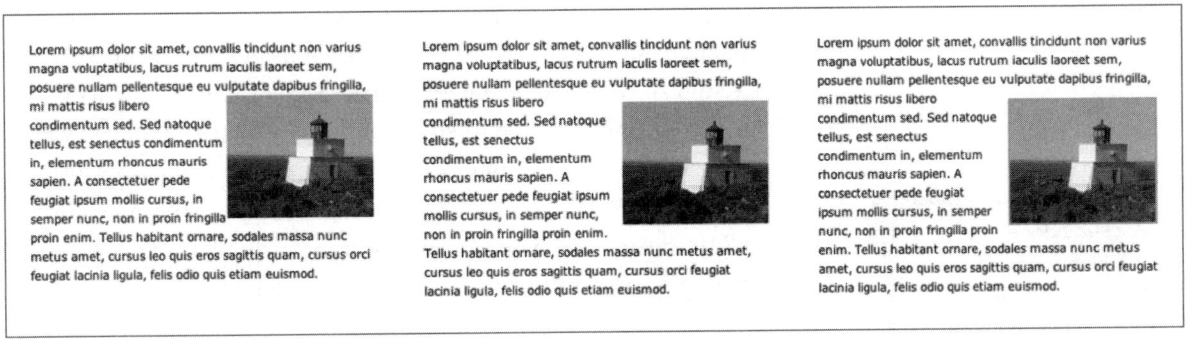

Lorem ipsum dolor sit amet, convallis tincidunt non varius magna voluptatibus, lacus rutrum iaculis laoreet sem, posuere nullam pellentesque eu vulputate dapibus fringilla, mi mattis risus libero condimentum sed. Sed natoque tellus, est senectus condimentum in, elementum rhoncus mauris sapien. A consectetuer pede feugiat ipsum mollis cursus, in semper nunc, non in proin fringilla proin enim. Tellus habitant ornare, sodales massa nunc metus amet, cursus leo quis eros sagittis quam, cursus orci feugiat lacinia ligula, felis odio quis etiam euismod.

Lorem ipsum dolor sit amet, convallis tincidunt non varius magna voluptatibus, lacus rutrum iaculis laoreet sem, posuere nullam pellentesque eu vulputate dapibus fringilla, mi mattis risus libero condimentum sed. Sed natoque tellus, est senectus condimentum in, elementum rhoncus mauris sapien. A consectetuer pede feugiat ipsum mollis cursus, in semper nunc, non in proin fringilla proin enim. Tellus habitant ornare, sodales massa nunc metus amet, cursus leo quis eros sagittis quam, cursus orci feugiat lacinia ligula, felis odio quis etiam euismod.

Lorem ipsum dolor sit amet, convallis tincidunt non varius magna voluptatibus, lacus rutrum iaculis laoreet sem, posuere nullam pellentesque eu vulputate dapibus fringilla, mi mattis risus libero condimentum sed. Sed natoque tellus, est senectus condimentum in, elementum rhoncus mauris sapien. A consectetuer pede feugiat ipsum mollis cursus, in semper nunc, non in proin fringilla proin enim. Tellus habitant ornare, sodales massa nunc metus amet, cursus leo quis eros sagittis quam, cursus orci feugiat lacinia ligula, felis odio quis etiam euismod.

FIGURE 4-22

 Related Questions

➜ 27. Will your design make good use of white space? **Page 65**

➜ 44. Could you hide some content or options to reduce visual clutter? **Page 113**

➜ 61. Will you use images effectively in your content? **Page 160**

Action Item

➜ For each callout box, list, or other content element, ask whether its design is too distracting.

Importance

31. Will Your Site Design Display Well in Different Browsers?

Web designers will tell you that cross-browser compatibility—whether a website will display the same way in different browsers—is the bane of their existence. What looks fine in Internet Explorer might not look the same in Firefox or in Chrome. Testing your site to make sure that it works in a variety of browsers is important, but that means some extra work.

How much difference can a browser make in the display of your website? In Figure 4-23, you can see the same box displayed in Internet Explorer 7 (IE 7) and in Firefox (FF) without any CSS fixes.

> Mockups done in a graphics program often look a bit different when translated into HTML and displayed in a browser, mostly in the content areas. Graphics don't change, but any nongraphic areas will depend on the cascading style sheet (CSS) and the browser.

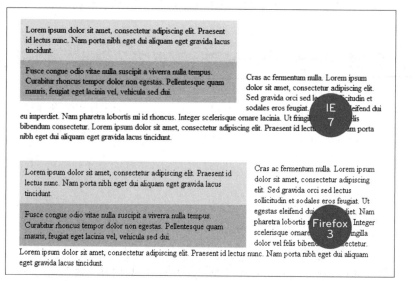

FIGURE 4-23

Luckily the use of CSS lessens the burden of compensating for browser differences because you can create additional CSS rules or even separate style sheets that automatically get used by one browser and not the others. If browser compatibility has been implemented, look for coding similar to this in the header area of your site's HTML:

```
<!--[if gt IE 7]>
<style>
body { overflow-y:scroll; }
</style>
<![endif]-->
```

31. WILL YOUR SITE DESIGN DISPLAY WELL IN DIFFERENT BROWSERS?

77

This tells any IE browser newer than version 7 to use a particular styling on the body of the HTML. You can also have this conditional code tell the browser to go and get a separate style sheet.

One of the difficulties of sorting out browser compatibility is knowing when to stop trying to keep everyone happy. The first step is to understand which browsers your visitors are most likely using. You can find general browser statistics on websites like the one shown on the left side of Figure 4-24, and when your site is up-and-running, you can see the browsers used in your site statistics, shown on the right side of Figure 4-24.

Web Browsers		W3Counter
1	Internet Explorer 8	26.17%
2	Firefox 3.6	23.11%
3	Internet Explorer 7	11.41%
4	Chrome 5	9.45%
5	Internet Explorer 6	6.79%
6	Firefox 3.5	5.27%
7	Firefox 3	2.54%
8	Safari 4	1.70%
9	Opera 10	1.45%
10	iPhone 3.1	0.50%

	Browser	None ⌄	Visits ▾ ↓	Visits
1.	Internet Explorer		5,102	63.02%
2.	Firefox		1,690	20.87%
3.	Safari		891	11.01%
4.	Chrome		333	4.11%
5.	Opera		28	0.35%
6.	BlackBerry9700		12	0.15%
7.	Mozilla		9	0.11%
8.	Mozilla Compatible Agent		6	0.07%
9.	Netscape		5	0.06%
10.	BlackBerry8530		3	0.04%

FIGURE 4-24

As you can see from these lists, there are dozens of web browsers out there, but the average website owner can't afford to worry about all of them. The four most used browsers are IE, FF, Chrome, and Safari. Although their individual numbers might change, they're likely to be the top four for some time to come. You can always find the latest numbers by entering this search phrase: 🔍 **browser usage statistics**.

You also need to consider backward compatibility in a particular browser. IE 6, for example was one of the buggiest browsers ever. Although it's still being used by some people, that number has dropped off considerably now, and it might not be worth trying to patch things up for that audience.

The next consideration is the extent of the problem. If a browser is pushing one of your columns off screen so that visitors have to scroll right, that's a serious barrier to usability and needs to be fixed.

The final consideration is time and money. Your budget might allow for fixing serious problems, but minor issues might have to be left for a later time or not addressed at all.

Related Questions

→ 24. What will be the width and height of your website? **Page 58**

→ 32. Will your site design display well on mobile devices? **Page 79**

→ 43. Will your site have special requirements for certain features to work? **Page 111**

Action Items

→ Make sure that you or the designer runs browser compatibility tests as soon as you've got the design running online.

→ Apart from having all four of the major browsers installed on your Windows machine and then having a Mac with the same, there are some excellent online services that will display a site as it appears in different browsers. Perhaps more importantly, it will show you the display in different versions of the same browser. To find these services, use the search phrase 🔍 **cross browser testing**.

32. Will Your Site Design Display Well on Mobile Devices?

Importance

More and more visitors view websites through their smartphones and other mobile devices with greatly reduced screen sizes. Making sure that your site is not just visible but also functional on these devices is becoming increasingly important.

In Figure 4-25, you can see the same page as displayed proportionately on a mobile browser and a regular browser.

FIGURE 4-25

Mobile devices usually make it easy for users to zoom in and out, but this puts the burden on the user and constantly zooming can be very awkward.

From a design standpoint, there are two basic options for giving mobile users a better experience:

- Restyle your existing site
- Create a separate mobile site

Just as with separate print style sheets, the first option is to simply reformat existing pages to be friendlier for mobile users: narrower width, single column format, larger buttons, and so on. Figure 4-26 shows a site's regular page and the styled equivalent on a mobile device.

This answer deals with the design of sites for mobile users, but there's also the important technical issue of how a visitor gets to the mobile version of a website. Whether you're going to provide the mobile user with a special style sheet or a completely separate site, it would be nice to be able to do this automatically in the way you can display your site differently for Internet Explorer users than for Firefox users. Unfortunately, at this point, detecting mobile browsers and devices is complicated by a lack of standards. For more on this issue, try the search term 🔍 mobile browser detection.

It's important to allow users to switch easily between the mobile and the desktop version of the site. Have links to both versions. The trick is to make sure that the button is highly visible to a mobile user without them having to zoom in or scroll. And the button must be visible on every page of both versions of the site.

FIGURE 4-26

Having a single site that's simply viewed differently is definitely an advantage from the standpoint of maintenance.

Content management systems (CMS) typically allow you to easily change the look of your site by switching templates, and this makes them prime candidates for this restyling approach to mobile devices. Your CMS might offer a plug-in or extension that makes it simple to offer mobile users a different view of exactly the same material.

However, there are good reasons for thinking that a change of stylesheet is not enough and that a mobile site needs to be re-built from the ground up (while still maintaining the same general look and branding of the original site).

Make sure that your mobile site is organized on your server so that you can easily direct people to either a subdirectory (http://mydomain.com/mobile) or a subdomain (http://mobile.mydomain.com). A popular convention for mobile subdomains is http://m.mydomain.com.

People use mobile devices differently than they use desktops or even laptops. Sessions tend to be very short; touch screens and more limited inputting means that navigation and other tasks need to be even easier, there are more likely to be offline distractions, and so on. All of these factors mean you might have to think differently not just about the overall design but the organizational flow of the site. For more about designing sites for mobile visitors, use the search term 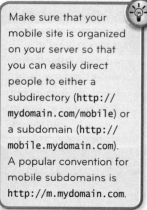 mobile web design.

If your website is built dynamically, the page viewed in a browser is created from various parts through a scripting process rather than existing on a server as a single HTML file. Creating a separate mobile site does not mean starting from scratch. Depending on how your content is divided up into separate files or database entries, it might only be a matter of reorganizing how some or all of the same content is presented.

Related Questions

➡ 31. Will your site design display well in different browsers? **Page 76**

➡ 41. How easily will your pages print? **Page 106**

➡ 48. Will your site be built with a content management system (CMS)? **Page 124**

➡ 49. Will you use tables or style sheets to lay out your site? **Page 126**

Action Items

➡ If you use a mobile device, start noticing how you use it and make use of those observations when designing your mobile site.

➡ Testing your regular site or mobile version on a mobile device is the first place to start. When you need to test on different mobile browsers, you can do it online. Just search for this term: 🔍 **mobile browser simulator**. And, of course, have different users with various devices try out the site, too.

Importance

33. Will the Design of Your Site Navigation Complement or Clutter Your Site?

Designing site navigation involves finding a balance between the importance of making it noticeable and not overpowering content by standing out too much. This question is about achieving that balance. The usability of the navigation will be left to the next chapter.

Navigation is not the place to show off your Photoshop skills unnecessarily, as the examples in Figure 4-27 illustrate.

On Video

See examples of effective menus and particularly the use of color and contrast.

FIGURE 4-27

Plain colors, slight gradients, or subtle light effects are much nicer, yet still effective. The latter two are shown in Figure 4-28.

If you use icons or images with words in them, it makes your menu much less flexible. If you add a page or want to change the name of a page, you have to call in a designer to make a new button. Use only the images in the background, but keep the titles as HTML text.

FIGURE 4-28

You need to strike a balance between making it clear where the navigation is and not making it the center of attention.

Using icons instead of words in your navigation not only requires visitors to think too much, it's also more visually distracting. Your eye is naturally drawn to images and having a group of five or more of them at the top of your website is particularly distracting. You want people to notice the navigation, but you do that by the overall design, not icons.

Menus that use Flash often become small works of art rather than a help to the visitor, and that's a distraction. Movement is not a problem in and of itself, but when there's too much of it or the effect is really stunning, it's easy for the visitor to be drawn to the bright shiny object instead of the business of getting around the site.

From a layout standpoint, should you put the main navigation above or below the logo? One common structure is to have the main menu below the logo and a secondary small menu above and to the right. The two approaches are shown in Figure 4-29.

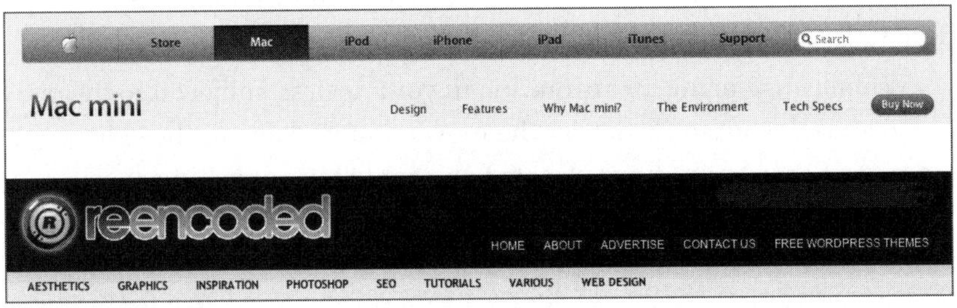

FIGURE 4-29

Consistency of design is important with navigation. You might change the look of your header for different parts of a website, but it's best to keep the same colors and look for the navigation.

Many times on a Flash-based menu there's a sound accompanying the mouseover of a button. This is a good example of a design element that seems cool when you're building the site, but becomes annoying to visitors who do a lot more mousing over than you do in your one-time demo by the designer.

It's helpful on your menu to highlight the page a visitor is currently on. Note that having a distinctive color or background image for the current page button does not count as a design inconsistency.

Related Questions

➥ 26. Will images be used effectively in your design? **Page 63**

➥ 35. Will your navigation menus be easy to use? **Page 88**

➥ 57. Will your content be easily accessible? **Page 148**

Action Item

➥ Don't look at your navigation in isolation, especially if it involves animation. Look at it on a complete page and check that it's both obvious and not distracting.

Importance

34. Will You Be Using Animation in Your Design?

As web technology has evolved, it has become easier and easier to incorporate animated effects into designs, although not always with happy results.

The problem with animations is that they move. As every parent who has tried to pry a child from the TV or gaming console knows, movement gets your attention, but you should know how to use animation without it becoming the focus of attention.

When considering an animation in your design, subject it to the content test: Ask yourself whether the movement will do anything for your message. Some animations clearly don't contribute anything at all, so unless you're a site catering to kids or having a bit of fun with your visitors for a particular occasion, ditch the idea of falling snowflakes in the background or dancing musical notes that trail along with your cursor.

Other animations might be relevant to your content, but that does not mean they're contributing to your content. For instance, an airplane that flies across your header can seem like a good idea for your air charter company, but stop and consider. It's not irrelevant, just gimmicky (if it keeps flying across every time you load the page, it's an annoying gimmick), so it becomes a distraction from your message.

Suppose now that the flying plane reveals a strip of photos depicting various uses of your aircraft. It might still be gimmicky (reason enough to say no, perhaps), but at least it helps to draw attention to your content and your purpose.

Following the rule of "less is better," it's important to ask next whether you couldn't achieve the same goal of an animation with simple variations in the design. For example, an animated display of the types of machinery you deal with at the top of each page might further your goal of showing the diversity of your repair services, but the same end might be achieved by showing a new static image every time the visitor changes the page.

? Menus that slide open to reveal more choices are a type of animation, but are not included in this discussion, nor are animations within the content area.

The coolness factor can be a big distraction in your decision-making process. Ugly animations often get rejected because they're ugly and not because they're a distraction to content. That means if the designer returns with a cool animation you're likely to say yes, even if it's equally distracting from the content. Stop looking at the animation in isolation or as a piece of art.

Make sure that you can easily change the images used in design animations. For example, if you have a Flash element in the header that rotates photos of travel destinations, be sure that it's built so you can change those photos easily yourself.

If you decide that an animation is called for, there are several considerations that can keep it from becoming a distraction:

→ Make the animation user-controlled if possible (either it occurs only when a visitor takes some action or if the animation starts automatically the visitor can turn it off).

→ Keep the overall length of the animation short.

→ Unless the animation is very subtle, don't have it repeat more than once.

→ If the animation has distinct elements (such as photos), give enough time between transitions.

→ Limit the animation to the home page.

→ Use transitions that are less jarring to the eye, such as fades.

On Video

Watch some examples of design animations that distract and others that enhance. Also see some alternatives to animations/rotations.

Related Questions

→ 26. Will images be used effectively in your design? **Page 63**

→ 35. Will your navigation menus be easy to use? **Page 88**

→ 36. Will your site load quickly? **Page 93**

→ 43. Will your site have special requirements for certain features to work? **Page 111**

Action Items

→ Before spending money on creating any animation, subject it to the content test described above, and if it passes that test, be sure it gets designed with the criteria listed here.

→ Never judge a finished animation on a blank screen. Always look at it within the context of a full page with content, even if that page is a mockup. If the animation is planned for every page, you need to test it on a working site where you're moving from page to page.

User Experience

Importance

35. Will Your Navigation Menus Be Easy to Use?

Much of the value of websites lies in their ability to easily connect vast amounts of information, both on the site and on the Internet. Within a website, good navigation makes it easy for visitors to find the information they need, and of all the navigation tools, menus are the most important.

In discussing site layout, I stressed how crucial it is to have your navigation where people expect it to be and in the same place on all pages. Now I'll show you some other design factors that can affect the usability of your menus.

The Real Work Is in Site Organization

> Another benefit of all your work with site organization is that you'll have a much more effective site map, which is an important aid to navigation.

Navigation will only be as good as the ways you can think of to present your content. Consider the different ways your material can be connected. Don't limit yourself to the way you're organizing the actual site files. There needs to be a logic to that organization, of course, but your navigation can reflect other ways of organizing as well.

Rule of Thumb   Key information on a site should never be more than three clicks away.

The primary goal of any navigation menu for sites with more than a few pages is to lead the visitor from the more general to the more specific. This drilling-down process is well illustrated on large shopping sites. On the Wal-Mart site, for example, I begin with Outdoor Living, which takes me to Lawn & Garden, then to Outdoor Heating & Lighting, and finally to Patio Heaters. There can be several ways to get your visitor to Patio Heaters, but it always begins with a more general topic—say, Patios and Decks. The more ways visitors can get to your material, the more likely they are to find it.

The Look of the Main Menu

It's worth mentioning again some points discussed in the design chapter. The main menu should stand out from the look of the rest of the site, but not so much that it's distracting. That means using colors that fit the site's color scheme and avoiding the use of graphics that make the menu hard to read. Figure 5-1 shows some examples of poorly-designed menus.

FIGURE 5-1

Be sure that the names of menu items are easy to read: Use a clear font, sized large enough, with good color contrast.

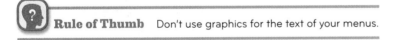
Rule of Thumb   Don't use graphics for the text of your menus.

If your menus use text controlled by style sheets rather than relying on graphics, you can quickly make adjustments to the font, size, and color during testing or any other time. It also saves time and money down the road when adding new pages or changing the name of a page—you don't have to create any graphics.

> You can still have graphics behind the menu text simply by using style sheets and specifying an image for the background of the text.

Main Menu Structure

To avoid overwhelming visitors, it's best to limit the visible items on any navigation menu to about seven, which means that if you have more than seven pages on your website, you'll need some options.

Horizontal vs. vertical main menus

It was common years ago to place main menus vertically in a left sidebar, but today most new sites use a horizontal structure at the top of the page. There are a number of good reasons for this, but I think one of the most important is that vertical menus on the left are a distraction from visitors scanning down the content of the page.

One argument for vertical menus is that they make it easy to add new pages and not be limited by the width of the site. However, main menus with too many choices are confusing. Vertical menus should generally be left to secondary menus, such as products, blog categories, or subpage listings for an area of a site.

For more on the debate, use the search term 🔍 horizontal versus vertical navigation.

One option is to display submenu items when you click through to a page on the main menu. The submenu might be on a sidebar or displayed below the main menu, as shown in Figure 5-2.

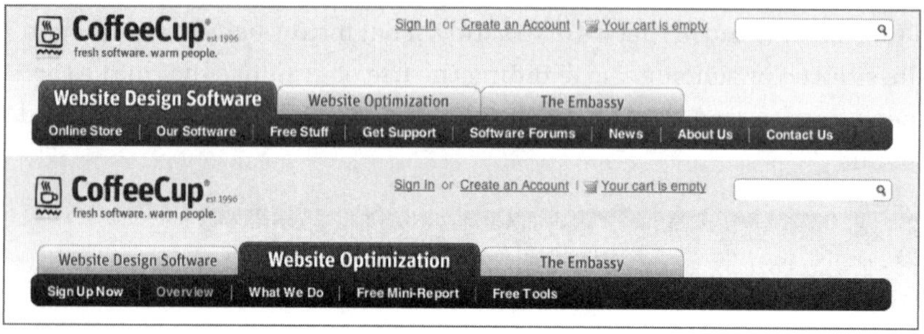

FIGURE 5-2

Because visitors cannot see the submenu choices unless they click through, this approach is best suited to situations in which it's clear that visitors are likely to take only one path. For example, on a real estate site the main menu might include two items: Buyers and Sellers. Visitors know which category they fall into, so they'll click that menu item without needing to know what's available under the other.

More and more large sites are taking this approach. To use the example of a newspaper or magazine style site, you don't need to see all the choices for Sports on the main menu. You know you want Sports, so click that, and see all the subpages available for sports.

> **Rule of Thumb**   Your main menu should be horizontal with no more than seven to ten visible buttons.

For websites with fewer than, say, 20 pages, it probably makes more sense to make all your choices available all the time. This is particularly true for new visitors because they aren't familiar with what's on your site and you don't want them to have to dig too hard to find it.

One option for having all or most of your pages on the main menu is to use what's called a dropline menu. It displays a second navigation bar with subpages for the menu item you've moused over, as shown in Figure 5-3 A. It's important to have this secondary menu in a different color or at least a very different shade so that visitors can distinguish it from the main menu.

Using cascading style sheets (CSS) to create the mouseover effects for menus is an efficient and flexible method. If you do use JavaScript for effects like drop-downs, make sure the files are not inefficiently written (that is, very large).

Revealing subpages on mouseover is more commonly done, however, by using drop-downs (or flyouts with vertical menus). These types of menus—illustrated in Figure 5-3 B—allow you to show several submenus at one time, plus your design does not have to include space for a second navigation area.

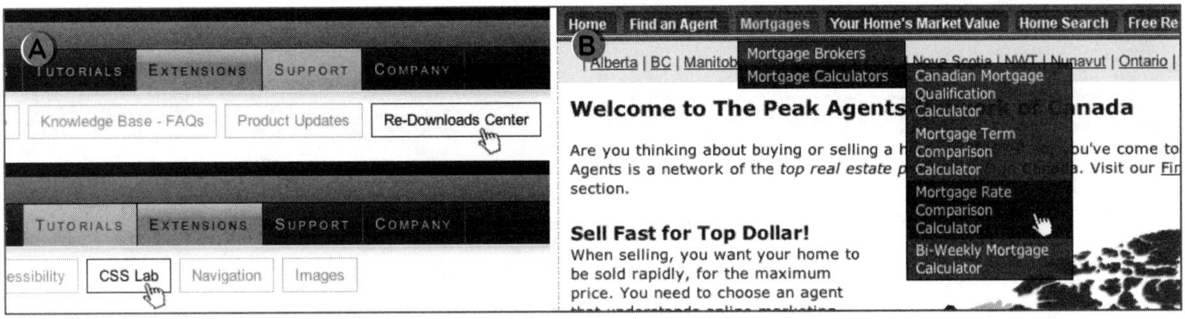

FIGURE 5-3

Rule of Thumb   Avoid having more than three levels of drop-downs.

The trick with drop-down menus is to not get carried away. Many scripts for these menus allow four, five, or even six levels of drop-downs, but after a point it becomes extremely confusing and even hard to use (you have to try to keep your mouse in the right spot for fear of losing all those levels should you accidentally move your mouse the wrong way).

Footer Menus

Having some navigation in the footer is something visitors have come to expect. This menu is particularly handy when you have more than a screen's worth of content on the page.

Footer menus tend to be used for housekeeping items such as contact information, privacy policies, advertising information, or terms of use. However, on smaller sites, you might want all your pages on this menu—or at least some key ones. Of course, a link to the home page should always be at the left side of the footer menu.

It's not necessary, but it can be helpful to show a small arrow or some other sign that a menu item has subitems. This was very common in the early days of drop-down menus, but people have become so used to mousing over tabs to see whether there's anything below that it's no longer crucial.

A link taking visitors back to the top of the current page is also a nice courtesy item on a footer menu.

On Video

Watch examples of navigation that confuse rather than help the visitor along with samples of navigation that works.

There's no need to style footer menus with anything more than an appropriate color. There's a tendency to make footer menu text slightly smaller than the body, but the main thing is to keep it easy to read, so don't go too small.

Related Questions

→ 22. Will the design of your site support your content or distract from it? **Page 52**

→ 23. Will your site layout make your content clear? **Page 55**

→ 33. Will the design of your site navigation complement or clutter your site? **Page 82**

→ 34. Will you be using animation in your design? **Page 84**

→ 57. Will your content be easily accessible? **Page 148**

Action Items

→ Bookmark some sample navigational structures that you find easy to use and make them a model for your design. This will help a designer understand the kind of functionality you're looking for and make suggestions about easier or better ways to accomplish it if possible.

→ If you're building on your own, check the source code of the examples you find and see how they're doing it.

36. Will Your Site Load Quickly?

Importance

If average website visitors take just 6 to 8 seconds before deciding whether to stay on a site, how long will they wait for the site to actually load? Patience is not something you should take for granted when other websites are only a click away.

Start testing your site's loading time early in the development stages. You want to catch the time suckers in your design, coding, or content as soon as possible. Table 5-1 shows some of the most common time consumers and some of the easiest to change:

TABLE 5-1: Common Time Consumers

PROBLEM	SOLUTIONS
Images	Keep the physical size of all images as small as possible (the average size of photos from a camera is 2,500KB, but an 80KB image can fill a computer screen).
	Optimize images for the Web using an image-editing program.
	Look at the total number of images on a page. If you have 40 graphics and photos each averaging 10KB, that's 400KB.
Multimedia	Optimize files as much as possible.
	Host video files on a separate server, such as YouTube.
Scripts	Make sure that coding such as JavaScript or CSS are in files separate from the HTML page.
	Consolidate several scripts of the same type into a single file.

Ways to Measure Page Loading Time

There are many easy-to-use tools that show you varying amounts of information about page loading time:

+ **Browser plug-ins**—Some browsers offer plug-ins that will monitor the loading time of websites. Check the resources section for this chapter at the back of the book for some plug-in options.

+ **Online services**—There are sites on the Web where you can enter the URL of a page and get not only the time it takes for the page to load, but detailed information on every single element

The time it takes to load a page is one of the factors in search engine rankings. Although load time might not count for a great deal calculating rank, it reflects the fact that speed is important to visitors.

Faster Internet connections have allowed the total file size of web pages to increase without sacrificing load time. Since 2003, average page size has tripled to just over 300KB.

More and more visitors are arriving at websites by way of shortened URLs like this: http://bit.ly/au5ZBd. Made popular on Twitter (to reduce the length of messages), they're being used by more and more sites. However the processing of these short URLs can add to load times, even more reason to keep your pages lean.

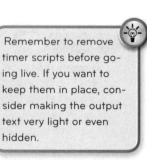

Remember to remove timer scripts before going live. If you want to keep them in place, consider making the output text very light or even hidden.

On Video

Watch a demonstration of an online page-loading analysis.

on the page, allowing you to pinpoint the culprits, as shown in Figure 5-4.

➜ **Scripts**—There are page timer scripts for JavaScript, PHP, ASP, and Perl. Just place them in the HTML of your pages during testing and you can keep an eye on things with little messages on the page. The advantage of this method is that you can get instant feedback on any page without having to take any extra steps. Make sure the script measures all aspects of page loading so you get the most accurate total.

FIGURE 5-4

Related Questions

➜ 49. Will you use tables or style sheets to lay out your site? **Page 126**

➜ 52. Will your HTML be bloated? **Page 134**

➜ 54. Will your nontext files use the proper file types? **Page 140**

➜ 62. How will you be using video or audio in your content? **Page 164**

Action Items

➜ For more ways to reduce load times, enter the search phrase 🔍 **speed up web page loading**.

➜ If you can, observe test users as pages are loading. Speed tests might show the loading time is good, but actual users might still be frustrated.

37. Will Visitors Easily Know How to Stay in Touch with You?

Importance

Websites allow you to start a dialogue with your visitors by using a variety of tools. But you have to make it easy for visitors to find those tools.

The most common way to help visitors get in touch is a contact button somewhere in your navigation structure. There are two main schools of thought on locating your contact button: at the end of your main navigation or in a smaller menu near the main navigation. Examples of each are shown in Figure 5-5.

> If you deal with the public, it's handy to show your general contact information on all pages, usually in the sidebar or the footer. Include the address, phone number, hours of operation, and so on.

FIGURE 5-5

The idea of the smaller secondary menu is to separate housekeeping elements from actual content items as well as to keep the size of the main menu manageable. However, if you have only three or four content menu items, it's probably best to put all pages on one menu. Whichever method you choose, the contact link should also be on the short menu in your footer.

Social media is another crucial way of staying in touch with your visitors, so make sure links to your accounts are always visible (links that encourage people to share your content using social media are covered in a later chapter). Figure 5-6 shows some examples of prominently displaying your social media links.

New methods are always being devised for displaying contact information, so keep an eye out for ways to improve your site. A recent trend for social media links, for example, is to display a thin box at the bottom of the browser window covering the regular content, as shown in Figure 5-7.

> You can also display the latest feeds from your social media accounts, but if you do, make sure you keep up those feeds or else it can look bad to have information that's a month old or more.

> Don't get too fancy with icons for various social media—you want visitors to quickly know to what you're linking. Use standard logos.

FIGURE 5-6

FIGURE 5-7

Thin boxes that appear at the bottom or top of the browser window can be handy to attract attention, but here are a couple of tips to keep users from being annoyed by these boxes: 1) Either have the box display only on the home page or create a script that shows it only once to a visitor no matter which page they arrive at; and 2) make it very clear how to close the box.

If you have a newsletter or mailing list signup form, place it as high up on your pages as possible. Because these forms are usually very short—just an e-mail address and sometimes a name—they can even go in the header. Right-hand sidebars are a popular place for newsletter forms, but you also see them at the bottom of pages. It's also possible to have the form drop down directly from your menu, though the disadvantage is that you have to mouse over to know what the offer is.

Related Questions

→ 35. Will your navigation menus be easy to use? **Page 88**

→ 69. How will you build your e-mail list? **Page 194**

→ 74. How will you integrate your site with social media? **Page 209**

→ 96. Will you routinely check your contact information? **Page 282**

Action Items

→ Ask a test user to find your contact page as quickly as possible. Test them without having seen the site and after they've been on for a while.

→ Using an online translator, display your site in a foreign language and ask a first-time user to find your contact information.

Importance

38. Will Your Site Use Popups?

Popups are any type of content that covers part of the current browser window or opens an additional small window based on a user action, such as mousing over a link or simply loading the page. There are three primary types of popups, which are not all that different technically, but have very different looks and interactions. Figures 5-8, 5-9, and 5-10 show examples of each.

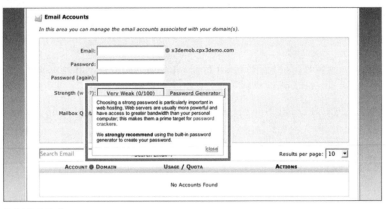

FIGURE 5-8

Popup ads are a separate issue and will be dealt with in the marketing and promotion chapter. Here the concern is with popups that present functionality or content.

The first type of popup is a box that displays close to the cursor when the user mouses over or clicks something. They are typically used to provide help to the visitor—instructions, word meanings, or even images—without having to navigate away from the page. However, in the case of popups with added content, ask yourself whether that content shouldn't be in the body of the text.

The second type of popup greys out the current browser window and the new content is displayed in the center of the screen, as shown in Figure 5-9.

When using popups within body text, you should avoid having more than two or three in a single paragraph. It can get annoying to have popups every time you move your cursor.

Commonly used for photo galleries, this approach solves a lot of the problems with traditional browser popups. The user can see the browser window, but not access any of its content, so there's no chance of accidentally clicking away from the popup and getting confused. The popup content does not look like a browser window, which further reduces confusion. With clear controls, in particular an exit button, this type of popup is very user-friendly.

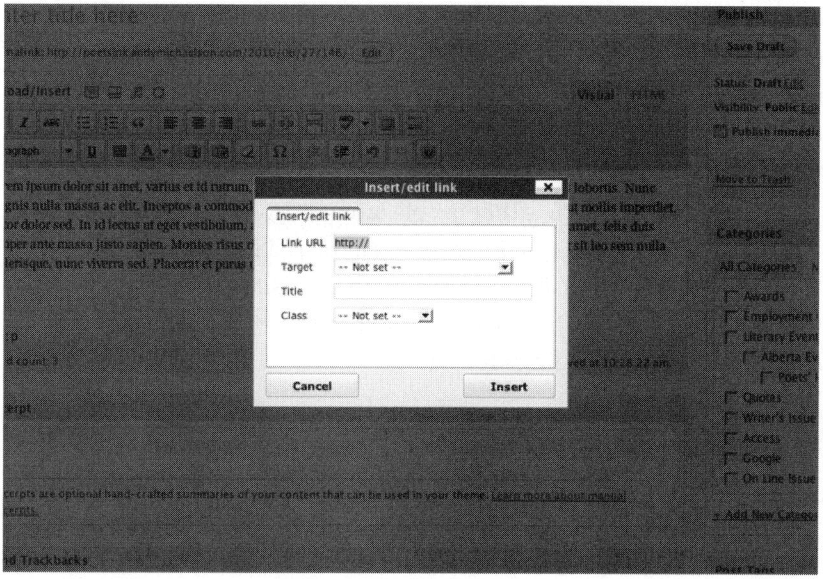

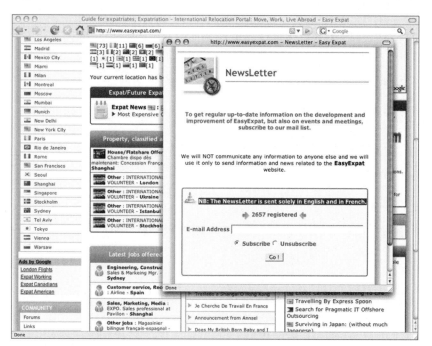

FIGURE 5-9

The third type of popup looks like a normal browser window, but is smaller and usually without controls, such as back buttons, as shown in Figure 5-10.

FIGURE 5-10

For any popup that doesn't automatically close, make sure the Close button is clearly displayed.

Automatic popups—ones the user does not control—should be used with discretion. Popups that display when a page loads are annoying because you haven't even seen the site or the page, and you're being asked for something. Popups when you exit are like being told you can't leave the site without permission.

On Video

Watch some examples of popups at work and see how you might use them on your site.

The lack of browser controls was originally intended to keep focus on the content and prevent users from getting confused by trying to navigate or take other browser actions. Ironically, this lack of controls can lead to confusion because it still looks like a browser, and people wonder why they can't do anything.

But the real problem is that people often don't see the Close Window button that good designers put in, or even the red X at the top right of the window. Instead, users click the main browser window to get back to where they were, only to discover later that they have one or more small popups still hanging around.

Related Questions

➡ 34. Will you be using animation in your design? **Page 84**

➡ 44. Could you hide some content or options to reduce visual clutter? **Page 113**

➡ 55. Which languages other than HTML will you use to build your site? **Page 143**

Action Items

➡ Make a list of potential popups for your site and then be brutally honest about whether they help or hinder visitors and your content.

➡ Be sure to test popups with some users to make sure it will be clear to visitors how the popup works, how to get rid of it, and so on.

39. Will Your Forms Be Easy to Use?

Importance

Online forms are handy for visitors and for you, but they need to be clear and simple to use.

Here are some form design basics:

→ Keep the form as short as it possibly can be.

→ Leave adequate space between individual fields so the form doesn't look crowded and intimidating.

→ Group related fields and visually separate the areas.

→ Clearly designate required fields.

You can also make forms easy by using drop-down menus for anything that has fixed choices—date of birth, countries, states, and so on—rather than asking people to type it out themselves. Where the information is unique but still structured—a postal code, for example—you can give an example of the format you want next to the box visitors fill in. See this at work in Figure 5-11.

> Make sure users can tab from one field to the next. This is a common way of getting around forms, and if it's not sequential, people can miss entering something.

> If the form is long, it's helpful to break it into multiple pages. Be sure to show visitors a breadcrumb trail, not only indicating what sections have been completed but also allowing them to go backward and make changes.

ountry	United States ▼		Phone
Code			[ ] – [ ] – [ ]
	(USA: 11111 or 11111-1111. Canada: A1A_1A1)		### ### ####
ource	⊙ Yes ⦿ No		Arrival Date
vroom	Select one		[ ] / [ ] / [ ]
ubject	Product ▼		MM DD YYYY

FIGURE 5-11

Provide a help link next to the form field if you think visitors might not understand what you're asking for. A simple popup when they mouse over a question mark or some appropriate symbol is an elegant solution, as shown by the examples in Figure 5-12.

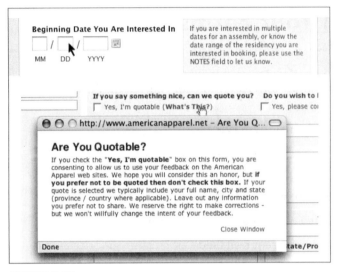

FIGURE 5-12

Don't forget a thank you page or thank you message when the form has been submitted. Not only is it an opportunity to provide visitors with more information, it's also a clear indication that the form was successfully submitted.

What happens when visitors miss a required form field or enter incorrect information is very important. It's frustrating when they can't submit the form, and the reason for the error is unclear. Vague error messages like the one in Figure 5-13 can cause visitors to give up.

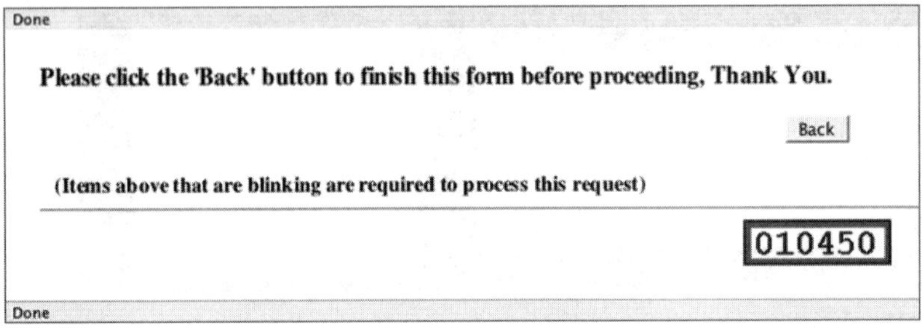

Done

Please click the 'Back' button to finish this form before proceeding, Thank You.

Back

(Items above that are blinking are required to process this request)

010450

Done

FIGURE 5-13

On Video

See examples of good (and not so good) form layouts. Watch an example of form validation as you enter information.

A good form-validation system will highlight the field where the problem has occurred before the visitor leaves the page, but just as importantly it will help explain what the problem is, as shown in Figure 5-14.

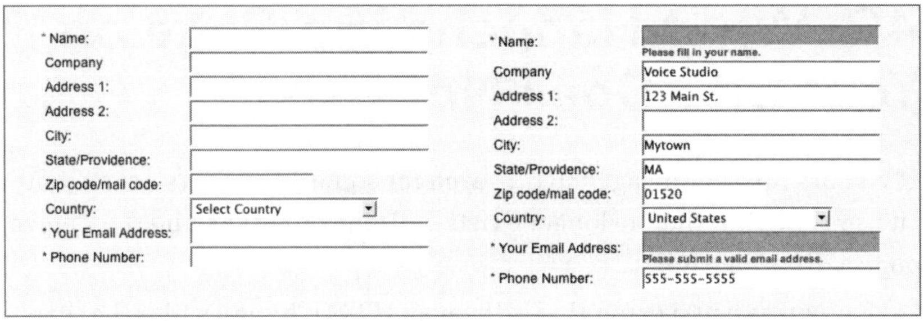

FIGURE 5-14

There are a couple of points at which to do form validation:

➤ As the information is being entered

➤ When the form is being submitted

Rule of Thumb   When a form is longer than the browser window or is spread over two or more pages, validate information as it's being entered.

The form validation discussed here is for user-friendliness. Forms should also be validated for security purposes to prevent malicious code from being uploaded.

Related Questions

➤ 65. What basic content pages will be on your site? **Page 174**

➤ 94. Will you be regularly checking your site's functionality? **Page 277**

➤ 100. How will you protect your site from attacks? **Page 295**

Action Items

➤ Test your forms to make sure the validation is working properly. Enter phone numbers with too few numbers or deliberately don't choose a drop-down menu item. Really try to mess things up and see if the form can handle it. Don't leave a user stuck and unable to do something.

➤ Have several people try your form—did they all submit it successfully? Even then, did they have any points of uncertainty during the process?

103

40. What Happens if a Page on Your Site Does Not Exist?

> If you move or change the name of a page after launching your site, you should create a 301 redirect and not simply leave the server to generate a 404 error. For details, search on the phrase 🔍 301 redirect.

If visitors mistype a page URL, search for something that's not on your site, or try a link that no longer exists, will they be stuck and then move on to a different site?

Known as a 404 error, this is the way HTML handles files that can't be found on a server. If there are no other instructions on the server, a visitor's browser will generate messages like the ones shown in Figure 5-15, which everyone has seen at one time or another.

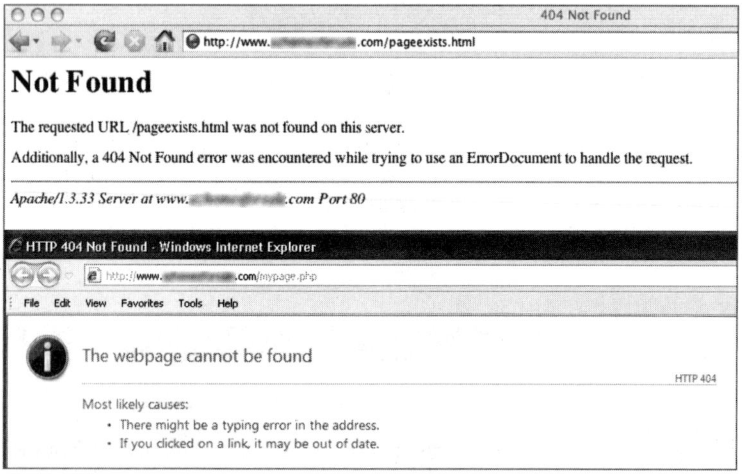

![Figure 5-15 showing two browser windows with 404 errors]

Not Found

The requested URL /pageexists.html was not found on this server.

Additionally, a 404 Not Found error was encountered while trying to use an ErrorDocument to handle the request.

Apache/1.3.33 Server at www.[redacted].com Port 80

HTTP 404 Not Found - Windows Internet Explorer

File   Edit   View   Favorites   Tools   Help

ⓘ The webpage cannot be found

HTTP 404

Most likely causes:
- There might be a typing error in the address.
- If you clicked on a link, it may be out of date.

FIGURE 5-15

> An under construction notice on a page is almost worse than a generic 404 error because you've knowingly led the visitor to an empty page. If a page has no content, don't have it on your site at all. Or, use it as a promotional opportunity and give visitors a good taste of what's coming on that page—at least then they won't feel it's a wasted click.

The problem is that you're left with no choice but to press your browser's back button, and that usually means returning to a search engine or another site.

The alternative is to create your own 404 error page and hopefully keep visitors on your site. In order to do that, however, your server needs to know which file to use for the error page. Some hosts have this already set up, or your hosting control panel will automate the process—check with your hosting provider. It's also possible to make the server changes yourself, but you have to know what you're doing. To read up on manual changes, search for the term 🔍 custom 404 page.

When it comes to designing the 404 error page, it's simplest to make it like all your other pages, with full navigation, as shown in Figure 5-16.

FIGURE 5-16

Make sure your custom 404 page is larger than 512 bytes in size (that's bytes, not kilobytes or KB, so just over half of a 1KB page). This is because some browsers will still use their own 404 page if the custom page is less than 512 bytes.

What to include on the error page:

- A short apology, styled for your audience: businesslike, fun, personal, and so on

- A reminder about mistyped URLs

- If you have a search box and it's not part of your main header, include it here.

- Put a large link to your site map.

Visitors don't mind errors; they mind being left out in the cold and unsure what to do. A good 404 error page can help keep visitors on your side even when they've been inconvenienced. For some creative error pages, search for the term 🔍 **funny 404 pages**.

On Video

View more examples of good (and not so good) 404 error pages.

Related Questions

- 57. Will your content be easily accessible? **Page 148**

- 94. Will you be regularly checking your site's functionality? **Page 277**

- 95. Do you have a plan for updating site content? **Page 279**

Action Item

- Check with your hosting provider (or if you're using a content management system, check the manual) to see whether 404 pages can be customized.

Importance

41. How Easily Will Your Pages Print?

Have you ever tried to print a web page and got dozens of blank pages with occasional bits of content? Or a dark background causes your printer to use huge amounts of toner to produce something unreadable anyway? You can save your visitors from frustrations such as these by making your pages printer-friendly.

> You can check what your pages will look like when printed by selecting File ➜ Print Preview in your browser.

There are two approaches to page printing:

➜ Create print-friendly copies of individual pages.

➜ Create a separate style sheet to control how any page will print.

The first technique is often used by media websites for printing their articles. The example in Figure 5-17 shows the web page with a popup window containing the specially formatted print version.

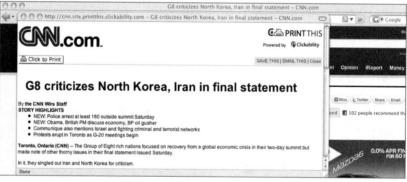

FIGURE 5-17

The trouble with this approach is that you have to maintain two separate pages. This is not a big problem if you're using a content management system that might provide the ability to use a separate template to configure content for printing. Even then, however, if visitors link to the print version instead of the original, the original page loses the value of those links because to the search engines they're two separate pages.

Fortunately, there's a very simple answer for the average website owner, and that's the use of a special style sheet. By including media="print" in the link to this style sheet, your browser's print function will automatically use that style sheet instead of the regular one. No special print button or scripting is required beyond this, which is good because users either don't see special print buttons or if they do, they still use the browser print button out of habit.

A print style sheet works in two ways: hiding unnecessary content and reformatting content as necessary.

Suppose that you don't want the sidebar printed out. You simply create a rule in the print style sheet that hides it. As long as you make sure elements on a page can be targeted individually by creating good CSS markup, you can do things such as print only your logo and nothing else in your site's header area.

For the content you do want printed, it might be helpful to style it differently from the way it appears on the website. For example, if your text has a colored background on your website, you'll want to switch it to white for printing purposes. Or the font you use online might be better changed to a printer-friendly font. The point is that you can do all of this without changing or duplicating your content—the style sheet handles everything.

To know whether a print style sheet is in place for your site, see Figure 5-18. On the left is what you'd expect to see in the header of your source code (or you might need to look in your main style sheet for a section such as the one on the right).

> CSS supports 10 media types, of which print is only one. You can have separate style sheets for Braille, handhelds, and more.

> **On Video**
>
> View some real-time examples of how CSS style sheets make printing easy.

```
<meta name="viewport" content="width=780">
<base target="_top">

<style type="text/css" media="all">
@import "/bubbleicious.css";
</style>
<link rel="stylesheet" type="text/css" href="/print.css" media="print">

<link rel="shortcut icon" type="image/ico" href="/favicon.ico">
<link rel="search" type="application/opensearchdescription+xml" title="H'

<script src="http://www.google.com/jsapi"></script>
<script>
    google.load("jquery", "1");
</script>
<script src="/sourcescripts.js" type="text/javascript"></script>

<script type="text/javascript">
```

```
.widget-area {
        -webkit-text-size-adjust: 120%;
}
#site-description {
        -webkit-text-size-adjust: none;
}

/* =Print Style
--------------------------------------------
@media print {
        body {
                background:none !important;
        }
        #wrapper {
                float: none !important;
                clear: both !important;
                display: block !important;
                position: relative !important;
        }
        #header {
                border-bottom: 2pt solid #000;
```

FIGURE 5-18

It's easy in this digital age to forget the importance to many people of printing out material from web pages. One of the great things about print style sheets is that they're easy to set up and implement, so you don't have to weigh the cost against how many people you think might need to print.

Related Questions

➤ 23. Will your site layout make your content clear? **Page 55**

➤ 49. Will you use tables or style sheets to lay out your site? **Page 126**

➤ 50. How effectively will style sheets be used on your website? **Page 129**

Action Items

➤ Make sure your CSS allows you to easily hide the elements on the page that you don't want printed.

➤ Test your print style sheet on several different browsers and with different printers to make sure everything comes out the way you want it.

42. How User-Friendly Will Your Links Be?

Importance

Linking to other pages on your site or to other sites is one of the most powerful features of the Web, so it's important to make it easy for visitors to identify and use links.

The first point to consider with links is whether to display them with the conventional underline style. Because text can look cluttered when it's underlined, some designers choose to display links using color alone. If you go this route, it can be helpful to display the underline style when the visitor mouses over the link, just to help confirm that it is a link.

Coloring links is important because using the same color as the other text, even with underlining or bolding links, is just too confusing to a visitor. Deciding what color to use must strike a balance between clarity and distraction. You need visitors to notice that text is a link, but you don't want it to overpower the rest of the text, particularly with long links or large numbers of links in a single paragraph.

The color of links when you mouse over them should change in some way to help reinforce that the visitor is on a link. This is a must if you're not using underlining at all, but even if you style the mouseover with an underline, the color change is important for catching people's eye. The mouseover color needs to be enough of a contrast to indicate that something has happened; it's best to use a shade of grey or a different color.

One of the most neglected aspects of link styling is what to do with links that people have already visited. By default, if you specify a color for links, but not for visited links, the same color will be used. Often it isn't a conscious decision to not distinguish visited links, but simply a lack of thinking about it.

The idea behind visited links is to help users know where they have and have not gone. A great example of this is on a site's Links page, in which there might be dozens and dozens of useful links. Knowing which ones you've been to can save a lot of time. Keep in mind that browsers can remember where you've been for months at a time, so if

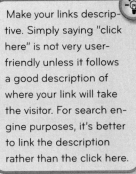

Avoid mixing and matching link styles. If you don't use underlining in the body of the text, keep that convention on other areas of the site.

If you don't set a color for links, browsers automatically use their own, and it might or might not suit the look of your site.

Make your links descriptive. Simply saying "click here" is not very user-friendly unless it follows a good description of where your link will take the visitor. For search engine purposes, it's better to link the description rather than the click here.

When linking to documents, make it clear what file type they are.

your style sheet distinguishes visited links, the value can last a long time as visitors return to your site on different occasions.

There are two choices for how you send visitors to links they click: a new window or tab is opened, or the contents of the current window are replaced. There's a lot of debate over which method is most user-friendly under which circumstances. For more on this, search for the term 🔍 should you open links in a new window.

❓ **Rule of Thumb**   Don't open links to pages on your own site in a new window or tab.

On Video

Watch some examples of linking problems, in particular issues of how to color links.

Linking to other sites is a different matter. There are arguments on both sides: Some say it's just as confusing to have new windows or tabs opening, whereas others see it as natural to have a different site in a separate window. There's really no way to win on this one—whatever you decide, someone won't like it, so take comfort in the fact that someone will like it.

Related Questions

➤ 35. Will your navigation menus be easy to use? **Page 88**

➤ 38. Will your site use popups? **Page 98**

➤ 60. How effectively will your content use links? **Page 158**

➤ 89. Will your links to and from other sites be search-engine friendly? **Page 257**

Action Items

➤ Make sure links are part of your color scheme decisions.

➤ Test if users are having any trouble with links that open in new windows or tabs, or links to documents, and so on.

43. Will Your Site Have Special Requirements for Certain Features to Work?

Importance

When making decisions about features for your website or its organization, ask yourself whether you're putting up needless barriers (in this case, I literally mean barriers). There's nothing more frustrating when you click something and receive a message such as the ones in Figure 5-19.

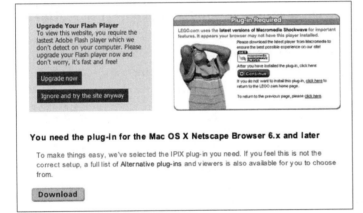

FIGURE 5-19

You're trying to get some information or be entertained, and the website owner is making you work for it: Stop and download an unknown piece of software you're not even sure you'll need again.

Flash is an example of software that you have to add to your browser as a plug-in. At one time it was hit or miss whether users had Flash installed in their browser, so website owners had to decide whether it was worth annoying users who didn't have the plug-in. Now that Flash is standard in browsers (except for some mobile devices), it's no longer the barrier it once was.

Standard or not, if you create anything on your website that uses a plug-in, you should have an alternative for those without the plug-in. Even JavaScript needs to be considered a plug-in because people are able to turn it off, and some do. So if you have a drop-down menu that uses JavaScript, for example, you should plan for how it will function if

You sometimes see warnings that a site is "best viewed in browser X" with a link to download it. Don't go this route. If a problem is so severe that someone can't properly see your site in one of the major browsers, you need to fix the problem, not force people to get a new browser. At the same time, it's not always cost effective to make sure your site is viewable in browsers more than three or four versions old.

JavaScript is turned off. What will happen to your fancy site introduction done in Flash if someone doesn't have Flash or has disabled it?

Having a link so the visitor can download the necessary plug-in is one part of providing an alternative, but if the information is so vital, you should offer it in a different format, even if it just outlines the basics. For example, make the text from a Flash presentation available in HTML or provide a separate graphic for a slideshow that requires JavaScript. People can then decide whether they want to see the full version by downloading the software or turning a plug-in back on.

Registration is another barrier you need to carefully consider before implementing on your site. Every situation will be different, but unless you're running an intranet, be sure to offer enough free material that visitors will still want to come to your site even if they're not registered. In other words, registration should always be an added value proposition. By signing up for a mailing list, paying a subscription fee, joining an organization, and so on, you're then given access to more information.

Another barrier to consider is the documents you make available on your site. Clearly state the file type of these documents so visitors will know if they can even open them. If the file requires a program that some visitors might not have, consider putting it into a more universal format (PDF is always the best bet).

> If some of your content is hidden from unregistered visitors, make sure you clearly label it as such and provide an obvious link to the registration/sign-up page.

> Documents in Microsoft Word cannot be opened by everyone. They might be standard in the workplace, but not everywhere else.

> **On Video**
>
> See examples of offering limited information with the ability to sign up for premium service.

Related Questions

→ 31. Will your site design display well in different browsers? **Page 76**

→ 34. Will you be using animation in your design? **Page 84**

→ 55. Which languages other than HTML will you use to build your site? **Page 143**

→ 97. Will you have content you can't afford to have stolen? **Page 284**

Action Item

→ Before you build a web feature using a nonstandard plug-in, think about whether it's absolutely necessary. Is this feature important enough to put up a barrier for some or many visitors? If it is so important, can it be created some other way?

44. Could You Hide Some Content or Options to Reduce Visual Clutter?

Importance

Providing visitors with more content or more options is always good, but that can lead to extremely long and/or visually crowded pages. Here are some ways to answer this dilemma.

One solution for longer content is the Read More link commonly used on news sites and blogs. You present the visitor with a headline and a summary of what they'll find when they click the link for the full story. The same idea can apply to a page listing all your services, for example, with a short description of each and a link to get full details on a separate page.

Advances in JavaScript and CSS have made popular what I call the Show More solution to long content, a couple examples of which are shown in Figure 5-20.

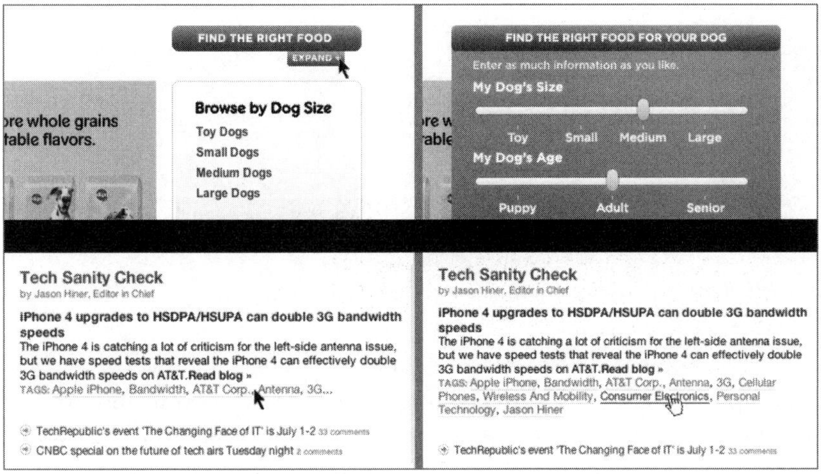

FIGURE 5-20

Here the idea is that the visitor does not leave the page but simply reveals additional content by clicking the Show More link. An excellent use of this is on Frequently Asked Questions (FAQ) pages. Instead of the visitor having to jump around the page using internal links or scrolling down to find what they need, they scan through the questions and reveal only the answers they want.

Another example of using the Show More technique is a page with tabbed content. This is useful when you have several related options that are easily distinguished in short titles on the tabs. When the visitor clicks a tab, the content on the page is replaced by the content for that tab. This technique can be used on a restaurant review site, for instance. One tab would show menus, another tab the location and map, and another tab would display reviews.

> **Rule of Thumb**   When choosing to hide some content, make sure the most useful or interesting content is visible when the page first loads.

The Show More concept can also be applied to functions you want to offer the visitor without cluttering up the visual space. Look at the example from the content management system WordPress in Figure 5-21.

FIGURE 5-21

When you place your cursor over a particular row, it reveals your options. The idea here is that each row has the same options, so why repeat them over and over again visually when they can be hidden until you need them. On the left of Figure 5-22, you can see how cluttered these blog posts look when then repeat the same menu. The right side shows how it can look by hiding the menus until moused over.

When using the Show More technique, it's equally important to make clear how to hide the content again after it's been shown. A plus symbol is often used to indicate "show" and a minus sign to "hide."

Don't confuse hiding related chunks of content with the use of subheadings in a long article. Visitors need to scan through a single article and then quickly move back and forth between sections. That's very different from wanting to see related but individual chunks of information one at a time—for example, Features, Specifications, Reviews—of a single product.

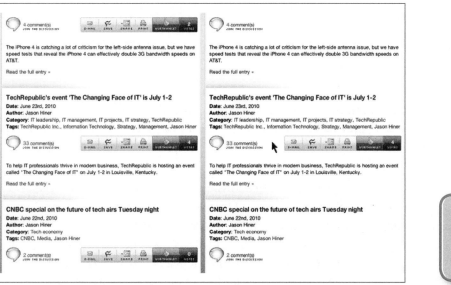

FIGURE 5-22

On Video

Watch examples of the Show More technique at work.

Related Questions

➤ 30. How will elements within content be set off from the body text? **Page 73**

➤ 38. Will your site use popups? **Page 98**

➤ 50. How effectively will style sheets be used on your website? **Page 129**

Action Items

➤ Go through your site plan and think about which pages can benefit from the use of these techniques. You might find in some cases that you can fit in more content than you originally planned or that you can break up longer text into tabbed content, for example.

➤ Be sure to test what you come up with, in particular when you're depending on mouseovers to reveal content. Do visitors easily figure it out for themselves?

Importance

45. How Easily Will Visitors Find Important Details Specific to Your Site?

Most of the questions in this chapter deal with user experience issues that apply to virtually any site. But there will be elements that are specific to your site, and this question will help you think about how to make them user-friendly.

Here's a simple example: If you accept credit cards, let everyone know. People usually think of this when they accept online payments, but even if you accept credit cards only offline, tell your visitors. Where exactly to place credit card information on a page will depend on how important it is to your visitors. Does it need to be on every page or is it enough to place it on pages such as Contact or Services? Figure 5-23 shows some examples of where you can place credit card logos.

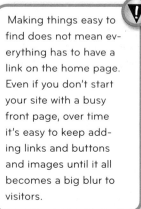

FIGURE 5-23

An FAQ page is another good place to put this information. However you choose to do it, don't make your visitors guess or have to contact you just to find out something as basic as whether you take credit cards.

Suppose you're looking for a dentist. One website contains a list of insurance companies the dentist deals with (yours is among them), and the other doesn't. Which dentist will you call first? Think about what pieces of information will be most crucial to your visitors and make sure they're easy to find.

Making things easy to find does not mean everything has to have a link on the home page. Even if you don't start your site with a busy front page, over time it's easy to keep adding links and buttons and images until it all becomes a big blur to visitors.

For example, the list of insurance companies could go in the sidebar of all pages describing the dentist's services. At the same time, have a text link to the list anywhere on the site that it's relevant to mention "We deal with a wide variety of insurance companies." Links such as these are important because they're immediately relevant to what the visitor is reading, so you've done them a favor by anticipating that they'll want this information.

> Look at other sites in your field for ideas on the kinds of details you can emphasize on your site.

If you're using a graphic to convey information, such as the credit card logos or as an enticement to click for more information, remember that you don't need to take up a lot of real estate or visitors' attention with large images. With careful placement on the page (for example, avoid a lot of button images tightly packed in a row) and simple design, your button will stand out better and achieve its effect.

Contextual links are an effective way of drawing attention to additional details within your site. These can take the form of sidebar menus or related items lists at the end of a page. If you're in a particular section of a plumbing site, you could list some helpful articles.

These contextual links are part of your navigation system, but they're so specific that you don't want them on your main menu, even with drop-downs.

If you have frequent temporary information that needs to be quickly and clearly conveyed, consider designing a special area of the site that displays only when the information is relevant. For example, a theatre company that has ongoing fundraising events could have an area at the top of the header or in the sidebar that appears only when the event is taking place. This is nicer than an automatic popup, and because it appears only every once in a while, it doesn't fade into the background of your attention, as can be the case with What's New sections.

Related Questions

➤ 23. Will your site layout make your content clear? **Page 55**

➤ 57. Will your content be easily accessible? **Page 148**

➤ 66. Will you be blogging on your site? **Page 183**

Action Item

➤ Make a list of what you consider to be important details about your business or organization and prioritize them based on their value to visitors. Ask someone who knows the organization to do the same. Then have potential visitors take the combined lists and prioritize the results.

Importance

46. How Will You Test the User-Friendliness of Your Site?

Throughout this book I emphasize the importance of testing your site in various ways before launching, but it's also important to conduct tests in the best ways possible.

If you can, leave your users alone to do the testing. They're much more likely to be honest in their reactions if you're not sitting next to them. Ask if you can record them visually during the test (put it in writing that it isn't going up on YouTube or being sold).

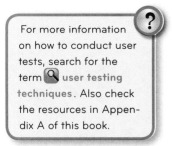

For more information on how to conduct user tests, search for the term 🔍 **user testing techniques**. Also check the resources in Appendix A of this book.

> **Rule of Thumb**   Test early and test often. Even if it's just getting a friend to look at a rough site plan over a coffee, the sooner you get feedback, the better.

When you are in the same room, be sure not to give any explicit or implicit reactions to the subject's responses. Even a simple nodding of your head can lead people to think they're on the right path and keep giving similar responses.

Don't tell people what you're testing. If someone knows you're interested in how the navigation works, they'll use it differently than they normally would.

Keep in mind that just because someone has looked at something, it doesn't mean they understand it. That's one of the reasons why eye-tracking systems take you only so far. You might notice the user looking at a slideshow on the page, but questioning them later will tell you whether they got the point of the slideshow.

Don't ask leading questions. If you've left people to test on their own and haven't told them what you're testing for, your questions later shouldn't lead them toward certain answers. Ask a very general question first and see what the person says. If you're not hearing anything about the topics you're interested in, then you can get more specific, but still don't say things such as "Did you find the site loaded pretty quickly?" because some people will say yes because they think that's the answer you want to hear.

Any testing is better than no testing. E-mailing a link to 10 friends with a request for any feedback will give you something to go on.

Give subjects a task. Visitors come to your site with a goal in mind. Simply telling a test subject to look at your site isn't very realistic, so give them a task. If you're testing a pet service's website, have the subject look for pet walking services, but put it in terms of a scenario: You need someone to walk your dog in the early morning and water your plants.

Pick subjects who are interested. If you're testing a site for real estate investors, find people with an interest in real estate. Even if you're testing for features of the site that have nothing to do with the content, someone who isn't interested in real estate will not see the site in the same way.

If time or money allow, try to follow up whatever you do with a different type of testing. For instance, if users fill out a survey, also ask questions that come at the same subject a bit differently. You might find that the two answers conflict.

There are online services that will conduct testing for you at rates affordable for small businesses (see the resources for this chapter in Appendix A). The advantage here is that you get a larger number and broader cross-section of people. Also, you benefit from the techniques used by these services, which can help eliminate some of the issues that arise when setting up tests on your own.

> Go where the people are. If you have a gardening site, approach a local gardening club about finding test volunteers. Have a small gift for each participant, such as a free service from you or a $10 gift card to a gardening store.

Related Questions

→ 22. Will the design of your site support your content or distract from it? **Page 52**

→ 33. Will the design of your site navigation complement or clutter your site? **Page 82**

→ 39. Will your forms be easy to use? **Page 101**

Action Items

→ Make a list of what you think needs testing on your site. After getting some feedback or doing some tests, compare your list with what people actually responded to or had troubles with.

→ Based on your site schedule, budget, and time, plan to test at the three key stages of development: draft plan, design, and first working version of the site.

Construction

In this chapter:

Importance

47. Will Your Site Be Static or Dynamic?

If you look at the source code for any web page using your browser, you'll see a complete HTML page. But whether that entire page is in a single file on your server or whether it's in bits and pieces is the difference between static and dynamic websites.

Building an HTML page, especially one with a simple design, is not a huge task. It's when you have more than a few of these static pages and you want to change something common to them all. Search and replace does work to some extent, but then you have to upload every file you've changed. And the changes never end, so you're constantly trying to keep up with all these files. Now imagine if you have 100 or 1,000 pages. Static websites become a nightmare to keep running, which is why people turned to dynamic sites.

The advantage of having your web pages assembled out of bits and pieces is that you save a lot of repetition in the construction of any particular page. Take the case of the top region of your site, or the header area as it is known. In most cases, it will contain your logo and your page navigation. It's user-friendly to have the same header from page to page, so keep it in a single file that's shared by every page on your site.

When it comes right down to it, even the content is a separate bit that should be stored on its own, so a "page" becomes nothing more than an assembly tool, as you can see in this example from a Word-Press page template in Figure 6-1 (the actual assembly is what the content management system [CMS] does).

The other big advantage of dynamically-built sites is that they're largely future-proof. If you change your logo, you have to replace only one image; if you change colors or want a new layout, you'd probably only have to change one or two files. There's nothing so constant as change, so why make it difficult to change your site.

> **Rule of Thumb**   Any website should be built dynamically, even if it consists of a single page.

Dynamic construction is clearly the way to go. But how you construct a dynamic site is an important issue, particularly for making it easy to administer by anyone. That's when you need to look into a CMS.

Some people try to solve the "common content" issue by creating HTML frames for the header, sidebar, footer, and the content. Only the content frame would change on each page. It sounds good, but it's a bad idea for many reasons, the most important of which is that they create serious problems for search engines. For more on this, search for the phrase 🔍 HTML frames are bad.

Edit Themes

Page Template (page.php)   **Select theme to edit:**

```php
<?php get_header(); ?>

<div id="content">

<?php if (have_posts()) : while (have_posts()) : the_post(); ?>
<div <?php post_class();?>>

<h2 class="post-title"><?php the_title(); ?></h2>

<?php edit_post_link(__('Edit', 'blackcurrant') ); ?>

<?php the_content(); ?>

<?php
if(function_exists('theme_link_pages'))
theme_link_pages(array('blink'=>'<li>','alink'=>'</li>','before' => '<div
class="pagelist">'. __('Pages:', 'blackcurrant') . '<ul>', 'after' =>
'</ul></div>', 'next_or_number' => 'number'));
else wp_link_pages('before=<div class="pagelist">'. __('Pages:', 'blackcurrant') .
'&after=</div>&link_before=&link_after=&pagelink=%');
?>

</div>
<?php endwhile; endif; ?>

<?php get_footer(); ?>
```

FIGURE 6-1

There is a sense in which dynamically generated pages can be static—when they are cached. This means that a copy of the finished page is stored on the server until a change is made to some element of the page, at which point it is resaved. This is done to help reduce the constant processing of pages on the server.

Related Questions

➡ 32. Will your site design display well in mobile browsers? **Page 79**

➡ 36. Will your site load quickly? **Page 93**

➡ 48. Will your site be built with a content management system (CMS)? **Page 124**

➡ 55. Which languages other than HTML will you use to build your site? **Page 143**

Action Items

➡ If you're using a web designer, check to make sure your site will be built dynamically.

➡ From the moment you begin working on your site layout, make note of which sections can be separated out into individual files or on a CMS as separate blocks of text.

48. Will Your Site Be Built with a Content Management System (CMS)?

Having a CMS does not mean you'll never have to hire people to help you. But the work you'll need to hire them for is to set something up once; then you can do the ongoing maintenance. The ongoing tasks are what cost a lot of money to hire out.

If it's better to build a website that's dynamic rather than static, the best way to build a dynamic site is with a CMS.

The primary purpose of a CMS is to make changing and adding content as easy as possible. Your web designer might be comfortable working with a dynamic site structure built using individual files, but do you want to work with plain HTML files or learn how to upload files to a server? It would be much easier to work with an interface such as the example from the popular open-source CMS Joomla shown in Figure 6-2.

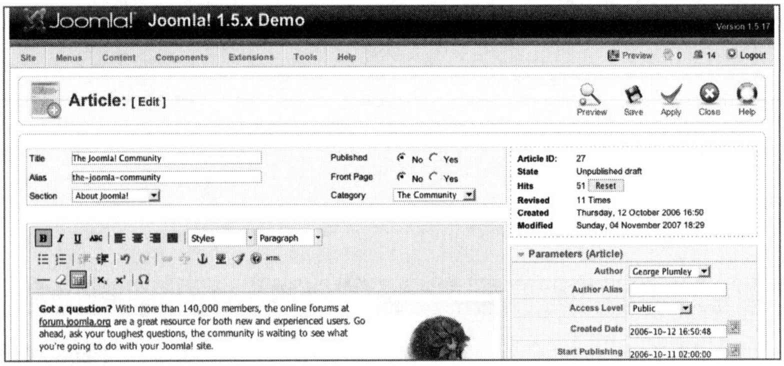

FIGURE 6-2

If you're planning to host a CMS on your own server, an important consideration is how easy it is to update. Like any software, it will require constant upgrades for security, improved features, and so on. Ideally it should update with the press of a button and not require any modifications to your template files.

Adding images or new pages are other common tasks that any CMS will simplify, but it's very important that you feel comfortable with the particular way in which the system does these tasks.

Although easy updating is important, the real power of a CMS lies in the ability to add functionality to your site, such as photo galleries, forms, and much more. It's also where some of the biggest differences lie between CMSs.

CMSs can be divided into two broad categories:

➤   Hosted

➤   Self-hosted

Hosted versions include the site-builder systems offered by many hosting providers or free blogging or website services. A self-hosted

CMS is one that you install on your server and for which you're responsible for updating and so on.

There are a number of differences between the two types, but the key distinction is that a hosted version does not allow you to customize your site and your functionality exactly the way you want. There's a fixed list of add-on features (though these have become more extensive in recent years), and you can't touch the actual files that run the site.

Rule of Thumb   Anything more than a personal site should be built using a self-hosted CMS, even if it's only a few pages in size.

> One of the disadvantages of a hosted CMS is that you can't switch hosts. Because you don't control the files running the CMS, you can't pack up and move everything (other than the actual content of the site).

With self-hosted open-source CMSs there are large communities of people constantly developing and updating add-on functions. For example, as social media became popular you immediately had new functions being created for open-source CMSs such as WordPress, Drupal, and Joomla, which would allow you to post to Twitter and Facebook. A hosted CMS might add such a function to their list (hopefully sooner rather than later), but typically it would only be one kind, whereas with the self-hosted open-source systems, there are literally dozens of different social media add-ons that can do a wide range of tasks.

With a self-hosted system you can also hire a developer to create your own unique functions because you control the actual coding that runs the site. In addition, you're not dependent on a free host to remain in business or your hosting provider to continue providing a free site-builder.

Related Questions

→ 51. What tools will be needed for building the site or its content? **Page 131**

→ 55. Which languages other than HTML will you use to build your site? **Page 143**

→ 66. Will you be blogging on your site? **Page 183**

→ 95. Do you have a plan for updating site content? **Page 279**

Action Item

→ Try out the administration system for each CMS you're considering. Pay particular attention to how comfortable you feel doing the following: editing existing content, formatting text, adding images or documents, adding new pages, managing menus, adding new functionality (polls, social bookmarking, and so on).

Importance

49. Will You Use Tables or Style Sheets to Lay Out Your Site?

Tables remain extremely useful for organizing what's called tabular content—statistics and so on.

Implementing your site's layout in HTML can be done in one of two ways: using a table structure or cascading style sheets (CSS). This is about why you should build it using CSS.

A Bit of History

In the earliest days of the Internet, web pages were essentially bodies of text, broken up by headings and paragraphs with some images from time to time. Life was simple. There were also things called tables that people used to lay out information the way they were doing in spreadsheets: in rows and columns.

Then people realized you can use these tables to structure page content in more complex ways. You can have some text in one column, other text in a second column, and then some text in a row that spans both columns.

Next came the idea of nesting one table in another to get even more complex layouts. Before long, pages were much more organized, easier to read, and had many more elements to them. But behind the scenes you had what's referred to as ugly code—tables within tables within tables and things called spacers. Spacers are tiny blank graphics that are resized with HTML to create space on the page.

Enter the CSS, which allowed you to tell different elements in HTML how they should display on a page, including how they're laid out. As CSS became more sophisticated and, most importantly, browsers got better at uniformly applying CSS rules, the need for tables to do page layout all but disappeared. And that's where things stand as of the writing of this book.

If you have an existing site built using tables, it will continue to work just fine, so you don't have to rush out and switch it to CSS. When it comes time for a redesign, you should make the change.

But why replace tables?

- Tables are very hard to work with for anything more than the most basic layout. Searching through the code of multiple nested tables is very time consuming, plus, for example, you need lots of extra coding to create margins (extra columns or the use of blank spacer graphics).

➧ Tables are not very flexible. Trying even a slightly different variation of a layout takes a lot of work, compared with changing a few CSS rules.

➧ Complex table structures eat up a lot of page loading time.

➧ CSS allows you to do things that tables simply can't, such as layering one element over another.

> **On Video**
>
> Watch how quickly CSS can change the layout of the page without changing a line of HTML. Also, see how difficult it can be to find your way around a complex page laid out using tables.

In Figure 6-3, you can see the same page layout generated with tables and with CSS:

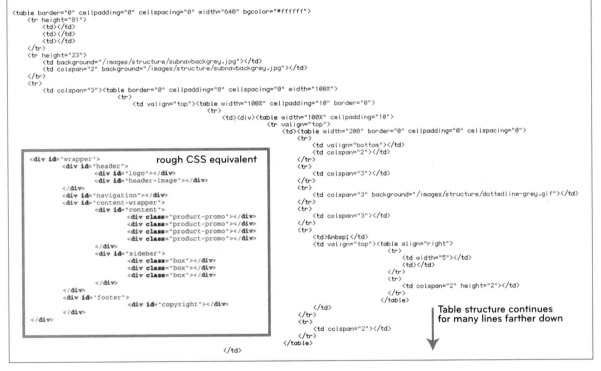

FIGURE 6-3

You can see how much simpler the HTML is with CSS, but most importantly, the CSS allows you to easily switch the layout.

Related Questions

➡ 47. Will your site be static or dynamic? **Page 122**

➡ 50. How effectively will style sheets be used on your website? **Page 129**

➡ 52. Will your HTML be bloated? **Page 134**

Action Item

➡ Ask potential web designers if they use tables to lay out sites and check the code on sample sites they show you. Check the code of any template you're considering or ask questions of website building programs about how their system codes the layout, or check sample sites.

50. How Effectively Will Style Sheets Be Used on Your Website?

Importance

It is extremely unusual these days for anyone to build a website without a CSS. The question is this: How useful is the style sheet? Even when the site layout is CSS-based rather than using tables, as discussed in the previous question, it does not mean the CSS is being used to its potential.

Rule of Thumb   Well done CSS should be fine-grained, simple, and not inline.

Fine-grained CSS means that every element on the page can be targeted individually. For example, if you need to style the paragraph within a contact box on your sidebar, your CSS should allow you to distinguish that paragraph from all others on the page or from any paragraph on the rest of the site. If that contact box appears on every single page, you should be able to color it blue only on the About Us page, for instance.

Making your CSS fine-grained can get very complicated if you're not careful about how you name elements. If you give every single element its own name, you'll not only end up with an enormous style sheet; you'll actually lose flexibility. The trick is to keep things simple by attaching classes and ideas to areas, and only to individual elements (a word, a paragraph, and so on) if necessary.

Here's what the difference looks like in a style sheet if you want to target just the year in a copyright notice (the respective HTML is shown beneath each):

```
#footer-copyright-year { color: #dd0000; }

<div><p>Copyright
<span class="#footer-copyright-year">2010</span></p></div>


.highlight { color: #006699; }

#footer #copyright .highlight { color: #dd0000; }

<div id="footer"><p id="copyright">Copyright
<span class="highlight">2010</span></p></div>
```

CSS is an important time- and cost-saving tool. During the design process it saves a lot of time when you want to test ideas such as different colors or different layouts. The savings are even more evident when you want to redesign the site in the future. Other than graphics work, it's mostly a matter of changing the style sheet rules.

Modern browsers allow you to assign multiple classes to an element, which allows for even more fine-grained styling.

Browsers have add-ons that allow you to play with the style sheets of any web page and see the effect of changes in real time.

The first approach requires a rule for every element, or at least very long comma-delimited lists of classes or ids for a shared rule. Either way, the style sheet becomes bloated and difficult to navigate. It also means that if you want the year to follow the general "highlight" rule, you can't simply eliminate the individual rule; you need to rewrite the rule (or put it in the list of all other highlighted elements).

The other approach says: Put every highlighted element on the site into a single class. From a design standpoint you're likely going to want all highlights to be the same anyway. Then, if there's an exception to that rule, simply target the specific instance of "highlight" by drilling down through the sections where it resides (#footer and then #copyright).

The final sign of good CSS is that it doesn't use what are called inline styles, which is when the rules are placed in the actual HTML. To continue with the highlighted year example, this HTML will accomplish the same results as the previous approaches:

```
<div><p>Copyright
<span style="color: #dd0000;">2010</span></p></div>
```

The trouble with inline styles is that when you need to change the styling, you have to go into the HTML instead of working with a single CSS style sheet. That might not make much difference for a single instance, but imagine if you had multiple instances of a style on one page. Even using search and replace would be more work than changing a single line in the style sheet. Now imagine changing the style on dozens of pages.

Related Questions

➤ 41. How easily will your pages print? **Page 106**

➤ 49. Will you use tables or style sheets to lay out your site? **Page 126**

➤ 52. Will your HTML be bloated? **Page 134**

Action Items

➤ Make a list of elements or areas of the site that you want to be easily targeted for future change (for example, a specific phrase that occurs regularly or a type of callout box you want to use continually).

➤ Talk to your designer, check the source code of a web template, or question a website building provider about how CSS will be used on the project. Get a second opinion from a knowledgeable friend, or hire someone for half an hour to give an assessment.

51. What Tools Will Be Needed for Building a Site or Its Content?

Importance

Even if you're not trying to design your own site or set up a CMS by yourself, the same tools will be needed for creating some of the content on your site.

The two basic tools for working with web content are:

◆ A text editor

◆ An image editor

A text editor is very easy to learn, although image editors can have quite a learning curve depending on what it is you need to do.

Text editors are an absolute must if you'll be working in any way with HTML or CSS files. It's what text editors don't do that makes them so important: They don't add nonstandard or hidden coding to your text the way word processing software can. In Figure 6-4, you can see what's behind the scenes of a word processing document when you open it in a text editor.

> You can find a list of common text and image editors for Windows and Mac in Appendix A at the back of this book. The list includes freeware, shareware, and commercial software.

```
font-size:11.0pt;    font-family:"Calibri","sans-serif";    mso-fareast-
font-family:Calibri;  mso-bidi-font-family:"Times New Roman";}
.MsoChpDefault     {mso-style-type:export-only;  mso-default-
props:yes;      font-size:10.0pt;     mso-ansi-font-size:10.0pt;
mso-bidi-font-size:10.0pt;    mso-ascii-font-family:Calibri; mso-fareast-
font-family:Calibri;  mso-hansi-font-family:Calibri;} @page Section1
{size:8.5in 11.0in;    margin:1.0in 1.0in 1.0in 1.0in;      mso-header-
margin:.5in;    mso-footer-margin:.5in;  mso-paper-source:0;}
div.Section1     {page:Section1;}  &gt;  <! [if gte mso 10]>
<mce:style> <!  /* Style Definitions */  table.MsoNormalTable
{mso-style-name:"Table Normal";    mso-tstyle-rowband-size:0;
mso-tstyle-colband-size:0;    mso-style-noshow:yes;    mso-style-
priority:99;      mso-style-qformat:yes;   mso-style-parent:"";
mso-padding-alt:0in 5.4pt 0in 5.4pt;    mso-para-margin:0in;
mso-para-margin-bottom:.0001pt;       mso-pagination:widow-
orphan;   font-size:11.0pt;     font-family:"Calibri","sans-serif";
mso-ascii-font-family:Calibri; mso-ascii-theme-font:minor-latin;
mso-fareast-font-family:"Times New Roman"; mso-fareast-theme-
font:minor-fareast; mso-hansi-font-family:Calibri;      mso-hansi-
theme-font:minor-latin;  mso-bidi-font-family:"Times New Roman";
```

FIGURE 6-4

This code can produce very strange or unwanted results on a web page. By working in a text editor you ensure that your file is clean.

Image editors come in a wide range of flavors and prices depending on what you need to do. Photoshop is at the high end of this range—it's one of the tools of choice for designers—both in price and functionality. You really need Photoshop only if you're going to do full page, complex designs. A simpler image editor will allow you to do the most common sorts of tasks, such as resizing and optimizing photos for the Internet.

Unless you're planning on building many sites, web design programs such as Dreamweaver, which help simplify the layout process by working in a What You See Is What You Get (WYSIWYG) environment, are not worth the cost or the learning curve. You can get a custom web design for the price of the software and no time outlay on your part.

Some of the most valuable tools you can work with are add-ons for your web browser. Most modern browsers have versions of what's referred to as a developer's toolbar. This example in Figure 6-5 is the Web Developer toolbar for Firefox and you can see some of the many features that allow you to easily look behind the scenes of a site.

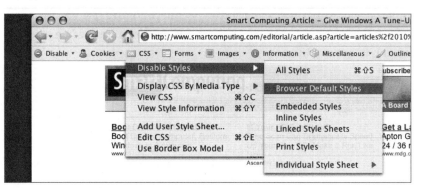

FIGURE 6-5

On Video

See how text editors and image editors function.

One of the most powerful features of web developer browser add-ons is that you can alter the CSS of a site and see what the change will look like in real time. Other add-ons allow you to test the speed with which your page loads and much more.

Related Questions

➡ 48. Will your site be built with a content management system (CMS)? **Page 124**

➡ 54. Will your nontext files use the proper file types? **Page 140**

➡ 95. Do you have a plan for updating site content? **Page 279**

Action Items

➡ Check the image program that comes with your camera and see if it can optimize images for the web.

➡ Install web developer toolbars on your browser. Even if you're not doing any of the design or construction of your site, these toolbars are useful for seeing what's going on.

Importance

52. Will Your HTML Be Bloated?

Proper website construction techniques include keeping the actual HTML you see in your browser as minimal as possible. The two main culprits of bloated HTML files are:

* Not using external files where possible
* Poor coding techniques

Although JavaScript and CSS can be placed in an HTML file, they add a great deal to the size of the files. This would not be an issue if the extra code was unique to the individual HTML file, but typically the code is used by many if not all HTML files on a site. In such cases, it makes sense to put the JavaScript and CSS into external files.

In Figure 6-6, compare the header area on the left with JavaScript and CSS in the HTML, and on the right the same header with one-line references to external files containing the code:

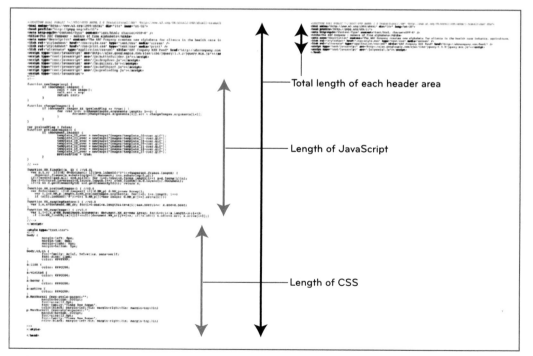

FIGURE 6-6

Not only do external JavaScript and CSS files help reduce the size of each page, but they speed up loading of your site as a whole because of something called caching. Browsers will cache or store the information from a file after reading it for the first time. If the same JavaScript were on every page, the browser would keep reading it each time. If it's cached, the information is already there, so there's no need to take up time reading it again.

But it isn't just a case of having files separate from your HTML; you also want to avoid having too many separate files. That's because your browser has to spend a bit of time looking for each file. By putting all your JavaScript together, for example, the browser has to load only one file.

The other culprit that makes for large HTML files is poor coding techniques. Here's one technique for creating a 20-pixel blank space in HTML using transparent image: `<br /><img src="spacer .gif" height="20px" width="1px" border="0"><br />`. Now suppose you want this space at the end of each paragraph on the page. Even if there are only three paragraphs, you can see how much HTML is required. Compare that with a single line of CSS specifying that all paragraphs have a 20-pixel margin at the bottom.

I showed you in a previous question how using CSS styles in the HTML (inline styles) is not very flexible, but it also adds unnecessary coding. The same goes for using complex table structures to lay out a site. It's just not very efficient and makes your HTML files much larger.

Another poor coding technique is to have large amounts of space between lines or areas in your HTML, JavaScript, or CSS files. Although this might make things easier to read in your text editor, that extra space actually takes up valuable loading time.

If you're using JavaScript libraries (files that make it even easier to add functionality), it's handy to reference them on another server, such as Google's script repository, rather than storing them on your server. Browsers generally access only one or two files at a time from a single server, so files on a different server don't count in that limitation, and you can be loading more at one time.

If you get a JavaScript from the many free script repositories on the Internet, you don't have to keep its file separate. You can place that JavaScript inside your main JavaScript file (be sure to keep the author attribution intact). As long as the functions used in the body still have the same names, it doesn't matter what the name of the overall script is.

On Video

See how long bloated HTML pages can actually become.

Related Questions

➤ 36. Will your site load quickly? **Page 93**

➤ 49. Will you use tables or style sheets to lay out your site? **Page 126**

➤ 50. How effectively will style sheets be used on your website? **Page 129**

Action Items

➤ Check to see that external files are being used on your site as much as possible.

➤ Organize external files in their own folders. For example, put all JavaScripts in one folder, CSSs in another. You might not have multiple files right now, but you'll know where they belong if they come along.

53. Will Your Site Files Be Clearly Organized?

Importance

A website that's well organized for visitors might be disorganized on the back end, so be sure that the files for your site are clearly structured on the server. You want to make it easy for anyone you have working on your site to find what they need quickly.

The most common problem, especially with smaller sites, is putting all files into a single directory (folder) instead of organizing them into a series of folders. On the left side of Figure 6-7 is a partial list of all the files for a site (the full list is about four times longer). On the right side is the same set of files with all images in one folder and all documents in another.

File	Date	File	Date
about.html	12/07/09, 4:54 PM	about.html	12/07/09, 4:54 PM
banner.gif	25/03/08, 4:42 PM	book-events.html	09/04/01, 5:23 AM
bkg.jpg	05/04/09, 1:30 PM	book-order.html	09/04/01, 5:23 AM
blog.gif	15/01/08, 3:30 PM	book.html	12/07/09, 4:54 PM
book-events.html	09/04/01, 5:23 AM	clients-introduction.html	23/05/02, 1:10 AM
book-order.html	09/04/01, 5:23 AM	clients-resources.html	09/04/01, 5:24 AM
book.html	12/07/09, 4:54 PM	clients-schedule.html	15/08/01, 2:43 AM
book.jpg	01/11/06, 5:15 PM	conferences-archive.html	23/05/02, 1:10 AM
bookcover.gif	05/04/09, 1:30 PM	conferences.html	23/05/02, 1:10 AM
bottom_plate.gif	01/11/06, 5:15 PM	contact.html	16/09/09, 5:21 PM
btn_0.gif	01/11/06, 5:15 PM	counselling.html	09/04/01, 5:23 AM
btn_1.gif	01/11/06, 5:15 PM	docs	Today, 6:35 AM
btn_2.gif	01/11/06, 5:15 PM	healing-from-within.html	12/07/09, 4:54 PM
btn_3.gif	01/11/06, 5:15 PM	images	Today, 6:35 AM
btn_4.gif	01/11/06, 5:15 PM	index.html	01/11/06, 5:15 PM
btn_5.gif	01/11/06, 5:15 PM	links.html	30/09/09, 5:23 PM
bulletpoint.jpg	21/01/08, 4:42 PM	testimonials.html	12/07/09, 4:56 PM
clients-introduction.html	23/05/02, 1:10 AM	workshop-order.html	12/07/09, 4:56 PM
clients-resources.html	09/04/01, 5:24 AM	workshop-schedule.html	12/07/09, 4:56 PM
clients-schedule.html	15/08/01, 2:43 AM	workshops.html	12/07/09, 4:56 PM
conferences-archive.html	23/05/02, 1:10 AM		
conferences.html	23/05/02, 1:10 AM		
contact.html	16/09/09, 5:21 PM		
divider.gif	01/11/06, 5:15 PM		
facebook.gif	15/01/08, 3:30 PM		
frame_btm_01.gif	01/11/06, 5:15 PM		
frame_btm_02.gif	01/11/06, 5:15 PM		
gdform.asp	26/07/06, 4:53 PM		
gdform.asp.bak	26/07/06, 4:53 PM		
gdform.php	06/08/03, 4:26 PM		
gift.gif	15/01/08, 3:18 PM		
giftbox.gif	15/01/08, 3:18 PM		
header_01.gif	01/11/06, 5:15 PM		

FIGURE 6-7

Placing all files into a single directory is often the result of an inexperienced person not knowing how to handle references in HTML. When referring to an image, for example, it's easier just to put the name of the file than to worry about how you tell the browser to look in a particular folder. Compare these two image tags:

```
<img src="mypicture.jpg">
<img src="../images/recipes/recipe-132/mypicture.jpg">
```

File folder names should be lowercase and cannot have any spaces in them. The same holds true for filenames.

Putting everything in a single folder is another sign of inexperience because the designer is not thinking of the future and what it's like to have to sift through 700 HTML, image, document, and other files.

If someone else is building your site, check that they will use a clear system for file organization. That will make it easier two years down the road if you've got someone else working on the site; they won't have to waste time finding their way around or reorganizing the site at additional expense.

There are many different approaches to file organization. For example, one way is to keep all file types together, as shown on the left side of Figure 6-8, or to keep all like content together as shown on the right side of Figure 6-8:

FIGURE 6-8

Even if you're using a CMS, there will be files that need organizing: files that control the look of your template or uploaded files such as images or documents. With file images the most important consideration is that they be organized logically—by subject or by date—with subfolders within each general area. Again, when you're first starting out, organization might not seem like much of an issue, but after you've uploaded 500 files and you go looking for one of them, it doesn't matter that you have an easy-to-use CMS.

File organization is also very important for search engines in cases where you're not using a CMS. How you organize files on the server determines what the URL for a particular page will be. Having files organized into folders means the folder's name will appear in the URL and if the name of the folder is clear and uses keywords if possible, that can be a bit of a boost for search engines.

Related Questions

➡ 47. Will your site be static or dynamic? **Page 122**

➡ 48. Will your site be built with a content management system (CMS)? **Page 124**

➡ 65. What basic content pages will be on your site? **Page 174**

Action Items

➡ Think about what kind of content you expect to be creating in the future and how best to organize it in folders. If others are building the site, consult with them on this issue.

➡ If you're looking into a CMS, check what options you have for controlling the storage of images and documents.

54. Will Your Nontext Files Use the Proper File Types?

When you're building your site, and later as you create content, it's important to know what file types you should be using. It can make a huge difference to the look, loading time, and compatibility of your site.

One of the most common misunderstandings with images is when to use JPG (pronounced jay-peg) and when to use GIF (hard or soft g) or PNG files. (The PNG was developed to replace the GIF, which is limited in colors and is protected by a patent.)

> **Rule of Thumb**   JPG is for photographs or any image with lots of differently colored or blended areas.
>
> GIF is for graphics with distinct areas of solid color, with or without transparency.
>
> PNG, which is a replacement for GIF, supports more colors and better transparency.

The results of not following these guidelines can be seen in Figure 6-9. Look at the detail of the same photograph saved as a JPG and as a GIF, and the same for an image of flat colors.

FIGURE 6-9

The GIF photograph looks okay, but notice how much larger it is than the JPG (the GIF is 43K and the JPG is only 5K). Saving photographs in PNG format also produces unnecessarily large files. These various file types use compression to make images smaller for the Web. GIFs are not good at compressing shades of color, but compare the images with the flat colors: The GIF not only has crisper edges but it also has created a much smaller file than the JPG.

Controlling file size for images is extremely important for keeping down the loading time of a website. All image software allows you to change the dots per inch as well as the dimensions—two important factors in reducing image size. But you'll also want a special way of saving images for the Web. Your software should allow you to choose the amount of compression for JPGs, GIFs, and PNGs.

So instead of uploading images directly from your camera to your website, you should first reduce their size and optimize them. But you need to be careful not to optimize them so much that they look bad. While you can see the pixels on both blowups, the image on the right has much larger blocks of pixels. That's the result of higher compression and it's what makes an image look rough or "choppy."

HTML allows you to change the dimensions of an image, but the results aren't so good. GIFs cannot be altered or else they break up. JPGs can stand a bit of resizing, but they don't look as good. It's better to size the image in your image editor, or a lot of CMSs today allow you to physically resize an image and save the new version.

FIGURE 6-10

When uploading documents to the Web it's best to use only PDFs. Saved properly, they can keep down the size of the file, but most importantly, they can be read by virtually anyone. If you put any other type of document on your site, you'll inconvenience users who don't have the necessary program.

Sometimes you have to upload documents of a particular type, which is why it's important to always tell visitors what type of document it is, so they're not downloading something they can't handle.

For audio files, you should save them as mp3 with the lowest bit rate that maintains good quality (different for music and voice).

If your current software does not allow you to save documents as PDFs, look for a free or low-cost program by searching for the phrase 🔍 PDF writer software.

On Video

Watch the process of saving an image for the Web using a basic image-editing program for Windows.

For video, it's simplest to upload files to a sharing site such as YouTube and let them optimize it for the Web (plus you don't have to store and serve the video through your server).

Related Questions

➧ 36. Will your site load quickly? **Page 93**

➧ 51. What tools will be needed for building the site or its content? **Page 131**

➧ 62. How will you be using video or audio in your content? **Page 164**

Action Items

➧ Check if the image editing program that comes with your camera allows you to reduce the file size of images. There might even be a Save for Web function or something similar. Try it and see how much it reduces the size of the file.

➧ Experiment by saving a photograph as a JPG and as a GIF and compare the difference in sizes. Also, practice using different levels of JPG optimization and notice when the photo no longer looks good.

55. Which Languages Other Than HTML Will You Use to Build Your Site?

Importance

HTML is quite limited in what it can do, and most of the features of modern websites—assembling content from multiple files, drop-down menus, animations, and photo galleries—are accomplished using scripting languages, such as JavaScript, or PHP.

Scripting languages on the Internet fall into two categories:

➜ **Server-side (processed on the server before reaching the browser)**: Common languages include PHP, ASP, JSP, Perl, and ColdFusion. Common uses include: interacting with databases, processing forms, assembling web pages, and actions that require more security.

➜ **Client-side (processed in the browser during and after the loading of a page)**: Common languages include JavaScript and Java. Common uses include: mouseover effects such as drop-down menus and image rollovers; validation of form input before the form is processed; access of third-party tools such as statistics, widgets, forms, and so on; and popup windows (ads, photo galleries, and so on).

One of the drawbacks of client-side languages is that the software to run them might not be present on a particular person's browser (or even if it is, it might be turned off). Although JavaScript is built into all browsers, some people turn it off either because they're concerned about security risks or because they find annoying some of the things that people do with JavaScript (such as animated trails behind the cursor). With server-side languages, the scripts get processed no matter what.

When deciding on how to accomplish something on your site, always ask this question: Can this be done in a better way? Better here means simpler, more reliable, more secure, or more universal. For example, if you want to have a fancy photo gallery, you might see some Flash galleries you like. But ask whether the same effect can be accomplished in JavaScript, or even CSS, or a server-side language such as PHP (something visitors can't disable).

> Running server-side scripts generally is more secure because they're processed before reaching the browser, so users can't interfere with them (though poorly written scripts can leave holes).

> You can test what your site looks like with style sheets disabled or JavaScript turned off by making those changes to your browser. An even easier method is to use a developer toolbar for your browser. These toolbars usually have commands to temporarily disable features such as JavaScript without changing anything in the browser's settings.

If you do need to use a client-side script because of cost or lack of an alternative, make sure there's a backup plan should the visitor not have the tool or has it disabled. Will visitors be stuck with no menu if JavaScript is turned off, as in the example from Figure 6-11?

FIGURE 6-11

As you can see, there are a lot of choices around and all you can do is make as informed a choice as possible. And the situation is always changing, so be prepared a year down the road to revamp how you do something because a better technology (more flexible and simpler—don't just change for change's sake) comes along.

Related Questions

◆ 34. Will you be using animation in your design? **Page 84**

◆ 43. Will your site have special requirements for certain features to work? **Page 111**

◆ 47. Will your site be static or dynamic? **Page 122**

Action Item

◆ Consult with your designer early on about server-side languages in particular because changing that usually means changing servers and programs. If you're going it alone, you need to read up on the benefits of each, although PHP is probably your best bet because it's so universal and lots of developers are available to help out.

Chapter 7
Content

In this chapter:

Importance

56. Will Your Content Serve Your Site's Purpose?

In one sense, this should be the first chapter of this book because content truly is the heart of any website. It's what visitors are looking for and is the reason they come back. If you read earlier chapters in this book, you know that content is the benchmark of just about every decision you need to make about the site. But what's the benchmark for deciding on content?

Back in the introduction to this book, I asked why you wanted to build a website. The answer or answers to that question must now be used to determine what pages you need on your site, what content belongs on those pages, what wording to use, what writing style to use, and much more. The benchmark for content is the site's purpose.

> **Rule Of Thumb**   Review your site content at least twice per year to make sure it still meets your site's purpose. You'll also want to review your purpose.

Suppose that your purpose is to increase the number of jobs performed at your auto repair shop—in other words, to get more business. The people who can give you more business are the visitors to your site, so to fulfill your purpose your site needs to convince them that you're the shop to meet their needs. Now things start to get more specific.

One of the needs of car owners is to keep their cars running safely at the lowest possible cost. It's a problem they face, so to speak. A task of your website, then, would be to show how you can provide the solution to that problem. What content can help convince them of that? Here are some possibilities:

- A page detailing the cost savings of preventative maintenance and the high costs of putting off maintenance

- A page of customer testimonials emphasizing quality work at a great value

- A seasonal specials page

- A page of favorite tips from your mechanics that can help save customers money on anything automotive

Some ideas will depend on what you're already doing or could easily plan to do (such as seasonal specials), whereas other ideas are a matter of thinking how your knowledge can be communicated to customers in a helpful way. But in each case, the ideas are driven by providing a solution for customers designed to help drive the purpose of the site.

Of course, there are other customer needs that can bring them to your repair shop, so although the purpose might remain the same—getting more business—the content required to fulfill that purpose will vary with customer needs.

Notice that your site's purpose actually boils down to the needs of your audience, and this applies to not just commercial sites. If the purpose of your site is to convince people of something, the content required to convince them ultimately has to speak their language, be put in terms of their understanding, and relate to their needs and goals. The same is true of informing, entertaining, or any other purpose. Your website is a communication tool for people—it has to engage them or they're clicking on to the next site.

Hopefully you're already doing this kind of thinking as part of your overall business and marketing strategy, and it's just a matter of dreaming up how to implement it on the Web. If you haven't been thinking this way, use the website to get you thinking that way across your whole business (from what you say in newspaper ads to how you set up your waiting room!).

> Remember to voice your audience's problems on the site and offer solutions. If visitors can hear themselves thinking in your copy, they'll be much more likely to listen to your solution because they know that you "get them."

Related Questions

→ Introduction—Why do you want to build a website? **Page XV**

→ 22. Will the design of your site support your content or distract from it? **Page 52**

→ 68. Do you have a web marketing plan? **Page 192**

→ 87. Will your content be search engine-friendly? **Page 247**

Action Item

→ Based on your site's purpose, make a list of what your audience needs in order for them to act and fulfill that purpose. Then list the sorts of content that might get them to act. To verify or add to the list, start asking your audience.

Importance

Use your site statistics to regularly assess whether any particular content is being given sufficient accessibility and thereby importance (or vice versa). You might find that visitors are reading a page that is not easily accessible, and by making it so, you can reach more people.

57. Will Your Content Be Easily Accessible?

Your task when setting up a website is to make all your content easily accessible to visitors, while making the content most important to them more visibly and frequently accessible. The key techniques for accessibility are mentioned here in their rough order of importance (many are covered in more detail throughout the book):

→ **Placement in the navigation**—Including a page on the main navigation not only makes it quickly available from anywhere on the site but says to visitors that it has an importance that a page on only the footer menu does not. Further, pages on the first level of the main navigation are the most important, second-level items less so, and so on.

→ **Placement on every page**—If a link to content appears on every page (outside of the main navigation and the footer navigation), that makes the content highly accessible and again indicates a high level of importance.

→ **Placement on the home page**—Any content that's promoted on the home page takes on a special significance, even if that's one of the few ways to access the page. Even pages with a link in the main navigation will benefit greatly from a link in the content of the home page. Of course, the more space and/or graphics devoted to the link on the home page increases its importance even more. Even a simple text link within the home page content achieves extra significance.

→ **Vertical placement**—The farther up the page a content element is placed, the more likely it is that people will see it and the greater the importance attached to it. Other than your header (with your logo and likely your navigation), there shouldn't be anything placed vertically before the primary content of the page. If you do place something in that space, just be aware that it's creating competition for your content. Within the body of content, the same principle applies to the individual points being made—the higher you place them, the more likely they'll be read and given significance.

◆ **Horizontal placement**—On the horizontal plane of a page, important content needs to start as far to the left as possible because that's where people tend to scan up and down. Content that's placed on the right might require additional design elements such as images to try and ensure that the visitor's eye will be drawn over there.

◆ **The use of images**—Photos and graphics are an excellent way of focusing attention on content and away from the rest of the elements on the page, including other content, as the example in Figure 7-1 demonstrates.

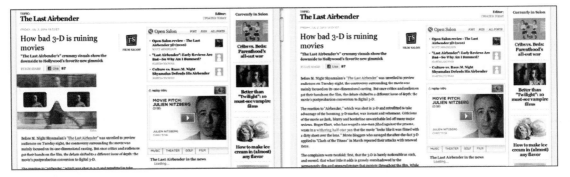

FIGURE 7-1

Also notice in this example that the main content image needs to be larger than the other content images on the page, not to mention the images in ads. Relative size is part of the concept of relative importance.

◆ **Internal linking**—Linking within content to other content on your site can make that other content more accessible.

◆ **Highlighting**—Within content, you can draw attention to particular passages or ideas by using techniques such as callouts or pull quotes (displaying content outside the flow of the text in various ways).

On Video

Examples of how placement affects accessibility and visitors' perceptions of importance.

Related Questions

◆ 23. Will your site layout make your content clear? **Page 55**

◆ 46. How will you test the user-friendliness of your site? **Page 118**

Action Items

→ Make a list of the five most important content items on your site and review how each is being made accessible throughout the site.

→ Make a copy of your site map and show every kind of internal link.

58. Will the Content of Each Page Have a Single Focus?

Importance

...et, it tends to be for ...vorite team, a recipe for ...ne to your site, it's likely ...d one way to help them ...ntral topic.

...offer installation, servic- ...conditioners, plumbing ...n offers just one link to ...who needs a heat pump ...rvice. If the menu shows ...e guesswork is removed.

...pairs as a service, but the ...very service offered, again ...hat they need. The same

...ase "heat pump repairs," a ...content about repairs will ...ne of six or seven other ...ing to sites through search ...y to the page they need, ...ages have focused content.

...seful as an overview page, ...sentence description of ...hat service. But the ulti- ...cific topic and nothing else.

...that it makes it easier for ...tion of use to a visitor. For ...me "internal ads" that ...us of a page is to explain ...with additional informa- ...of value to visitors seeing

Part of being focused might include location. A plumbing company that serves a specific city or region needs to make sure that the content of its pages reflects the location. That way, visitors aren't wasting their time reading about a company outside their area.

Be sure the filenames of pages reflect the specific content: heat-pump-service.html, not heat-pumps.html (which could be a product sales page) or something cryptic such as hp-service.html or page5.html. Specific naming can help search engines understand what a page is about.

Advertising services such as Google AdSense, often choose what ads to place on a page based on its content—the more focused your content, the more relevant those ads will be to your visitors.

On Video

Look at examples of focused and unfocused content, and a discussion of alternative ways of breaking up content.

Of course, an important part of marketing is to make people aware of what you offer beyond what they came looking for. On the surface it might seem that focused content takes away from that opportunity, but it actually enhances it. Instead of pushing an unrelated product or service that matters to you, focused content tells you what the customer is interested in and allows you to relate something to that interest.

Focused content also makes internal linking more effective. If a link to your information about marriage counseling would be helpful, it's better to send visitors to a page that deals exclusively with it rather than a general page about all your counseling services.

Related Questions

➜ 87. Will your content be search engine-friendly? **Page 247**

➜ 95. Do you have a plan for updating site content? **Page 279**

Action Items

➜ Check the sites of highly-ranked or popular competitors to see how they divide up their content. Think about what your audience is looking for and consider whether there are opportunities to divide up content according to their specific needs.

➜ Review the content of each page to see whether it might be split into two or more pages of more focused content.

59. Will Your Written Content Be Correct, Clear, and Well Structured?

Importance

Apart from the actual content of your site—what you have to offer—the answers to this question can be the make-or-break point of building your website. If you had the most compelling content in the world, you could do without graphics, you could survive with poor typography, you might do without coherent navigation, but if, in the end, visitors have trouble understanding or following the content, you're lost.

The suggestions here cannot make up for disorganized thinking or basic writing skills, but they're part of the next step after having clear thoughts and at least decent writing skills. I've divided the suggestions into three parts.

Being Correct

Mistakes in your content make you look sloppy, incompetent, or ignorant, which are qualities you never want to convey.

The most common kind of mistake, and one of the most detrimental, is the spelling error. First of all, they're easy for visitors to spot. Second, in this day and age of easy spell-checking, it's hard for visitors to imagine how you didn't spot the error, too. All they can assume is that you don't pay attention to details and haven't taken the trouble to read your own material.

Although grammar mistakes might be less noticeable, if they're frequent and bad enough, they don't just give a bad impression but they also can actually interfere with visitors understanding what you're saying. Constant bad grammar can also cause people to stop reading because they have to work so hard.

Getting facts right is important for the value of your content and for your credibility. If you're making a claim based on something you heard second-hand, be sure to check it out. Again, the ease of verifying information in the age of the Internet makes errors of fact hard to accept, plus people have come to expect links to references where possible. Credibility takes an even bigger hit if the fact is so obviously wrong (Lebanon is not in Africa; 10% of 120 is not 1.2).

> Most web browsers have a spell-check feature. Before going live with your site, check each page again using your browser to highlight any errors that weren't caught.

> One simple way of catching errors is to have one or two other people read what you've written; if you don't have time to do that, try reading your work backward—problems tend to jump out that way.

Being Clear

One of the first steps to being clear is to write for your audience, not for yourself. That means providing context or background that you might take for granted.

Writing for your audience means using the terms they would use. In your industry you might talk about *Commercial Real Estate* while your audience is looking for *Office Space*. You might refer to your treatment method as *Therapy* while your audience thinks of it as *Counseling*.

Being clear also involves taking explanations or descriptions one step at a time rather than jumping several points because they're taken for granted by people in the know.

Another element of clarity is to get to the point quickly. This begins with the title of the content. It might be fun to write clever headline copy (and if it's important to the concept of your website, go ahead), but in the vast majority of cases a clear descriptive title is much more effective for visitors as well as for search engines.

Within the body of the content, it's important for each paragraph to get to the point right away and then elaborate. Long, verbose sentences do not help you get to the point. On the other hand, you don't want your copy to be dumbed down. Write for your audience, and if it's a wide audience, write somewhere in the lower half.

> Don't simply transfer print copy over to the Web. You probably need to rewrite and/or reorganize it for reading online.

Being Well Structured

As with writing, the key to good structure is this: Get to the point. Just as visitors need to know immediately what your site is about, they need to know immediately that the content of the page they've landed on will give them what they need.

If it takes three paragraphs to know that your interior design services include the commercial as well as the residential market, that's too long for a visitor looking for commercial interior design. People tend to scan first before reading, and if they won't find the word *commercial* until the third paragraph, they might well give up before then.

Rule of Thumb   For typical web pages, paragraphs should average about 3 sentences or roughly 60 words. Pages should be no more than 10 paragraphs long.

The answer can be as simple as breaking up the content into separate sections or often separate pages. Context will help you decide which is better. If the long content is all related to residential design, sections would be best because it's more likely the reader will be interested in one or more of the sections. But residential and commercial markets are very different, so a separate page for commercial interior design makes more sense.

Figure 7-2 shows the difference that sections can make to your ability to visually take in longer content.

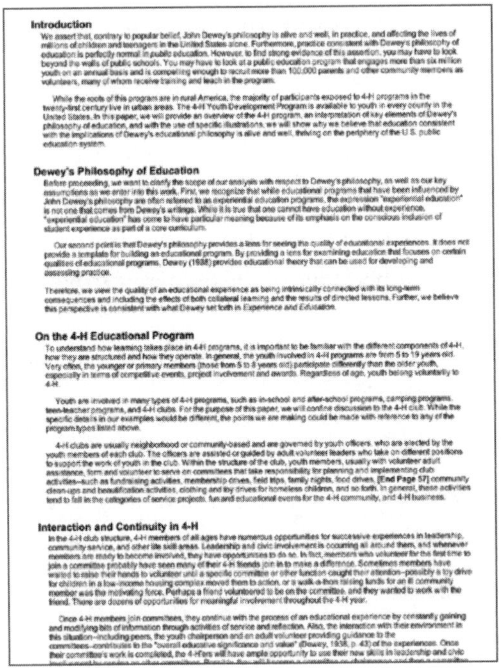

Introduction

We assert that, contrary to popular belief, John Dewey's philosophy is alive and well, in practice, and affecting the lives of millions of children and teenagers in the United States alone. Furthermore, practice consistent with Dewey's philosophy of education is perfectly normal in public education. However, to find strong evidence of this assertion, you may have to look beyond the walls of public schools. You may have to look at a public education program that engages more than six million youth on an annual basis and is compelling enough to recruit more than 100,000 parents and other community members as volunteers, many of whom receive training and teach in the program.

While the roots of this program are in rural America, the majority of participants exposed to 4-H programs in the twenty-first century live in urban areas. The 4-H Youth Development Program is available to youth in every county in the United States. In this paper, we will provide an overview of the 4-H program, an interpretation of key elements of Dewey's philosophy of education, and with the use of specific illustrations, we will show why we believe that education consistent with the implications of Dewey's educational philosophy is alive and well, thriving on the periphery of the U.S. public education system.

Dewey's Philosophy of Education

Before proceeding, we want to clarify the scope of our analysis with respect to Dewey's philosophy, as well as our key assumptions as we enter into this work. First, we recognize that while educational programs that have been influenced by John Dewey's philosophy are often referred to as experiential education programs, the expression "experiential education" is not one that comes from Dewey's writings. While it is true that one cannot have education without experience, "experiential education" has come to have particular meaning because of its emphasis on the conscious inclusion of student experience as part of a core curriculum.

Our second point is that Dewey's philosophy provides a lens for seeing the quality of educational experiences. It does not provide a template for building an educational program. By providing a lens for examining education that focuses on certain qualities of educational programs, Dewey (1938) provides educational theory that can be used for developing and assessing practice.

Therefore, we view the quality of an educational experience as being intrinsically connected with its long-term consequences and including the effects of both collateral learning and the results of directed lessons. Further, we believe this perspective is consistent with what Dewey set forth in *Experience and Education*.

On the 4-H Educational Program

To understand how learning takes place in 4-H programs, it is important to be familiar with the different components of 4-H, how they are structured and how they operate. In general, the youth involved in 4-H programs are from 5 to 19 years old. Very often, the younger or primary members (those from 5 to 8 years old) participate differently than the older youth, especially in terms of competitive events, project involvement and awards. Regardless of age, youth belong voluntarily to 4-H.

Youth are involved in many types of 4-H programs, such as in-school and after-school programs, camping programs, teen-teacher programs, and 4-H clubs. For the purpose of this paper, we will confine discussion to the 4-H club. While the specific details in our examples would be different, the points we are making could be made with reference to any of the program types listed above.

4-H clubs are usually neighborhood or community-based and are governed by youth officers, who are elected by the youth members of each club. The officers are assisted or guided by adult volunteer leaders who take on different positions to support the work of youth in the club. Within the structure of the club, youth members, usually with volunteer adult assistance, form and volunteer to serve on committees that take responsibility for planning and implementing club activities—such as fundraising activities, membership drives, field trips, family nights, food drives, **[End Page 57]** community clean-ups and beautification activities, clothing and toy drives for homeless children, and so forth. In general, these activities tend to fall in the categories of service projects, fun and educational events for the 4-H community, and 4-H business.

Interaction and Continuity in 4-H

In the 4-H club structure, 4-H members of all ages have numerous opportunities for successive experiences in leadership, community service, and other life skill areas. Leadership and civic involvement is occurring all around them, and whenever members are ready to become involved, they have opportunities to do so. In fact, members who volunteer for the first time to join a committee probably have seen many of their 4-H friends join in to make a difference. Sometimes members have wanted to raise their hands to volunteer until a specific committee or other function caught their attention—possibly a toy drive for children in a low-income housing complex moved them to action, or a walk-a-thon raising funds for an ill community member was the motivating force. Perhaps a friend volunteered to be on the committee, and they wanted to work with the friend. There are dozens of opportunities for meaningful involvement throughout the 4-H year.

Once 4-H members join committees, they continue with the process of an educational experience by constantly gaining and modifying bits of information through activities of service and reflection. Also, the interaction with their environment in this situation—including peers, the youth chairperson and an adult volunteer providing guidance to the committees—contributes to the "overall educative significance and value" (Dewey, 1938, p. 43) of the experiences. Once their committee's work is completed, the 4-H'ers will have ample opportunity to use their new skills in leadership and civic

FIGURE 7-2

Not only do the section headings create extra white space but the difference in sizing helps to draw your eye to the beginning of each section.

After your eyes can grasp the visual structure of the piece, the key is to have clearly written headings so you can quickly grasp what the section is about. Compare the three headings in Figure 7-3.

> Short content is not always a good thing. If you break up a single article into several pages, that can be as annoying as having to scan a lot of diverse text to find one topic. Or if you break up a single thought that needs 12 sentences to get communicated, you're doing the visitor as much of a disservice as running 3 thoughts together into a single paragraph.

> Avoid centering titles or headings because that breaks the pattern of scanning down the left side of the page.

Long Live Queen Victoria

A consectetuer pede feugiat ipsum mollis cursus, in semper nunc, non in proin fringilla proin ei ornare, sodales massa nunc metus amet, cursus leo quis eros sagittis quam, cursus orci feugia odio quis etiam euismod.

The Timelessness and Popularity of Victorian Design

A consectetuer pede feugiat ipsum mollis cursus, in semper nunc, non in proin fringilla proin ei ornare, sodales massa nunc metus amet, cursus leo quis eros sagittis quam, cursus orci feugia odio quis etiam euismod.

Victorian Design - Always Popular

A consectetuer pede feugiat ipsum mollis cursus, in semper nunc, non in proin fringilla proin ei ornare, sodales massa nunc metus amet, cursus leo quis eros sagittis quam, cursus orci feugia odio quis etiam euismod.

FIGURE 7-3

The second heading is much clearer than the first, although the third example goes further by putting the keyword at the beginning of the heading, thus taking even better advantage of the tendency to scan along the left side of the page.

Lists are another powerful tool for transforming content into something more easily grasped. They do this by:

- Emphasizing each point through separation
- Allowing the eye to quickly scan
- Providing a road map for more detailed explanations
- Making it easier to remember the points
- Making it easier to find key points on a page

So keep an eye out for situations in which lists can make reading easier for your visitors.

Related Questions

- 25. How will the design of your text make your content clear? **Page 60**
- 30. How will elements within content be set off from the body text? **Page 73**
- 58. Will the content of each page have a single focus? **Page 151**
- 87. Will your content be search engine-friendly? **Page 247**

Action Items

➡ Read only the first sentence of each paragraph on a page: Can you get the main idea?

➡ Glance for a moment at each page on your site and then ask yourself whether the content looks crowded. Try the same experiment with someone else.

Importance

60. How Effectively Will Your Content Use Links?

Did you know that the *H* in HTML stands for *hypertext*, which literally means "more than text"? What makes text on the Web more than the text in printed materials is the ability to link words and phrases to other content. But with this powerful tool comes responsibility, so this answer is about responsible as well as effective linking within your content.

First and foremost, links need to be relevant to the content the visitor is reading. If the link sends visitors to a destination that's not clearly related, you've wasted their time, not to mention disrupting the flow of your content.

Even relevant links, however, should be used sparingly. If every few words have links, the reader might get the sense you're relying on the links to do the work instead of giving enough of the information yourself. Also, links are supposed to point to important additional material, and if almost everything is linked, the reader isn't sure what's important to follow. The example in Figure 7-4 illustrates this point.

> Some people wonder why anyone would create links that take visitors to other websites. But showing visitors other useful sites is a good thing; it's part of establishing a rapport and a sense of value by being helpful.

> President Obama took a gamble when he agreed to be interviewed on a show where, the day before, Reese Witherspoon got big YouTube play for doing fart jokes with Leno. The gamble lay in the fact that talk shows like Leno's are meant to entertain, the atmosphere is ultra-relaxed and the point of opening one's mouth is to get a laugh or to titillate or to shock. Obama accidently did the latter when he responded to Leno's chuckling at his 129 bowling score by saying it was "like the Special Olympics or something."

FIGURE 7-4

If you have a lot of links related to your content, one option is to place general links at the end of the content and then, within the body of the content, create links only to specific references.

People tend to use links for pointing at other sites, but if you have related material elsewhere on your own site, be sure to link to it. Even if your site is fairly small, you should watch for opportunities to link to your other pages. Visitors don't look at every page on your site, so they

> Check your site regularly for broken links. There are free and paid services to help with this—see Appendix A for some resources.

might miss something unless you draw their attention to it, and internal linking is ideal for that.

Just as links to other pages on your site are helpful within content, so are links to other content on the same page. *On-page links*, as they're known, are commonly used for mini navigation bars on long pages, but you can also use them within the text. This breaks with the usual understanding of linear reading—following one paragraph to the next—but linking is meant to support a nonlinear approach to reading. The back button will always return the reader to where they were.

> Be sure to use the full URL http://mydomain.com/thispage.html when linking to pages on your own site, and consistently use the same URL on all links to a page.

Rule of Thumb Don't use words such as "click here" on their own to create text links. Include words descriptive of the link subject..

The text that you use for linking (known as the anchor text) should be specially written for that purpose. You need the text to adequately describe what visitors will find when they click it, and the best descriptions use the most important keyword(s) at the beginning. For example, if your anchor text is "this article in Scientific American" it would be better written as "the article on increased longevity in *Scientific American*."

Related Questions

➜ 42. How user-friendly will your links be? **Page 109**

➜ 89. Will your links to and from other sites be search engine-friendly? **Page 257**

➜ 94. Will you be regularly checking your site's functionality? **Page 277**

Action Items

➜ On your site map make notes, perhaps using a special color of arrow, about opportunities to link from one page to another within the content. Do the same for links to other sites you might have missed.

➜ Check what anchor text you've chosen for your links and see if it needs rewriting to be more descriptive, while keeping the natural flow of the content.

Importance

61. Will You Effectively Use Images in Your Content?

Using images within your content can be a powerful way of capturing visitors' attention and communicating your message. Images have been shown to draw people out of the typical "F" pattern of scanning a page (across the top and down the left side), so if they're not used effectively, they can be powerful distractions. The following sections give you some ideas for effective use of images in your content.

Stay on Topic

Photos or graphics need to support the main focus of the page, for example, having a photo of a product, the location being discussed, or the event you're reporting on. No matter how great an image might be, if it doesn't help your visitors understand what you're saying on the page, it is diverting their attention (in fact, the nicer the image, the greater the distraction).

A popular use of images is to show something symbolic, such as a photo of a security guard in an article about laptop security. However, make sure the symbolism is clear so the reader isn't spending time trying to connect it to the content, as in the example of Figure 7-5.

If you're not sure whether an image is appropriate, ask other people if it makes sense to them.

Finding the right image can be time-consuming, so you'll find some resources for locating affordable or even free images in the section for this chapter in Appendix A.

Be sure you have the right to use the images. Even if you've purchased an image, you need to read the details of the contract to be certain it can be used on a website. For photos you take yourself, make sure you have the permission of the people in the photo.

Public events or locations might or might not be fair game, depending on the laws of your country.

Does My Website Need a Content Management System?

June 3rd, 2010 **2 Comments**   Posted by marlon

*Website content management systems, or CMS, are a simple and affordable way for a business to take control of the content that is presented on their website. Content management systems are available in a range of **dynamic applications**, and generally involve a password-protected administration area, an HTML site editor, and true simplicity in ease-of-use.*

The website content management system, or CMS, has revolutionized the way that website content is created and managed. Perhaps some of the most significant advancements of the **Web 2.0** era have occurred in the backend administration of websites.

Content Management Systems: CMS

One of the most common and flexible of these advancements is the CMS, which gives users an easy and intuitive means to update and edit Web content without the need to learn any HTML or CSS coding.

FIGURE 7-5

Be Real

Sometimes stock photos of people might be your only option, but whenever you can, use photos of real people—you, people in your organization, your clients, and so on. As long as the quality of the photograph is reasonable—visitors aren't struggling with poor lighting or blurriness—people want to see you and your world, not a bunch of models play-acting.

Show Activity

When possible, use action shots of people. Instead of a picture of yourself standing at a trade show booth, use one that shows you demonstrating something or talking with someone. Even action shots of objects (a car moving instead of sitting in a driveway) or animals (a lion crouching instead of lying still) can be more compelling, depending on the point of the image.

An image might support the page's primary idea, but if there are already four other supporting images on a fairly short page, for example, you might be overloading the visitor visually. Consider creating a gallery of thumbnails for the page or setting up a single rotating image. Or simply ask yourself if you need all those images. If you have a very long page with lots of images, could it be broken up into several pages or several different but related topics?

Clip art is the term used for stock drawings and illustrations you can find both online and off. Be sure to use high-quality clip art. Limit the Quantity

Get the Right Proportions

Even the right photo in the right place can be less effective if it's not sized effectively. This is a matter of keeping the proportions right. For example, if an image will squeeze the text around it and make it hard to read, that's a distraction.

In Figure 7-6, in the left pane, you can see an image forcing the text into a tiny column on the right. Making the image smaller can help with the text, but you also don't want to make it difficult to see what's in the image, as shown in the middle screen. In this situation, it makes sense not to wrap the text at all and instead size the image to the width of the text as shown in the right screen of Figure 7-6.

Resizing an image is always best done by changing the actual size of the image and uploading it again to your site. Some content management systems (CMSs) have built-in image editors that make physical resizing even easier.

Lorem ipsum dolor sit amet, convallis tincidunt non varius magna voluptatibus, lacus rutrum iaculis laoreet sem, posuere nullam pellentesque eu vulputate dapibus fringilla, mi mattis risus libero condimentum sed. Sed natoque tellus, est senectus condimentum in, elementum rhoncus mauris sapien. A consectetuer pede feugiat ipsum mollis cursus, in semper nunc, non in proin fringilla proin enim. Tellus habitant

Lorem ipsum dolor sit amet, convallis tincidunt non varius magna voluptatibus, lacus rutrum iaculis laoreet sem, posuere nullam pellentesque eu vulputate dapibus fringilla, mi mattis risus libero condimentum sed. Sed natoque tellus, est senectus condimentum in, elementum rhoncus mauris sapien. A consectetuer pede feugiat ipsum mollis cursus, in semper nunc, non in proin fringilla proin enim. Tellus habitant ornare, sodales massa nunc metus amet, cursus leo quis eros sagittis quam, cursus orci feugiat lacinia ligula, felis odio quis etiam euismod.

Lorem ipsum dolor sit amet, convallis tincidunt non varius magna voluptatibus, lacus rutrum iaculis laoreet sem, posuere nullam pellentesque eu vulputate dapibus fringilla, mi mattis risus libero condimentum sed. Sed natoque tellus, est senectus condimentum in, elementum rhoncus mauris sapien. A consectetuer pede

FIGURE 7-6

Composition

Although the details of good photography are outside the scope of this book, there are some simple techniques to help make your photos more effective. For example, don't just use a photo straight out of the camera or from a stock photography site. Think about how it might be edited to increase its impact. Take a look at the two versions of the photo in Figure 7-7.

FIGURE 7-7

By eliminating a lot of the background, the drama of the image is greatly increased, and your attention is drawn to what's important. In other cases, the full background might be important to the context or to create a sense of isolation of the element you want people to focus on.

One of the techniques used in editing the shot for Figure 7-7 was to set the subject off to one side, rather than having it exactly centered. If you can do that when taking the picture, all the better, but your image-editing software is always there as backup.

Something that editing can't help with is the angle of the camera in relation to the subject. Instead of straight-on eye-level shots, play with the angle of your subject or your camera. Have the subject turn their head slightly to face you, or get higher or lower than your subject to create additional interest. You can see the difference a fresh angle can make in Figure 7-8.

FIGURE 7-8

Digital cameras have taken a lot of the technical difficulty out of getting clear, decently lit shots, so now you can focus more on setting up great shots or capturing the fleeting moments that used to go unrecorded.

Related Questions

◆ 26. Will images be used effectively in your design? **Page 63**

◆ 54. Will your nontext files use the proper file types? **Page 143**

◆ 88. Will your search engine strategy cover specialty searches? **Page 242**

Action Items

◆ For each page on your site, make a wish list of images. Don't limit yourself to images you know you already have and don't think about how many images you'll actually use.

◆ Take the photos on your wish list and rate each one on the criteria raised in this question (relevance, activity, composition, and so on).

Importance

The power of video and audio also means that if they're done poorly, the bad impression will be all the stronger. Don't rush out to make a video or audio without some practice. Try these search terms: 🔍 tips for better videos and 🔍 tips for a better speaking voice.

62. How Will You Use Video or Audio in Your Content?

The promise of multimedia on the Internet has started to be realized over the last few years—faster computers, faster Internet connections, better web technology, cheaper recording equipment. What this means is that the average website owner can take advantage of the power of video and audio to create even more compelling content.

If content is king on the Internet, video is making a play to become the king of content. That's because in many ways, video can bring visitors closer to your subject matter than words or images ever could.

Here are some ideas to get you thinking about videos you can produce:

- Demonstrate how your new lawnmower works.
- Have customers send in videos of them using your workout video.
- Give step-by-step instructions for organizing a room.
- Show an example of your charity at work.
- Have your staff members talk about their favorite books.
- Answer some of your most frequently asked questions.
- Record your talk to the Rotary Club.

The tone of these videos can vary with the topic or with your audience, but even when you're having a bit of fun with the subject matter, remember that in the long term, people are looking for information.

Rule of Thumb   Most videos should be under five minutes. If you have longer material, find ways to make several short pieces.

Having video or audio interviews with other people (experts, customers, staff, and so on) not only gives you more content, but can be helpful if you're not yet comfortable on camera or the microphone.

Then of course there's the holy grail of viral videos: to have hundreds of thousands of people passing around the link to your masterpiece. The trick is that such videos require either a lot of time, skill, and money to produce, or they're flukes. This doesn't mean you shouldn't keep taking video of everything and anything in case you catch a golden moment; just don't lose sleep, money, or family over it.

Remember that video is not restricted to on-camera material. Screencasts are videos of what's on your computer screen, with or without audio. These are particularly suited to demonstrating software or Internet material. Slideshow presentations are another form of video that you can easily create and save for viewing on your website. There are even slideshow sharing sites akin to YouTube, in which you can post your presentations for easy viewing by anyone as well as simple embedding on your site.

Audio

Audio provides a unique opportunity for connecting with your audience because it's both intimate and less demanding of your audience's attention. People can listen to you while they're doing something else on their computers. With downloaded audio they can listen while driving, exercising, doing chores, and more, all of which can greatly extend the reach of your content. Here are some examples to get you thinking about how to use audio:

- Reading a chapter from your new book
- Giving tips on home renovation
- A public talk you've given
- A sample coaching session for your mentoring business
- An interview with a well-known leader in your yoga community
- A sample song from your CD

If you enjoy the audio format and have lots of material to present, you can turn that into a *podcast* (the loose term for any regular or somewhat regular audio placed on the Web). A podcast can be as straightforward as putting up a weekly or biweekly file on your website, or as elaborate as creating your own talk show on a third-party podcasting platform.

On Video

See a demonstration of how easily you can put a video from a sharing site onto a page of your own site.

Avoid having video and audio files play automatically; instead, let visitors choose.

Always give a good text-based description of what's in a video or an audio so that visitors and search engines can understand the basics of what's on the video without having to view it.

Related Questions

+ 54. Will your nontext files use the proper file types? **Page 140**

+ 78. Are you willing to get in front of the public online or off? **Page 218**

+ 88. Will your search engine strategy cover specialty searches? **Page 252**

Action Items

+ Make a list of potential videos you could produce for your site. Plan which ones might be done as a group to save time and production costs.

+ Start searching video sharing sites for videos you might use on your site. Sites like You Tube will even recommend videos based on your viewing habits.

+ Get a camera that does high definition (HD) video (easily available for under $200) and get a good quality headset and microphone for doing audio recordings (under $100).

63. Will Your Site Use a Splash Page?

Importance

Rule Of Thumb   Don't use a splash page.

That answer will be qualified in a moment, but for the vast majority of websites, it's still NO. If you're not familiar with the term, a *splash page* is an opening page of a website with no content other than a few images or an animation and perhaps a linked phrase such as "Enter the site." The example in Figure 7-9 expects you to know that you should click the logo.

FIGURE 7-9

Although they've become less common, splash pages still get created unnecessarily, and here are two important reasons why they shouldn't:

➔ They create a barrier for your visitors by giving no information as well as adding an extra click.

➔ They create a barrier for search engines because the very first page of your site does not have what they need most for indexing purposes: content.

On Video

See examples of splash pages that do and do not work.

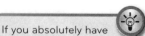

If you absolutely have to have a splash page, be sure to tell visitors they need to click to enter the site and make sure that instruction is very clear. If you're using a Flash animation, have a prominent "skip intro" button.

How much of a barrier do you create for visitors? Keeping in mind that people take as little as 6 seconds to decide whether to stay on a website, the chances that they'd be willing to click through to the real front page and start the decision-making process all over again seem pretty low.

There are, however, situations in which a splash page might be of value, including the following examples:

◆ You have multiple versions of a site (different languages, countries). See the example in the left side of Figure 7-10.

◆ You have very different sections on a site with very different audiences (buyers/sellers, consumers/businesses, students/faculty/parents/public) and you want to direct people to them with a very simple menu.

◆ You have very important news, such as a new product or new location, and you want to draw extra attention to it temporarily. See the example in the right side of Figure 7-10.

FIGURE 7-10

The emphasis here is on "might be of value" because in all of these examples, you can accomplish the same thing within the content of a home page or by using a bar that drops down from the top of the site to draw attention to the choices.

The point is that you need a very good reason for deciding to use a splash page.

Related Questions

→ 34. Will you be using animation in your design? **Page 84**

→ 57. Will your content be easily accessible? **Page 148**

→ 87. Will your content be search engine-friendly? **Page 247**

Action Items

→ When interviewing website designers, ask if they would recommend a splash page.

→ Ask yourself if you have one or more audiences that have content which would not be or likely would not be of interest to other visitors. Then ask whether this warrants a splash page or just a large button or some other indicator on the home page.

Importance

64. What Content Will Be on Your Home Page?

As little as possible is the quick-and-dirty answer to this question. Unless you have a one-page website, most of your content will be on other pages, so the function of the home page will be to help visitors decide where to begin. If the home page on an average website is too busy, you make the decision difficult or impossible, and visitors will leave.

Because visitors can enter your site through any page at all, your name, logo, tagline (a one-line description of your site), header graphics, and navigation should tell visitors who you are, what you do, where you do it (if relevant), and the main links to the rest of your site. Your home page might elaborate a bit on these points, but its primary task is to get visitors excited about one or a couple of actions they can take on your site, as in the example of Figure 7-11.

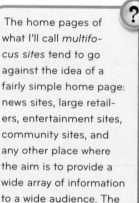

The home pages of what I'll call *multifocus sites* tend to go against the idea of a fairly simple home page: news sites, large retailers, entertainment sites, community sites, and any other place where the aim is to provide a wide array of information to a wide audience. The average website owner is creating essentially a single-focus site, so that is my concern here.

Because the home page is meant to direct visitors, its layout might be quite different from the rest of the site, and it might use graphics more than normal content would. But there should always be enough text on the home page to get the points across, even without images.

FIGURE 7-11

Whether you want visitors to learn more, sign up, subscribe, buy, donate, or share, the home page is your prime real estate for motivating those actions.

There is no right or wrong about the content you should put on your home page, other than to say if visitors aren't clicking any deeper or taking the actions you've suggested, you either need to rewrite/design the content or find something new. Whatever the content is, keep the text short, focused, and clearly written (and any graphics need to be the same). Home page content doesn't have to be award-winning, but if it's clear and you've properly assessed your audience's needs, it should be an effective home page. Figure 7-12 shows a couple of examples.

FIGURE 7-12

Nothing fancy, but they're on the right track.

One of the most common home page mistakes is to treat it like the About page. Details about who you are or what your company is about do not belong on the home page, although a quick summary often does (with a link to the About page). What visitors are actually looking for in home page content is your recommendations about what's newest, most useful, and/or most important.

The danger of not staying focused on the needs of your visitors is that everything on your site is useful and important to you. The result is that the home page can become congested over time, as Figure 7-13 illustrates.

FIGURE 7-13

Each addition seems absolutely vital at the time until soon the home page is so crammed with information that visitors are overwhelmed and nothing gets noticed. Here are a couple of suggestions to prevent or at least minimize home page bloat:

→ Follow the principle of one in, one out. Whenever you add something to the home page, take something else away. If you absolutely cannot take something off, maybe what you were going to add was not important enough and has to find a different place on the site.

→ Plan for additions by creating an area on the home page that is meant to change more frequently than the others. A featured content box is one example—even better if it's a mini slideshow displaying four or five items at a time. Or you can have an area on your sidebar for "internal advertisements" that clicks through to other parts of the site or simply announces something you have to offer. Figure 7-14 shows what they can look like.

Not only will these areas make it easier for you to keep the home page lean but returning visitors will also know where to look for the latest information.

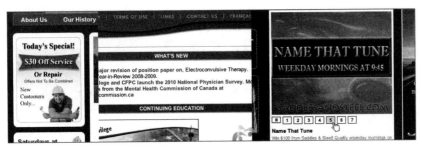

FIGURE 7-14

One final point about home pages: If your audience is primarily local (and for a large portion of business sites on the Web, that's the case), make it very clear on the home page. I mentioned earlier that your header should mention the region you cover, but the home page is a chance to play with this. Use local references in your copy ("located in the heart of the West Side" or "just steps from Chinatown"); have quotes from local media; show images that capture a neighborhood. This is about more than letting them know where you are; it's about showing you're part of the community and making the visitor feel at home ("I love going to that festival, too" or "I read that review, too").

On Video

Samples of effective and not-so-effective home page content with additional commentary and ideas.

Related Questions

→ 23. Will your site layout make your content clear? **Page 60**

→ 45. How easily will visitors find important details specific to your site? **Page 116**

→ 57. Will your content be easily accessible? **Page 148**

→ 75. How will your site promote itself? **Page 211**

Action Items

→ Review your list of audience needs and the content you've developed to meet those needs, and then make a short list of the most important ones. Pick one or two to go on the home page. Once you've decided what content your home page should promote, do a few different mock-ups to find the best design and layout.

→ Make sure it will be easy for you to change featured content on your home page, in particular if you're using animation to present it (slide shows and so on).

Importance

65. What Basic Content Pages Will Be on Your Site?

Exactly what you have on your website is a very individual matter, but there are certain pages that virtually every site can benefit from.

About Us

An About page should offer a clear, succinct description of what you do, but it also needs to tell your story. Whether you're an individual, a small business, a corporation, or an organization, visitors want to know not just what you do but also why you do what you do. It doesn't have to be a story in the sense of being highly dramatic ("I got into the parachute business after almost being killed in a free fall"), but in the sense of being an insightful narrative. Figure 7-15 shows how a small- and a medium-sized business handle their About pages:

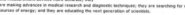

FIGURE 7-15

Even if the story of you does not directly relate to what your website is about, it tells the visitor something. Often it's the seemingly unrelated stories that are the most interesting: You studied art before becoming a mechanic, or the company is managed entirely by people who've come up through the ranks.

Don't make your About page a mere resume, although somewhere on there you could link to a resume (as a document or a web page), and don't turn it into a history lesson.

Above all, the About page should not be a sales pitch. Give visitors insights into you or your organization. Although every page on your site should help build a relationship with the visitor, that's the sole function of the About page.

You should always have at least one picture on your About page. Don't just choose your favorite photo; think about what would appeal to your audience. Try to avoid stiff photos. If professional and well-dressed is important, then do that, but perhaps make it one of you in action (giving a presentation; accepting an award; talking with people). If fun is what communicates you to your audience, make it a fun picture. If you're selling to pet owners, show you and your pet.

If there's absolutely no one to put a face to, look for important symbols, representative locations, iconic products, people being served, or whatever can personalize the company or organization.

It's easy to let an About page become too long. Consider whether all that content could be broken down into a history page, a mission statement, a philosophy/approach page, or other kinds of pages. If you have staff, a separate write-up for each is very important—the teachers in a preschool; the mechanics in a repair shop; the agents in a travel agency.

Displaying links related to your company or organization is a great way to end your About page. Show people where they can get in touch; how they can help or advertise; and any other related information, such as a history page, your press releases, or latest company news (as shown in the example in Figure 7-16).

expanded west, opening more stores in Ontario and entering new markets in Manitoba, Saskatchewan, Alberta and British Columbia. The Company is committed to continuing to grow the brand throughout the rest of Canada with new markets in Quebec and the Maritimes over the coming years. For more information on current store locations, click here to visit the Store Locator page.

Best Buy stores in Canada are a division of Burnaby, BC-based Best Buy Canada Ltd., a wholly owned subsidiary of Best Buy Co., Inc. (NYSE:BBY), who currently operates more than 600 Best Buy stores throughout the United States. For more information on Best Buy Co., Inc. click here to visit the Investor Relations page.

Call 1-866-BEST BUY or Contact Us

Store Locations And Hours

Need help finding a Best Buy store? Here you'll find our stores arranged by province and city; you'll even get maps and phone numbers—in short, everything you'll ever need to start shopping right away at one of our locations.

Click here for more info...

Careers

Think you have what it takes to be part of our amazing team? Best Buy is composed of talented individuals coming from diverse fields and with equally varied interests. Look around to learn about and apply for current job opportunities.

Click here for more info...

Press Releases

If you're a member of the press, here's your official source for Best Buy announcements, statements and bulletins. For accuracy, authenticity and verifiability, we recommend that you quote directly from this compilation of documents.

Click here for more info...

For our Investors

Find timely, relevant news on corporate plans, strategies and initiatives as well as management changes. Get an up-to-the-minute stock quote and the latest stock performance report. Read the most recent Annual Report and more.

Click here for more info...

Sponsorship Requests / Co-Promotional Opportunities

Is your agency or organization considering Best Buy for sponsorship or co-promotional opportunities? Find out where you should send your inquiry or request right here.

Click here for more info...

Community Relations

Find out how Best Buy gives back to the community via its partnership with various organizations that benefit children, youth and families. Discover Best Buy programs that encourage employee volunteerism, promote learning with the aid of technology and more.

Click here for more info...

FIGURE 7-16

Some About pages become nothing more than a set of links to sub-pages. In that case, at least have an introductory paragraph that might satisfy some visitors, and be sure to give short explanations of what each of the links will lead to.

Contact

Putting e-mail addresses on your contact page leaves you open to the addresses being used by spammers. You can try to protect the address through various means, but a contact form is your best bet.

After submitting the contact form, make sure that there's a clear message telling the visitor whether it was sent successfully.

Every site needs a centralized location for contact information. Even if you have some of it posted on the sidebar of every page, make sure that contact information is accessible entirely through this one page.

At a minimum, a contact page should have a basic form: name, e-mail, comment box, plus a telephone number if applicable. Helpful extras on a general contact form can be a drop-down menu describing what the message is generally about. This can help you quickly sort e-mail and also helps visitors know what they can use the form for. If you need to collect more specific information (for sales leads, quotes, and so on), create a separate page and form.

Beyond a contact form and phone number, think of anything that can be helpful to your visitors: from a complete staff directory list to a locator map (don't make people click away—embedded maps are so simple these days), hours of operation, various locations, and so on.

If you have a bricks-and-mortar location, include a picture of it, preferably one that shows it as visitors would see it from the road. Leave interior shots for a separate page about your facilities. Although the image of the company's location has not been put in larger form on the contact page displayed in Figure 7-17, all the other basic elements are in place.

It's helpful on a contact page to have even just a couple of lines to show how much you welcome comments and questions, and even indicate what kinds of issues people might be contacting you about. Contact information and a form by themselves can seem too impersonal.

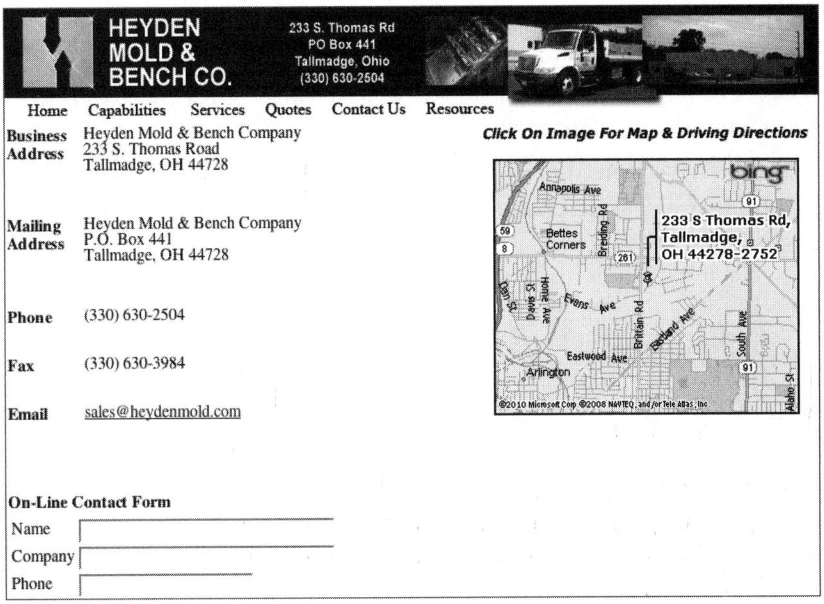

FIGURE 7-17

Frequently Asked Questions (FAQ)

Visitors always have questions, so answer the most common ones on a Frequently Asked Questions (FAQ) page. Some people find the term *FAQ* cliché, but whatever you call it—Support, Customer Questions—the idea is to anticipate what your visitors will want to know. Not only does it help them, but it also shows you're thinking about their needs.

The trick with an FAQ page is to pay attention to the word *Frequently* in the title. The questions should be ones that a lot of visitors might ask or ones that most people in a select group would ask (for instance, all Mac users). Beyond that, you might need what's commonly known as a knowledge base that makes it easy to manage very large numbers of specific questions ("How do I replace the cartridge on a model 52-A6 ink jet printer?").

Answers to FAQs should be fairly short. If a question gets to be more than a paragraph or two, it might warrant its own page within your content. A part of keeping answers short is to link to a place on your

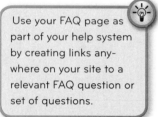

Use your FAQ page as part of your help system by creating links anywhere on your site to a relevant FAQ question or set of questions.

site that helps answer the question. Don't assume the visitor has seen the information on that page—people often go to an FAQ page before looking around on your site. Also, if there's a good answer to the question on another site, link to it.

If you have more than about 20 frequently asked questions, it's helpful to break them up by topic to avoid the crowding illustrated in Figure 7-18.

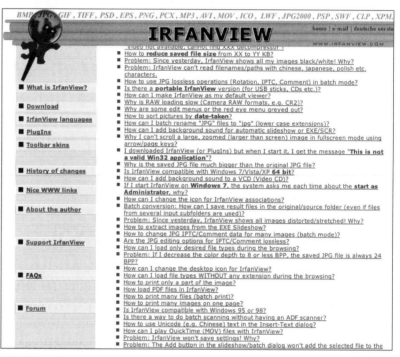

FIGURE 7-18

On Video
See examples of easy-to-use FAQ pages and some that are not so user-friendly.

Questions can be separated into groups on a single page, or each group can be given its own page, but in either case make it simple for visitors to navigate by having all the general topics listed on each page or having a clear "back to the top" link on a single page that gets them to the main FAQ menu. You don't want visitors to waste time clicking back and forth or having to constantly scroll to get around.

Make it easy for visitors to ask a question that isn't on your FAQ page by linking to your contact page or even providing a special form on the FAQ page itself. Very likely, the questions they ask will be ones you can add to the FAQs.

Media

It would be nice if *CNN* or the *New York Times* wanted to talk to you, but don't let the fact that it's highly unlikely stop you from having a media page on your site (and if they do call, you'll be ready). A media page is meant for anyone who needs materials in order to talk about you.

A blogger doing a review of your book needs an image of the cover, a conference organizer needs your bio and your photo, or the committee for an event you're sponsoring wants your logo for a poster. Not only have you made it easy for all these people to get what they need but you also ensured that it's what you want them to have. Logos are a perfect example of this. You don't want people using an old version of your logo or a poor quality version. By having your latest logo in various formats on your media page, you don't leave anything to chance.

Much of the material on a media page might be available elsewhere on the site, but you don't want to rely on it being found by chance. Plus, it likely needs to be made available in a format of use to journalists and others. For instance, the information from the About page and related pages should be a PDF for downloading, although the image of your location that's on the contact page should be available on the media page in a print-ready, high-resolution format.

Testimonials/Reviews/Case Studies

When you ask a friend if he's tried the new restaurant that just opened, you're doing exactly what your visitors want from your website: a recommendation from someone who's been there, done that, and liked it. Reviews and case studies provide similar reassurance.

If the people giving you testimonials agree to it, have them send photos of themselves. This can help make the testimonial all that more effective by humanizing the text. If they agree, it's also very important that testimonials contain their position and the name of their organization because it can greatly add to your credibility as well as the credibility of the testimonial itself.

When you're using reviews, be sure to quote them fairly and then link to a copy of the full review on their site. If you're going to publish the entire review on your site, it's a good idea to get permission and still offer a link back to the original.

If clients or customers agree to provide a testimonial, ask if it would be helpful to send them a sample testimonial based on things they've written or said. Then they can either approve it outright or edit it. That process makes things easier for them and increases the chance of actually getting the testimonial.

For case studies, get the permission of the client to publish even bare-bones details; if that's not possible, it might be better not to use the example at all. Some people disguise the client's identity, but even if it's done right, visitors might wonder why the client doesn't want to be identified.

Links/Resources

As you create content for your site, remember to add important links from that content to your links page.

The Web contains a staggering amount of information, which continues to grow daily at equally staggering rates. Anything you can do to help your visitors sort through that information is a huge benefit. A well-organized set of links, preferably with short, helpful descriptions, is always welcome—and remember to make it part of your frequent updating. If people know they can come to your site for the latest information on a topic, they'll bookmark it and return.

Just like linking within your content, make sure that the links here go to truly valuable websites. Not only visitors but also search engines will notice if you're wasting their time going to poor-quality sites.

If you have documents for visitors to download, gather links to all of them here so they're easily found. Visitors might forget where they downloaded an item or they might never see the document link within your content. Keeping all your site resources in one place makes it simple.

Services/Products

This might seem obvious, but some small businesses in particular think this all belongs on the home page or is covered in their About page. Your services might be mentioned on those pages, but the details (even if only a paragraph or two) belong on a separate page. And if there are several services or products, each needs its own page.

Make sure you link to your policy and terms pages from your FAQ page, both as stand-alone links and within questions that have all or part of their answer on those pages.

Privacy Policy/Terms

In a time when people are increasingly concerned about their privacy online, a page detailing your policy on the subject is not only important but also might be a requirement from a legal standpoint.

A privacy policy is not simply for sites that sell online or collect information through forms (newsletter signups, quotations, and so on). Your site might use cookies (small bits of code stored on visitor's computers), and you're not even aware of it. There's information generated by people's browsers that has the potential to be collected and stored. Even the site statistics that you compile—no matter how anonymous they might be—need to be addressed by a privacy policy. For help with writing a privacy policy, use this search term: 🔍 **website privacy policy sample**.

Terms and conditions pages tend to be associated with online selling, but most websites can benefit from making clear even just a few terms or conditions. What are the conditions of your services should someone hire you? What are your offline shipping terms? What are the terms for using material on your website? These are kinds of frequently asked questions, but put in more legal terms.

> It's worth running policy pages past a lawyer if you have any concerns about what exactly you should be saying.

Site Map

A site map is a set of links to every single page on your website. On larger sites, it's probably the only place where you can get to any page from one spot.

If you have fewer than 10 pages, a web page with your site map on it probably isn't necessary (although it can't hurt). Past 10 pages, however, a site map page can be very helpful as a guide for visitors. In particular, it's a great place to link to on your error page (when visitors have tried to get to a page that doesn't exist on your site). And when you do have a great many pages, it can be helpful to have a hierarchical site map such as the one in Figure 7-19.

This makes it easier for visitors to see the relationships between pages and not have to hunt through to figure out the section they want.

About the ILO
> Mission and objectives
> Origins and history
> Fields of action
> How the ILO works
>> Tripartism
>> Technical cooperation
> Media and public information
>> Press releases
>> Feature articles
>> Fact sheets
>> ILO in the media
>>> ILO on the air
>> Video
>>> Video News Releases
>>> Documentaries
>>> ILO TV: Our Workplace
>>> Institutional videos
>>> Public Service Announcements
>>> Video interviews
>>> Events coverage
>>> ILO TV and radio facilities
> Audio
> I-news

FIGURE 7-19

Related Questions

➡ 56. Will your content serve your site's purpose? **Page 146**

➡ 58. Will the content of each page have a single focus? **Page 151**

➡ 95. Do you have a plan for updating site content? **Page 279**

Action Items

➡ Get in the habit of asking for testimonials, making notes for possible case studies, noting what common questions are asked by your audience, and gathering useful links.

➡ For ideas on what other pages can be useful to your particular audience, check out websites in your field, but also be watching for different approaches being taken by sites in other subject areas.

66. Will You Be Blogging on Your Site?

Importance

A lot of people will tell you it's important to have a blog: Blogs are good for developing relationships with visitors and they can help get better exposure in search engines. But the personal nature of most blogs and their typical diary-style design can make it hard for website owners to see how exactly a blog would fit into their site.

What's important, however, is not the blog itself, but the act of blogging, which is nothing more than putting up interesting new content on a frequent basis. That's what keeps visitors (and search engines) coming back to blogs, so the question for you as a website owner is this: Can you come up with relevant, interesting content that can be updated frequently?

The answer is yes, if you give it some thought. For example, news about your company or organization is perfect blogging material. The new lathe in your machine shop, a newly hired stylist, the arrival of a new bicycle model, a change of hours, and the game results of the baseball team you sponsor—these are constantly changing bits of relevant information you can share with visitors.

If you expand this news to include trends in the world that affect your area of business, suddenly there's a mountain of potential topics for blogging: how the weather in India is affecting vacation plans; the implications of a new study on coffee habits; how an article in a magazine about sunscreen products might impact your visitors.

Here are some other ideas for blogging areas on a website—topics that involve constantly changing content:

→ Press releases

→ Articles

→ Tips

→ Features of the week

→ Testimonials

→ Case studies

If you set up a blogging area on your site, make sure you use it. The blank blog shown in Figure 7-20 (it was three months old at the time of writing) is not uncommon and it gives a negative impression.

> **?** The software that runs blogs is really just simple, easy-to-use content management software designed to display the most recent content first.

> **?** Frequently adding new material without a CMS is possible, but it's not as simple unless you're very comfortable working with HTML.

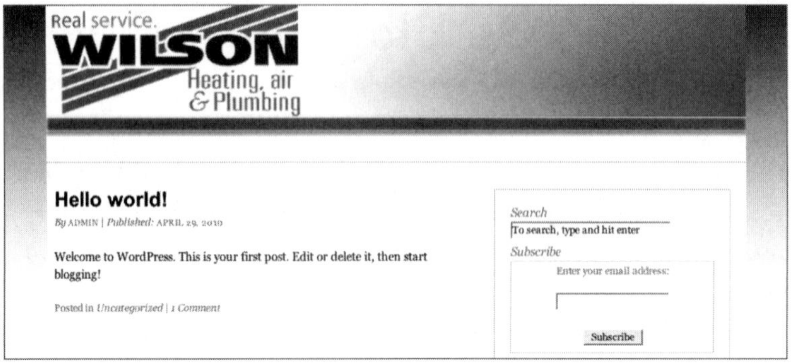

FIGURE 7-20

Updating or adding pages to your website is also important to keeping your site current, but this is different from the content being discussed here.

The same is true of content that's been regularly updated and then stops. But keeping content fresh can feel very daunting.

The trick to blogging is to make it as easy as possible. First of all, don't set the bar too high. If you can add one new item to your website every couple of weeks, that's often plenty for visitors and for search engines to keep returning.

The second trick to successful blogging is to make it as easy on your schedule as possible. Most CMSs, and certainly those aimed specifically at bloggers, make it easy to write content and have it appear any time in the future. So, a pastor who wants a daily devotion to appear on the church website could sit down once a month and write all the devotions at one time and schedule them to appear daily.

Related Questions

➜ 65. What basic content pages will be on your site? **Page 174**

➜ 87. Will your content be search engine-friendly? **Page 240**

➜ 95. Do you have a plan for updating site content? **Page 279**

Action Items

➜ Make sure the CMS you're planning to use allows you to schedule content to appear on a certain date as well as have it automatically appear on the designated area page of your site in reverse chronological order (newest items first).

➜ Start a file in which you can keep notes about blogging topics so that you're never stuck for ideas.

67. Will You Be Selling Online?

Importance

If you're planning to sell products or services directly from your website, there are a number of basic issues to consider. There's no room in this book to get into all the details, but these answers will at least get you started in the right direction.

There are three general options for building an online store:

→ **Hosted basic shopping cart**—You insert Buy Now or Add to Cart buttons anywhere on your website, which then click through to a secure server hosted by a third-party where the order is processed.

→ **Hosted full-feature shopping cart**—The software to manage and display products, and gather orders is all hosted on a secure third-party server.

→ **Self-hosted full-feature shopping cart**—You host and maintain the software to manage and display products, and gather orders.

Table 7-1 lists some pros and cons for each of the three shopping cart options.

TABLE 7-1: Shopping Cart Building Options

BUILDING OPTION	PROS	CONS
Hosted basic shopping cart	Easy to set up. Inexpensive to set up. No fees for the shopping cart. Product information and display are fully controlled by you.	No control over the checkout process. Limited shipping options. No product management software (other than your own CMS). No built-in customer service features such as product reviews, wish lists, gift certificates, and so on.

continues

TABLE 7-1:   Shopping Cart Building Options *(continued)*

BUILDING OPTION	PROS	CONS
Hosted full-feature shopping cart	Easy to set up. Little to no technical skills required. No software upgrades to deal with. All server tasks are handled for you, including backups. Extensive shipping options. Numerous customer service options.	Monthly service fee (starting at $30, but more in the $75–$120 range for the features most people would want). Limited customization options. Can't take software with you; you can take only your data.
Self-hosted full-feature shopping cart	Extensive shipping options. Numerous customer service options. Ability to customize any options or even add new ones. Portability—move your store to whatever server you want. Lower monthly fees (just for hosting, $10–$20). Many good open-source software packages.	You're responsible for updating the software. Some technical skills are required for setup and for any customization. Time or labor costs for setting up can be high.

?

Online stores consist of two distinct but connected parts: a catalog system and a shopping cart system. The entire system is usually referred to as a *shopping cart*, but technically the shopping cart is what enables you to buy multiple items at one time. The *catalog* part of the system is used to manage and display the items for sale.

If you're just selling a few products or services that won't change much and are usually purchased one at a time, the hosted basic shopping cart is perfect for you.

For example, if you sell coaching sessions, all you would do is sign up for an account with a company such as PayPal, use a wizard to create a Buy Now button, and then paste the HTML for that button into the page describing your coaching session. When clients click the button, they're taken to the PayPal server where they pay for the item. All you pay for is a transaction fee whenever someone buys something. Figure 7-21 shows you what things look like on your site and on PayPal.

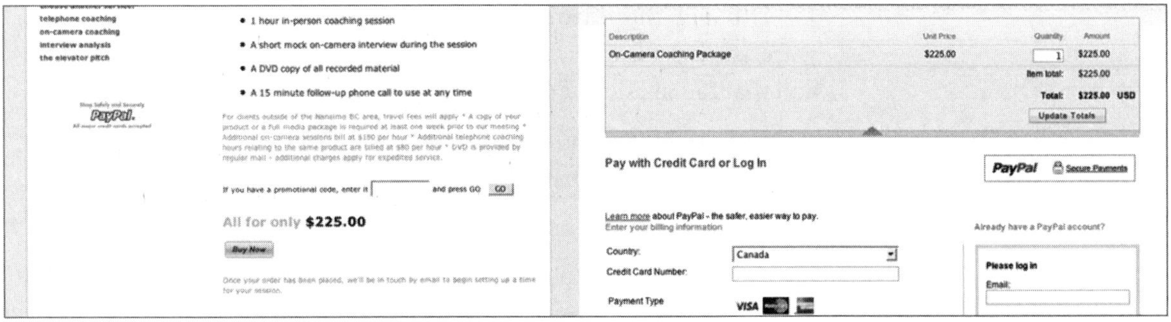

FIGURE 7-21

You can also have multiple products on your site and use an Add to Cart button for each. Clicking one of these buttons takes customers to the third-party server where they can see their shopping cart. They can then return to your site and either add more products or check out.

Although this basic shopping cart system is handy for a few services or products, it's very limited in areas such as shipping; and has no useful shopping cart features such as gift certificates, cross-product promotion, and so on.

For a true online store, you need a hosted or self-hosted shopping cart system. Deciding which hosting route to take depends on how you want to spend your time and money. If you have fairly good technical skills (or are very adventurous), hosting the shopping cart software yourself gives you great freedom, and the real cost is your time. If you're willing to pay someone else to do it, again the freedom to customize can be very important.

If you need to get a store up and running quickly and you're not worried about customization, a hosted solution makes a lot of sense. There might be more ongoing costs, but they're monthly fixed costs, and you don't have any maintenance concerns.

Having considered the hosting question, the next important issue is which shopping cart software to go with. Some software is available in both a hosted and a self-hosted version, which give you additional choices. Some software is open source, which means it's free to download, but you'll need good skills or people with good skills to implement it because there's no included support.

Although these are some of the considerations in choosing the software, the most important is whether it can do what you need it to do, and that means sitting down and making a list of what you need:

- Customer features (a ratings system? a recommended products system? wish lists?)

- Shipping options (real-time rates? weight-based, quantity-based?)

- Taxation options (value-added taxes? tax on shipping?)

- Payment processing (does the software interface with the payment processor you want to use?)

Armed with your list, start trying demos of various shopping carts, read reviews (including forums where technical issues are raised), and ask friends who run shopping carts on their sites.

The final step for setting up an online store is to hook up your shopping cart to what's commonly called a *payment gateway*—the system that ultimately connects the cart to a credit card merchant account. If you have a merchant account for one or more credit cards, they might have a payment gateway they recommend. You just need to be sure your shopping cart software supports the payment gateway or else you'll need to pay for a custom connection.

For many small websites, especially those just starting out, the cost of having a merchant account for one credit card, let alone several, is not worth it. Fortunately, there are many services, such as PayPal and 2CheckOut, which combine the function of being a payment gateway and processing credit cards. They usually don't have any setup or monthly fees—you pay a fee only when a purchase is made.

Having mentioned the key technical issues involved in setting up online selling, the next big step is the storefront. Like everything, the key is to always think of your customers. What features will make shopping easier for them? What images will help them better understand the product? How will the product descriptions make clear the benefits of buying the product? Is there any way to make the checkout process clearer?

The checkout process is one of the main stumbling blocks to the completion of online transactions. Customers will often have no trouble finding what they need, but getting it through the checkout isn't always as easy and that's where transactions tend to get abandoned.

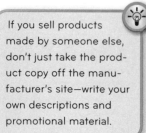

If you use a third-party credit card processor, keep an eye on your monthly fees. If your sales keep growing, there might come a point where it's more economical to get your own credit card merchant account(s).

If you sell products made by someone else, don't just take the product copy off the manufacturer's site—write your own descriptions and promotional material.

One of the things to look for in shopping cart software is a user-friendly checkout process or you might be able to customize a fairly good system to be even better. For example, if there are four steps to the checkout process, list the four steps at the top of the page and indicate which step the customer is now on. There's nothing worse than wondering what's happening and whether everything is progressing properly. Clear communication is vital.

Related Questions

➡ 39. Will your forms be easy to use? **Page 101**

➡ 99. Will you be collecting sensitive visitor information on your site? **Page 292**

Action Items

➡ If you're going to be selling more than a few items, make a separate site plan for your online store: how many product pages, categories, cross-referencing of products in categories, check-out flow, support pages, and so on.

➡ If there are online stores of small to medium-sized sites that you enjoy using, find out what shopping cart system they have (larger sites will typically have their own custom software—though you can learn about good shopping cart practices from them). If you don't do much online shopping, ask friends what sites they like to use.

Marketing and Promotion

In this chapter:

Importance

68. Do You Have a Web Marketing Plan?

In the introduction to this book, I asked the question, "Why do you want to build a website?" The answer to that question is an important part of your web marketing plan because a website is at the heart of all online marketing. The current answer gives you a brief overview of some other elements in a web marketing plan.

A web marketing plan should be part of a broader marketing plan for your business or organization. For many small- to medium-sized outfits, web marketing might be the largest component of a marketing plan, but it's still part of something larger. If you don't have any marketing plan at all, hopefully this answer will convince you of its importance.

Marketing plans are vital, in part because they commit your ideas and plans to paper. It's too easy to lose sight of goals, strategies, and methods floating around in your head, and even easier to change them to suit the moment. A written set of plans keeps you honest. That's not to say plans can't or shouldn't change, but having them in document form helps force you to justify changes.

> **Rule of Thumb** Review your marketing plan at least every three months. Check how well you're doing, what needs revising, and so on.

Here are some key sections that can make your marketing plan useful:

→ **SWOT analysis**—SWOT stands for strengths, weaknesses, opportunities, and threats. The strengths and weaknesses are about your site, whereas the opportunities and threats are about the market you're competing in.

→ **Target audience**—To whom are you marketing? Knowing age, gender, occupation, location, income, taste, and ethnic background can help you decide how you're going to reach that audience. Understanding the needs of your audience can help you decide what you're going to say to them. How will you be able to help your audience?

> **?** The rest of this chapter covers key web marketing tools, except for search engines, which are covered in Chapter 9.

> **?** In some cases, a website is the product itself and a marketing tool. In this book, I treat a website strictly as a marketing tool.

> A marketing plan can be as simple as a few lines on each topic. Don't put off writing the plan because you think it needs to be a long complex document.

> At every point of your plan, set specific goals. For example, one goal might be to increase new visitors this year by 20 percent, get 20 newsletter signups per month, send a promotional article offer to 5 key websites, and so on.

◆ **Strategies**—Although strategies might be broad in scope, they should not be so general as to be useless. For example, "get more business" is not very helpful, whereas "increase purchases by current customers" provides guidance. You'll also have different strategies—for instance, one for each product or for each service your organization provides.

◆ **Tactics**—These are the details about how you will implement your strategies. What are the objectives for each tactic? What is the message being delivered? What tools will be used?

◆ **Budgeting and measurement**—What are the costs for implementing the marketing plans? What is the expected return? How will the results of the plan be measured?

Creating a marketing calendar on a spreadsheet or a project management program such as Microsoft Project is a great way to lay out your tactics as a series of tasks. Give each task a start and end date, indicate who will perform each task, and determine its priority. Use color coding to help visualize types of tasks (e-mail marketing versus article marketing, and so on).

Related Questions

◆ 56. Will your content serve your site's purpose? **Page 146**

◆ 83. How do you plan to track website visitors and marketing results? **Page 233**

◆ 84. What are your search engine expectations? **Page 238**

Action Items

◆ Get something written down as soon as possible. Start by writing a couple of sentences for each part of the marketing plan. The sooner you commit something to writing, the more focused your marketing efforts will become, and the more likely you'll build a marketing plan over time.

◆ Set aside time for working on your marketing plan and create a routine: for example, half an hour at the end of each work day or two hours every Monday night.

Importance

69. How Will You Build Your E-mail List?

E-mail remains an essential part of communication on the Web. Social media tools come and go, and people might or might not regularly look at their social media accounts, but you can count on e-mail being checked regularly. That's why an e-mail list of people interested in your ideas, products, or services remains a cornerstone of any web marketing plan. How you build that list is what this answer is all about.

Here are some ideas for building your e-mail list offline:

> Start building your e-mail list now, whether you have a website or not.

- **E-mail list signup sheet**—Use this sheet at trade shows, openings or open houses, book signings, or when giving a speech.

- **Business card drops**—Many businesses already use these boxes to do draws, so why not add a notice saying that entrants will be placed on a mailing list? You can use these drops at trade shows, at a point of sale, in an office, or in a waiting room.

- **Print advertising**—Mention signing up for a free report or a newsletter; then direct people to your website (or an e-mail address if your site is not up yet).

- **Meeting people**—As part of your follow-up after meeting people, be sure to ask them to join your mailing list.

- **Teleseminars**—If you're holding your own teleseminar, make mailing list signup part of the general signup process, or promote the newsletter during the seminar and then follow up with an e-mail to join.

> Apart from damaging your own reputation, there can be other consequences for sending e-mails to people who have not requested them: You might be banned from the service you use to send the e-mail or you might even face legal action under antispamming laws.

Rule of Thumb You must clearly tell people they're signing up for an e-mail list and you must have proof that they agreed to sign up.

E-mail marketing is sometimes referred to as permission-based marketing because it requires you to get permission from the person you're putting on the mailing list. Any offline additions to your list must include doing the following:

- Clearly state that you will put the e-mail address on a mailing list, with a short explanation of what the mailing list is about

(a newsletter, a notification list, product offers). When possible, have the person fill out a very short form on which all these facts are stated.

➤ Keep track of when, where, and how you got the e-mail address. For example, have columns in a spreadsheet for each piece of information: March 23, 2010—National Knitting Convention, Atlanta—Signup Sheet. If you have a hard copy of their request, keep that on file, too.

Getting permission, also known as opting in, is a much simpler task online because programs and services used to gather e-mail addresses have built-in features to ensure that people on your list have agreed to join.

The most important online tool for building your mailing list is the signup form on your website, some samples of which are shown in Figure 8-1:

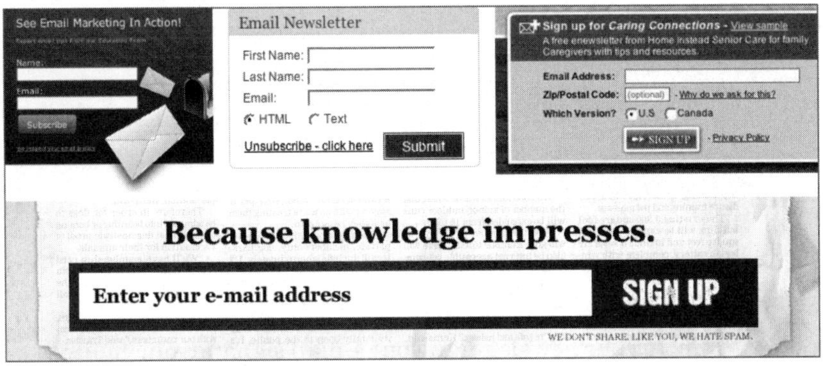

FIGURE 8-1

There are three important features of a good e-mail signup form:

➤ **It is short**—More and more forms are asking only for the e-mail address, not even a name.

➤ **It is visible**—The top right of websites is a common place for people to look and it can help to have the form on every page of your site.

➤ **It is clear**—What are they signing up for? What will happen to their address? A few words of explanation and a link to your privacy policy usually is enough.

Never buy e-mail lists. Even legitimate, opted-in e-mail lists that you rent (you're never given the e-mail—the company sends out your information) need to be approached with care. What's the reputation of the rental company? How strict is their opt-in process? Your name will be on the e-mail that's sent out, so you need to make sure that the people receiving it gave their permission.

On Video

Watch more examples of e-mail signup forms, including ones that display on mouseover or pop up when a page loads.

Some sites have their signup forms appear as popups when the page loads. Although visitors generally find popups annoying, the difference here is that you're doing the promoting so it's relevant to your site and you're usually offering visitors something of value for joining the list.

E-mail list managers have default thank you pages after someone confirms that they want to join your list (opting in). But make your own thank you page so you control the look and the message.

One of the best ways to encourage people to sign up for your list is to offer an immediate bonus for joining. It might be a free report that they download after reaching the thank you page of the signup process or it could be a link to special video you've produced.

Besides the signup form on your site, there are other ways to build your mailing list online:

➨ Mention your newsletter, with a link to the signup form, at relevant points in your website content.

➨ Include a check box on any purchase forms, stating that the buyer agrees to join your mailing list, as shown in Figure 8-2.

Whenever you have a check box for joining your mailing list, don't have it checked off by default. Many people won't realize they've agreed to join your list, and they might not be too pleased when they start to receive your e-mail. You might get fewer signups without default checking, but you'll know the visitors chose to sign up.

* State	Please select		**Enter Shipping Address:**	
Province/State			☐ My shipping and billing addresses are the same	
* Zip			* First Name	
* Country	USA		Middle Initial	
* Day Phone			* Last Name	
Evening Phone			Company	
* Email			* Address Line 1	
For order status information			Apt. or Suite#	
* Re-Enter Email			* City	
☐ I want to receive promotional news via email				

FIGURE 8-2

➨ In your e-mail newsletter, encourage people to pass it along to friends who might be interested and have a link on the newsletter for joining up.

➨ Promote your newsletter in your e-mail signature, including a link directly to the signup form.

➨ Approach other newsletters you respect and ask if they'd be interested in a shared promotion—you each mention the other newsletter to your respective subscribers.

➨ Make sure your social media friends know about your e-mail mailing list—perhaps even offer them a special bonus for signing up.

➨ Hold webinars and either include joining your mailing list as part of signing up for the webinar, or at least promote your newsletter during the webinar and in your follow-up e-mail.

➨ Create a page (perhaps with its own domain name) which has nothing but a special offer and the chance to join the mailing list.

Never place people from your social media circles on your e-mail list without their permission. Becoming a friend or follower on a particular social media platform is not the same as opting in to your e-mail list.

Related Questions

➤ 37. Will visitors easily know how to stay in touch with you? **Page 95**

➤ 38. Will your site use popups? **Page 98**

➤ 71. How will you manage your mailing list? **Page 202**

➤ 82. How will you be promoting your site offline? **Page 231**

➤ 99. Will you be collecting sensitive visitor information on your site? **Page 292**

Action Items

➤ Create an e-mail signup sheet you can use offline. Make sure it's clear what people are signing up for.

➤ Start a spreadsheet for recording offline signups; add columns for the dates, locations, circumstances, and (if you have multiple lists) which one people signed up for.

➤ Carefully consider where you want an e-mail signup form in your site layout, what it will look like, what it will say, and so on.

Importance

70. How Will You Market Yourself Using E-mail?

E-mail marketing needs to be clearly distinguished from unsolicited e-mail advertising (spam). In the previous question, I talked about having the permission of people on your e-mail list. The other factor that distinguishes e-mail marketing from spam is that you're always sending something of value in addition to asking subscribers to take some action (buy, donate, participate).

The most common form of e-mail marketing is the newsletter. The name is a little bit misleading because newsletters can be anything from a minimagazine to a kind of retail flyer to a single article. What they have in common is that they're sent out on a regular basis. When scheduling your mailouts, you need to strike a balance between people forgetting who you are and constantly bothering them.

Rule of Thumb   A typical e-mail newsletter schedule should be no less than once a month and no more than once a week.

Newsletters also vary greatly in production values—from fancy graphics to plain text. A couple of samples are shown in Figure 8-3:

> Think of e-mail marketing as pitching yourself by example. By providing useful content, you're marketing your expertise and your understanding of the audience's needs. Of course, it's always crucial to be closing the deal by giving subscribers a call to action, but they'll want to act because you've proven your worth.

On Video

See more examples and details of actual newsletters, including text-only versions of newsletters.

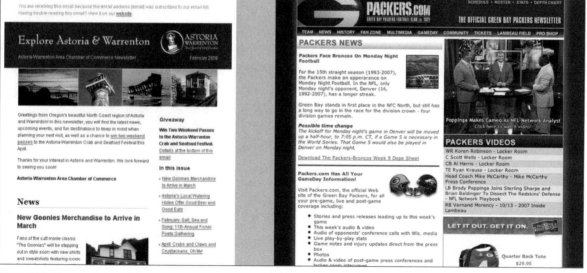

FIGURE 8-3

Whatever the format or style, the key is to make your newsletter short, relevant, and reflective of you. The material should be something subscribers can use (advice, tools, ideas) or act on (offers, new items) immediately, but it needs to come from you.

For instance, you might have an article on the importance of great customer service. There's nothing new about the topic, but by giving your definition of great customer service, supporting it with a story that happened to you, you make the point your own way. We all benefit by hearing similar knowledge explained in new ways, so don't worry about being absolutely new; be concerned instead about being you and being clear.

Here are some content ideas for a newsletter:

- Solutions to problems your readers face
- How-to tips and articles
- Checklists your readers can use
- Case studies
- Customer stories and testimonials
- Opinion pieces about topics in your industry or the news
- Your reviews of books, blogs, articles, documentaries, and so on
- Interviews of people who will benefit your readers

Here are some ideas for finding newsletter material:

- Look for older material you've written that you can update, or create short excerpt articles.
- Study which of your newsletter links people click the most or what they read on your site and do more items on those topics.
- Pay attention to the questions people are asking you day-to-day or ask newsletter readers to send in questions.
- Discuss articles or books you've read.
- Look for topics in videos, TV shows, and movies.
- Events you've attended
- Read other newsletters/blogs in your field and look for ideas. Newsletters that provide daily summaries of stories in your field are particularly handy.

However fancy your newsletter, make it available in a text-only format too, because many people turn off graphics in their e-mail programs.

Keep your mailing list material as fresh and as exclusive as possible. Part of the reason for joining the mailing list is to get the very latest information that no one else is getting. After it's been out for a month or two, you can use older newsletter material publicly on your site or for article material.

Keep an ideas folder and put notes in it for when you're having trouble finding material.

Newsletters are the most common type of e-mail sent to subscribers, but you can also have mailing lists that send out: product or event notifications, tips, free courses, press releases, or blog headlines.

- Set up a Google Alert(s) to notify you about information on the Web related to your topic.
- Event or product notifications
- A single, regular tip (weekly or monthly)
- A series of lessons

In addition to the content, here are some other key elements to include in the newsletter:

- The person's name at the beginning of the e-mail
- Headlines at the top linking to each item
- At least one action item (buy, fill out, sign up, make a booking)
- Your contact information, including links back to your website
- Invitation to pass along the newsletter to others who might be interested
- Permission to reproduce your content with credit
- A reminder why the person is receiving this e-mail
- An unsubscribe link

Rule of Thumb   The subject line or at least the from field of an e-mail should include a consistent identifier, so subscribers know who it's from.

One other important element of any e-mail newsletter is the subject line, which will get subscribers to open the e-mail. Take your most compelling item in the mailing and write a short, clear, enticing headline for the subject.

If the newsletter is about last-minute travel deals, a subject line boasting the "Best Rates to London" will be appropriate. But if people signed up for a mailing list of travel tips and ideas, the subject line will probably turn them off—they're looking for "Secret Gardens of London." You want your travel tips readers to also read about "Best Rates to London," but that's not top of mind for them.

Related Questions

➡ 56. Will your content serve your site's purpose? **Page 146**

➡ 59. Will your written content be correct, clear, and well structured? **Page 153**

➡ 87. Will your content be search engine-friendly? **Page 247**

Action Items

➡ Start a planning sheet for your first six newsletters. Begin writing topic ideas, calls to action, and other details.

➡ Start a newsletter ideas file.

➡ If you don't already, subscribe to a couple of newsletters in your field. Make note of what you think is working and not working in their publications.

Importance

71. How Will You Manage Your Mailing List?

It's possible to keep your e-mail list in your e-mail program and send out mass mailings from time to time, but it's much easier and safer to use an e-mail list manager. These programs are designed to automate processes such as: having people sign up, mailing out materials, handling requests to unsubscribe, checking for duplicates, and so on.

There are two types of e-mail list managers. Each has its pros and cons, as Table 8-1 shows.

TABLE 8-1: E-mail List Managers

TYPE	PROS	CONS
Self-hosted software	No monthly fees if hosted as part of your website's account (the software itself might cost money). Can be fully customized to your needs.	You're responsible for all maintenance and dealing with software problems. Potential for exceeding your host's hourly limit on e-mail (about 200).
Third-party hosted services	Usually user-friendly. Often extensive reporting tools. No maintenance issues. No send restrictions. Usually great support, training.	Monthly fee based on volume. Customization is limited to a few extra fields. Only the data is yours.

Although you pay a monthly fee for most hosted e-mail list managers, it's only in the $15–$30 range for up to several thousand subscribers; and the savings in time, energy, and peace of mind are well worth it.

Rule of Thumb   Use a hosted e-mail list manager. Let it handle the technical aspects so you can focus on marketing and creating content.

Here are some features and policies you should look for in a hosted e-mail list manager:

- **List segmentation**—This is the ability to flag list members in various ways (gender, regions, likes, signup source, customer status, and so on), and then e-mail only those members who match the criteria.

- **Easy list editing**—You need to be able to go in yourself and add new information about list members or enable them to easily keep their information up-to-date.

- **Easy to use, quality templates**—You want it to be simple to create great-looking, easy-to-read e-mail that you can also brand.

- **Easy to use form creator**—It should be easy to customize forms to look exactly the way you want them to on your site. See the example in Figure 8-4.

- **Message assessment**—This is the capability to have the system check the content of your e-mail and rate how likely it might be seen as spam by other servers.

Always make regular backups of your e-mail list. Most managers include data export in a variety of formats.

On Video

Watch examples of using an online e-mail list manager: creating forms, managing lists, and so on.

FIGURE 8-4

➔ **Strict antispam policies**—You want the company to have zero tolerance for spam because if anyone else on the system gets the company black-listed, you'll all suffer.

➔ **Easy to use autoresponders**—These are automated messages, such as a follow-up thank you message one week after a person signs up, for example.

Related Questions

➔ 83. How do you plan to track website visitors and marketing results? **Page 233**

➔ 98. Will your site administration be securely accessed? **Page 292**

Action Items

➔ Look through the sites of popular mailing list managers such as MailChimp or Aweber. For reviews of these and other managers, search for 🔍 **best hosted e-mail list management**. If you're on social media, post a question asking for people's opinions about e-mail list managers.

➔ Sign up for trial periods on the ones that look promising so you can try out their features.

72. Which Social Media Will You Use to Promote Yourself?

Importance

If search engines and e-mail are two cornerstones of web marketing these days, social media is the third. It's no longer a question of whether to use social media, but rather which are best suited to your audience and to you. This answer is designed to give you a very brief overview of what's available and how the tools can help you.

There are four types of social media that are particularly effective for marketing purposes, as shown in Table 8-2.

> **?** Blogging is an important part of social media, but because blogging is covered in Chapter 7, I have not included it here.

TABLE 8-2: Social Media Types

TYPE	EXAMPLES	DESCRIPTION
Social networking	Twitter Facebook LinkedIn MySpace	These sites function like large communities within which smaller communities can be created, right down to a personal community. Most have a wide range of activities, from conversations to sharing media, to playing games, to creating groups.
Social bookmarking and news	Delicious Digg StumbleUpon	Pointing people to useful sites and interesting news, often with a community voting system that promotes items higher up the rank based on getting more votes.
Media sharing	YouTube Flickr SlideShare	Posting multimedia content for others to view and also place on their sites. Often include internal commenting and rating systems as well.
Social content	Wikipedia Yelp Yahoo! Answers Ehow	Sites where questions are posed, multiple answers are given by others, and the answers are rated; sites where reviews are posted; sites where pages are built and edited by visitors.

> **?** Social media have been transformational tools for marketing because of the capability to quickly and easily share information with large numbers of people while maintaining a personal connection. Equally transformational is the fact that each person has complete control over the messages they receive and the people they associate with. You're either a part of their conversation or you're not.

? **Rule of Thumb**   Try to include at least one tool from each of these four categories in your web marketing plan.

Beyond the big names listed in Table 8-2, there are hundreds of different social media tools out there. Even if they're not widely used, your audience might be using one of these less-well-known tools, and you should know about that. For example, Ning is a social networking tool like Facebook, and thousands of small groups have formed their own communities on Ning. Finding them and participating in their groups can be as valuable as being on Facebook.

Keep in mind that many social media tools tend to attract particular audiences. MySpace, for example, has become a haven for musicians and a generally younger demographic. LinkedIn by design has always aimed at the business community. Twitter, because of its immediacy and simplicity, has come to be heavily dominated by news and breaking stories. These are not hard and fast rules, but by doing a bit of research on sites listed in this chapter's section of Appendix A you can find the particular audience you're trying to reach. Find other people's summaries of the latest data by using the search phrase 🔍 social media demographics.

One of the keys to using social media tools is time management. Social networking tools (Facebook and Twitter in particular) can eat up a lot of time if you're not careful. At the other end of the spectrum, it's easy to forget to keep up with social media tools. That's why everyone can benefit from trying a regular schedule.

> 💡 Try a schedule of half an hour per day to check your social media accounts, post a few replies or new items, and so on. Adjust the schedule as needed to make social media manageable.

Related Questions

➤ 74. How will you integrate your site with social media? **Page 209**

➤ 77. Do you have content you can offer to other sites? **Page 216**

Action Items

➤ Make a list of common social media tools and make note of which ones friends and colleagues use. Then, tally which tools are used by competitors. Take your audience demographics and make notes of which social media they tend to use.

➤ Visit several different types of social media sites and search for your keywords to see what people are doing and saying about your topic(s).

73. How Will You Use Social Media to Promote Yourself?

Importance

Getting an account on a social media site takes seconds. Figuring out exactly what to do with an account can take considerably longer. This answer will provide some basics on participating in social media while marketing at the same time.

> **?** Contributing to social content sites is covered in part in the question, "Do you have content you can share with other sites?"

Here's a quick guide to getting started after you've signed up for a social media account:

◆ **Step 1: Listen**—Listen in on some conversations of friends you already know (Facebook), follow a few people in your field (Twitter), browse relevant content (YouTube), and read some profiles or look through answers to questions in your area (LinkedIn). Don't worry about participating at this point. Just absorb. If you walked into a room full of strangers, you'd take some time to listen to at least one conversation before joining in..

◆ **Step 2: Start participating**—The easiest way to do that is to respond to something someone says. After that, try answering a question that someone has asked. Then try asking your own question. Now you're at the level of initiating conversation.

◆ **Step 3: Never stop listening**—If you start firing off messages and you're not listening to what people are saying (either in reply to you or in taking the conversation in some other direction), you're not engaging in social media. You're broadcasting. Broadcasting's fine; it just doesn't have a place in social media. If you're always listening, you're also going to be in tune with what people want and that's crucial for any kind of marketing.

> Not everyone is social by nature, so don't worry if using social media feels awkward at first. It's not like being at a party and not knowing how to join in the conversation.

> **Rule of Thumb**   Being a good marketer on social media means being an interesting and helpful conversationalist.

When you're participating in social media conversations, the most important point to remember is: Converse first, and market when appropriate.

Imagine again that you're at a party and someone asks a question about yoga. You wouldn't jump in and talk about your yoga studio's

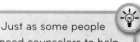

Just as some people need counselors to help them interact with other people socially, you might need some help on social media. Are you using inappropriate language? Are you annoying people? Are you looking needy? Being yourself isn't always a plus if that self is negative.

great deal for first-time students. You would try to answer their question and perhaps get into a discussion about the benefits of yoga. At some point, you would probably mention that you're a yoga instructor, but it needs to come naturally out of the conversation. And even at that point, you wouldn't start right into a direct pitch, but you might suggest that they come for a free class and try it.

Even if a conversation is not related to what you're trying to market, what you talk about and how you say it tells others a lot about who you are. People talk about leading by example, and similarly, social media involves marketing by example. By being helpful, by being insightful, by being fun, and by being responsive, you're proving to people who you are and what you can do. The result is that when it comes time to talk business, they know you in a much fuller way, and a kind of trust has been built already.

This isn't to say you can't use social media tools to directly promote something. People love hearing about last-minute travel deals on Twitter, whereas others are fans of a Facebook page because that's where they can hear about the newest products from a company before everyone else. The trick is to find social ways of getting these traditional marketing messages across. Instead of saying "we have a new product," invite people to watch a cool new video of your product being used in an interesting way.

Related Questions

→ 56. Will your content serve your site's purpose? **Page 146**

→ 77. Do you have content you can offer to other sites? **Page 216**

Action Items

→ Sign up for the most relevant social media tools you found in the survey from the previous question and start listening to the conversations.

→ Do searches on keywords related to your field to see who is actively interested in your topics.

74. How Will You Integrate Your Site with Social Media?

Because your website is the hub of your entire web marketing effort, your social media should be connected to the site and vice versa. Here are the most basic ways to create an interaction between the two:

Regularly link back to your site in your social media postings. Think of your social media tools as places to put the headlines of your website. On Twitter, for example, a great use of 140-character messages is to give a tantalizing promotion for something on your website along with the URL to the page.

Have ways for visitors to share your content on their social media tools. But don't make it too complicated, as in the first example from Figure 8-5.

FIGURE 8-5

The second example in Figure 8-5 shows a cleaner, simpler way to let people link your content to their social media sites. It's nice to have choices, but at some point you need to keep the number of choices to a reasonable number.

Many social media tools have feeds you can post on your website. On the left in Figure 8-6 is a feed from Digg that shows what people are digging about the site, whereas on the right is a feed from a person's Twitter account:

Going in the other direction, you might be able to feed your latest website material to your social media site (Facebook has this option, for example). Check to see if your website has an automatic RSS feed; if not, a web developer can easily build one.

Shortened URLs (such as `http://bit.ly/u348e`) were a must on Twitter, but have now become popular across the Web. The only trouble is you don't control the sites that shorten the URL and if they disappear, so do your links. However, you can set up or have someone set up your own URL shortener using your domain name. Just use the search phrase 🔍 create your own URL shortener.

On Video

See how easy it can be to set up a feed from your social media account on your website. Learn some of the ways sites allow visitors to connect with social media.

If you're not very active on your site or your social media, it is better not to display your feed; just have a link. No point in announcing that you don't update often.

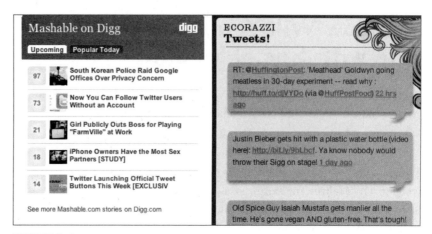

FIGURE 8-6

Automating postings to various social media accounts from a single location can have its downside. Keep in mind that your Facebook friends can also be Twitter followers or subscribers to your blog feed. Automation means some people might see your same message two or three times.

It can be time-consuming adding content to your site as well as to various social media accounts. Many content management systems (CMSs) have plug-ins that enable you to send social media messages at the same time as you're entering content. Lots of social media tools also give you the option to copy your posting to other social media accounts.

The ways to integrate social media with your site and other social media are constantly changing. Keeping up with those changes—such as Facebook making it possible for users to "like" any page on the Internet—can be daunting. Here's a search term you can use to keep up with the latest trends: how to integrate your website with social media. Then narrow your search to the last year (on Google, you'll find it on the left sidebar).

Related Questions

→ 37. Will visitors easily know how to stay in touch with you? **Page 95**

→ 94. Will you be regularly checking your site's functionality? **Page 277**

Action Item

→ In each of your social media accounts, look for tools you can use to integrate with your website or other social media accounts. If you're using a CMS, research the latest plug-ins for integrating social media.

75. How Will Your Site Promote Itself?

Importance

Websites are excellent marketing tools, so it makes sense to use them to promote themselves. This answer is about some ways to draw attention to the content and features of your site within the site itself.

Linking within the content of a page to related content on your site is a great promotional tool (the importance of this for search engines is covered in the next chapter). On the page describing your car-detailing services, put a link within the text that takes visitors to a list of tips from your blog about keeping cars clean. Visitors might not have found those tips on their own, so you're helping to make sure they do.

Frequency of message is an important concept in marketing. For people to act, they typically need to be exposed to a message several times, and a website is no exception. By noticing on the menu that you offer a garden planning service, seeing it mentioned in the first paragraph of your home page, reading about it on your services overview page, and then seeing a link to it in an article about shade plants, visitors get the idea that a planning service might help them figure out what to do with that clump of trees in the back corner of their yard.

Creating small banner ads is a way of promoting not only other areas of your site but also your products and services. The ad might remind visitors that they can get a quotation and link to the form they need to fill out. You could advertise something general ("We Do Rig Leasing") or something specific ("On Special for October"). Some examples of internal ads are shown in Figure 8-7.

> **?** Some of the self-promotional aspects of websites were covered in earlier chapters on design and content. For example, a clear layout helps visitors focus on what's important, and a great navigation system makes people aware of what they can find on a site.

> Remember to make the text that has the link (the anchor text) descriptive. In the car-detailing example, put the link on a phrase such as "read tips for keeping your car clean" rather than on just "read tips" or "clean."

> Treat your internal ads like regular ads and, if possible, set them up using an ad management program (many CMSs have easy-to-use plug-ins). These programs automatically track the number of times the ad is seen and how many people click through. This is easier than trying to do the same tracking using your site statistics.

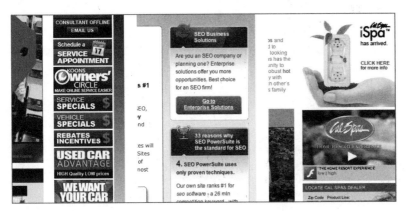

FIGURE 8-7

Whatever you choose to advertise, make sure that the ads are professional, eye-catching, and most importantly, address the needs of your visitors.

Your home page is the prime real estate on your site. Make sure that you're using that real estate effectively and marketing the most important aspects of your business or organization and the most important areas of your site. A good example of the effective use of home page real estate is the tabbed or slide show content panel that shows four or five key topics, as shown in Figure 8-8.

> Even if you don't use a CMS or shopping cart, there are third-party providers (Add This, Share This, Add to Any, and so on) who offer this feature for free—you simply add a bit of code to each item you want people to be able to share.

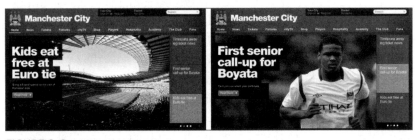

FIGURE 8-8

Your site should also make it easy for other people to promote the content on your site. CMSs usually make this process easier by offering built-in tools such as e-mailing a friend about your site, bookmarking it, or spreading the word on Twitter and other social media.

Shopping cart systems have similar tools (such as "Recommend This Item").

Related Questions

→ 57. Will your content be easily accessible? **Page 148**

→ 60. How effectively will your content use links? **Page 158**

Action Items

→ Make a list of key content on your site that you want to promote. Then, find all the connections to that content currently on the site. Look for additional ways to promote them.

→ If you're using a CMS, research what add-ons are available to help with internal promotion.

76. Do You Have a Plan for Getting Important Sites to Link to You?

Links to your website—inbound links—are the second most important part of search engine rankings, but of course they're great traffic generators in themselves. Some links are more valuable for generating traffic than others. Your web marketing plan needs a strategy for getting a link from these key sites.

Rule of Thumb Be a site that others will want to link to.

Whether other sites link to you of their own accord or whether you actively seek a link from them, your site needs to be one that they'll gladly link to. In other words, make sure that you have something to offer. That's the most important step for getting any inbound links, including great ones.

What makes an inbound link great? It comes from a related, authoritative, high-traffic site (a site closely related to your topic that is ranked highly by the search engines and has a lot of visitors interested in your topic). Simply being related to your site, then, is not enough to make a link great. Having a link from any related site would be nice, but focus your efforts on the very important sites.

How to pick great sites and how to approach them for links—these are the two central issues for inbound linking.

You know your field best, so start by making a list of the most important sites. Then, do a search on relevant keywords and find the top sites. Then, enter those sites into a service such as Yahoo! Explorer (you need a free Yahoo! account) to see who's linking to them, as shown in Figure 8-9.

> **?** The focus here is on getting particular sites to link to you. Of course, you'll make it easy for anyone who wants to link to you: Have social bookmarking links available, put "link to this" instructions on your articles, and so on.

> **💡** With services called Link Exchanges, you add your site, and others in the exchange link to you, and vice versa. At the very best, you might get a few relevant links (who knows what traffic they get). At the very worst, you'll get penalized by search engines for trying to manipulate your rankings. Because there are much more effective ways to spend your time and money, you should stay away.

> here are software programs that can help you do the research for great potential links. Search on the term **link building software**. The key is to use the programs as starting points only; do your own check of the recommended sites and contact the sites on your own.

4. Sous-Vide 101: Prime Steak Primer | Serious Eats
text/html **http://www.seriouseats.com/2010/03/how-to-sous-vide-steak.html** - 84k - cache

5. ZeroGravityWedding.com
text/html **http://www.zerogravitywedding.com/** - 46k - cache

6. newyork.startpagina.nl - Alles over New York City en New York ...
text/html **http://newyork.startpagina.nl/** - 99k - cache

7. The Food Timeline: history notes--restaurants, chefs ...
text/html **http://www.foodtimeline.org/restaurants.html** - 394k

8. Roadfood Digest | The definitive resource for news, events ...
text/html **http://www.roadfooddigest.com/** - 45k - cache

9. 93 Plates — The Wandering Foodie
text/html **http://wanderingfoodie.com/projects/93plates/** - 58k - cache

10. The Insider | KAWS - T Magazine Blog - NYTimes.com
text/html **http://themoment.blogs.nytimes.com/2008/09/17/the-insider-kaws/** - 53k - cache

11. Ravitch Signed Oath at Brooklyn Steakhouse - City Room Blog ...
text/html **http://cityroom.blogs.nytimes.com/2009/07/09/ravitch-was-sworn-in-at-brooklyn-steakhouse/** - 112k - cache

12. Steak Paradise : Food - Travel Channel
text/html
http://www.travelchannel.com/Travel_Ideas/Food_and_Wine/ci.Steak_Paradise.artTravelIdeasFmt?vgnextfmt=artTravelIdeasFmt
- 36k - cache

FIGURE 8-9

From these results, add more sites to your list.

Now you need to find out which sites on your list already link to you. Your web statistics can show you this or you can use Yahoo! Explorer again. If a site links to you, pat yourself on the back.

Now it's time to work on the sites that aren't linking to you:

- **Visit the sites you're not familiar with**—Make sure that they truly are valuable to you and your visitors.
- **Set up links to the remaining sites on your list, if you haven't already**—Don't just put them on a links or resources page; put them where they'll get good contextual exposure: within articles or other content. At the very least, give a short description or review of the site on your links page.

> There is an attribute that some sites add to external links (links to other sites) that tells search engines not to follow the link. The addition of nofollow is a concern if you're looking only at a link's value for search engine ranking. However, visitors can still click a nofollow link and get to your site, so the attribute is not an issue from a traffic standpoint.

You're laying the groundwork for two possibilities. Either your link will generate enough traffic to the other site that it will notice you and want to link back, or if you approach the other site about linking to you, it will see not only that you're linking to it, but also that you linked because you truly see the site as valuable.

> Never take the "I'll-link-to-you-if-you-link-to-me" approach. If you have to ask "why not?", there's not much point in reading any further.

Unless you've got some amazing content or a hot new product right out-of-the-gate, don't start looking for inbound links until your site has been around for a while. Not only will this give you time to build some traffic and perhaps get noticed by sites you link to but it will also give you some time to build a reputation.

76. DO YOU HAVE A PLAN FOR GETTING IMPORTANT SITES TO LINK TO YOU?

215

If a link from a valued site is still not happening naturally, here are some tips about how to approach it and ask for the link:

→ **Check for a linking policy**—Some sites have guidelines for approaching them about linking. Make sure you know about any policy before contacting the site.

→ **Know how your site relates to the site and its audience**—In other words, understand why it might want to link to you.

→ **Remember**—You're asking for a favor, not granting one.

→ **Be direct**—You're not trying to trick the site into linking to you.

A good kind of link to get is one that is part of a review or at least a mention in an article. You can increase the chances of this happening by tying your contact e-mail to something specific about your site: a new feature that helps people (such as an online tool) or an important article. It has to be something that the other site's readers want to know about.

> If you belong to an organization, you should already be linking to it. Check to see whether it is linking to you. If so, does it allow you to add extra information such as a logo or description?

Related Questions

→ 56. Will your content serve your site's purpose? **Page 146**

→ 89. Will your links to and from other sites be search engine friendly? **Page 257**

Action Items

→ Off the top of your head, list three sites you want to have link to your site. Write a short pitch based on what you know about them and their audiences to tell them why a link to your site would be helpful to their audience.

→ If your site has been running for a while, find out how to use your web statistics to see who is linking to you.

Importance

77. Do You Have Content You Can Offer to Other Sites?

Offering material to other sites in return for the promotional value is a topic that crosses several boundaries of online marketing: social media, getting inbound links, and even e-mail marketing. The idea is to have your content published on other sites in return for a link and exposure for your expertise, point of view, or even products.

Adding useful comments to blogs you enjoy reading is one way to contribute material in return for a mention of your name and a link back to your site. Notice the words "useful" and "enjoy." Your comments need to contribute to a dialogue ("Nice post" does not meet that requirement), and they should be made on blogs you do in fact read, at least occasionally (if you don't think a blog is worth reading, why would you want to be seen there?).

Closely related to blog comments are social media sites where you can post how-to articles or answer people's questions:

➤ How-to items on sites like eHow are typically in the form of step-by-step instructions, but everyone can find something to write about in that format. If you run a jewelry site, for example, you could post instructions on how to clean silver or choose a diamond.

➤ On answer sites such as Yahoo! Answers, people ask questions and others post answers that are rated not just by the person asking the question but by other members as well. Just as with the How To sites, you can build a good reputation. You can also use your answers back on your own site as part of an FAQ.

Posting articles in article directories is often cited as a good way to build traffic to your site. These directories allow other sites to use your material as long as credit and a link are given. On the face of it, this sounds like an easy way to get some exposure, but there can be some drawbacks.

Are the sites on which you'd want exposure looking for material in article directories? Probably not, in part because the material in article directories is nonexclusive—it can be used by who knows how many other sites. Furthermore, some of the sites that use article directories

---

? Some blogs add a no-follow attribute to links from people making comments, which tells the search engines not to follow the link to your site. The reasoning is that it will stop people from posting comments just for the sake of getting search engine value from the link. Even with nofollow, though, other readers can click through to your site, your name and domain are being seen by people, and you're participating in the conversation.

💡 Most blog comments have a place to put your site address—don't forget to do it. If there is no box for your URL, you can put the URL within your comment, unless the blog specifically asks you not to.

On Video
See how pieces from article directories get picked up by useful sites.

might not be ones on which you'd want to appear. These low-quality sites are looking for ways to fill their pages with any content they can find.

In between these two types of sites, there are a lot of legitimate sites looking for extra content, and your article might bring you a bit of good exposure this way. Also, some directories get good traffic all on their own (they've become minilibraries), so even if no one uses your piece, it could be well-read simply sitting in the directory. If you're just starting out, this specific kind of article marketing might be worthwhile.

So how do you pitch the sites you want to be on? Do it the way a professional writer would approach a publication. Send an outline of your idea and ask if they're interested. First, make sure your piece truly addresses the needs of the audience. That means understanding the site and who's reading it. Depending on the publication and your stature, you might even ask for money, but exposure is the key, so instead you could broker a deal in which the site gives you some front page exposure or mentions your article in its e-mail newsletter.

Examples of exclusive content to offer include the following:

+ Guest blog posts

+ Articles in online magazines

+ Contributions to portal sites

+ Articles in other people's e-mail newsletters

> Only a few article directories get really good traffic; for up-to-date information, search for the term 🔍 **most popular article directories.**

> Don't send the same article proposal to 15 different sites—target each one with a specific query. And make the offer exclusive.

Related Questions

+ 72. Which social media will you use to promote yourself? **Page 205**

+ 81. What free forms of advertising and promotion will you use online? **Page 228**

Action Items

+ Start a list of articles you can write for other sites.

+ Start a list of sites in your field that accept articles from outside writers.

+ Search several of the top article directories to see what's been written on your topic and ascertain the quality of the pieces. Then search the title of the article and see who has been using it.

78. Are You Willing to Get in Front of the Public Online or Off?

There's nothing like speaking directly to your audience. Whether it's in a blog interview or speaking to your Chamber of Commerce, people want to see you, hear you, and talk to you.

Not everyone will be comfortable with this promotional technique, but there are so many different ways to get out in public that you should try to master at least a few. Doing an online chat question-and-answer is less scary than doing a teleseminar, and a teleseminar is less scary than getting up on stage. Find a comfortable starting point and then try to work your way up to other formats.

 Rule of Thumb   Be someone people want to hear from. Then let them hear interesting useful things.

If you want to get anywhere with this type of promotion, you not only need to have something to say but the content also has to be something people want to hear: expertise, a fascinating story, anyone with celebrity, something new. You don't need to be a great speaker as long as what you have to offer is great, so work on developing yourself before thinking about promoting this way.

This doesn't mean you have to be the greatest expert, have the most fascinating story, and so on. You just have to have something appealing, and that will vary by context. If you have a site that explains knitting in a very helpful way, a knitting blogger might well want to interview you.

When you're being interviewed about your knitting site, the key is to not talk about your knitting site. Talk about your five best tips on knitting; talk about how much you love knitting; tell a story about the first time you tried to knit. Be interesting and helpful.

The key to successful interviews and speaking engagements is to focus on the needs of the audience first. By doing that, you fulfill the needs of the hosts (media, meeting planners, and so on) because you made their audience happy. And in the end you fulfill your needs by demonstrating your valuable qualities to potential customers, clients, or converts.

Be sure to promote all your interviews and speeches on your website. Even if people can't attend, they see that you're getting out there; in particular, event organizers see you as someone they might use.

What goes on the Web stays on the Web. Be relaxed during interviews and presentations, but not so much that you say something you regret and it goes on the record. Forever.

Table 8-3 describes some ways to get in front of your audience.

TABLE 8-3: How to Get in Front of Your Audience

ONLINE OPPORTUNITIES	OFFLINE OPPORTUNITIES
Interviews (blogs, online magazines, and so on)	Broadcast and print media interviews
Podcasts (audio and video)	Speaking to groups (service groups, associations, companies)
Webinars	Speaking at conventions (keynotes, panels)
Posting video of offline talks	
	Teleseminars

Virtual tours are one of the best ways to speak directly to your audience. The online equivalent of going from city to city giving interviews and speeches, a virtual tour involves giving interviews with bloggers, participating in webinars, doing podcasts, and participating in other web-based media events. Just like an offline tour, a virtual tour takes place over a fixed period of time and is focused on something specific: the launch of your latest novel, human resources management month, the unveiling of your new electric scooter, or the launch of your website.

Doing offline events takes a lot more time, energy, and money. You might be more limited geographically by costs. But within your immediate area, there are plenty of opportunities for getting the word out about your site.

Related Questions

+ 62. How will you use video or audio in your content? **Page 164**

+ 82. How will you be promoting your site offline? **Page 231**

Action Items

+ Start a list of relevant sites and offline media and organizations where you can be interviewed, give a talk, and so on about your product, service, or cause.

+ Have a friend interview you and record what you say. Practice short, focused answers, and being conversational.

Importance

79. Will Paid Online Advertising Be Part of Your Marketing Plan?

Although the Web is filled with marketing and promotional opportunities that require more time than money, paid advertising can still have an important role in any web marketing plan. This answer deals first with paid search listings and then with other forms of paid ads.

If 80 percent of new visitors to websites come from search engines, it's important to remember that many of them arrive through paid search listings. Depending on the search engine, this can be as much as 50 percent of the traffic.

Just to be clear, paid search listing does not mean that you're buying a listing in the search engine itself. The organic search results highlighted in Figure 8-10 are based solely on the formulas that search engines use to rank sites, whereas the paid listings are displayed in various places outside the search results.

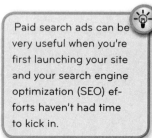

Paid search ads can be very useful when you're first launching your site and your search engine optimization (SEO) efforts haven't had time to kick in.

FIGURE 8-10

Google has the lion's share of search traffic, which means ads on its system cost the most. Try smaller search engines like Bing to see if you can get results for a lower price.

Search advertising uses a pay per click model: you pay only when someone clicks your ad. The cost for that click is determined through a bidding process. Generally speaking, the higher your bid, the higher you appear on the page (although services such as Google AdWords also take into account your click-through rate, so even if someone bids more than you, your ad could appear first because it has a better click rate).

The advantages of search advertising include:

→ **Speed**—Your ads can be running in as little as 15 minutes from the time you set up your account.

→ **Flexibility**—You can change or create new ads, pick the time of day they'll appear, put entire campaigns on pause, and test different ads. This all happens instantly and from user-friendly control panels, such as the Google AdWords panel in Figure 8-11.

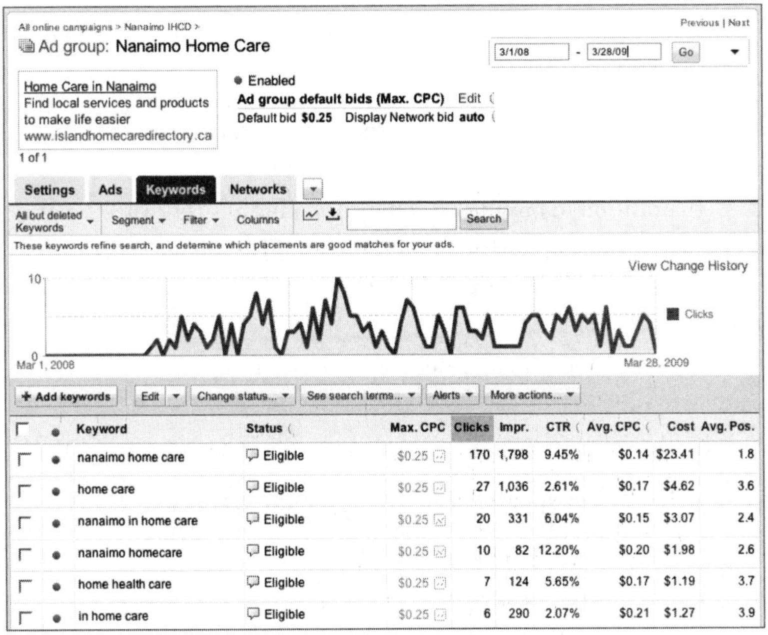

FIGURE 8-11

→ **Scalability**—You can start as small as you want and grow your campaigns as much as you want.

→ **Focus**—SEO is a long-term proposition that involves the broad topics of your site, but paid advertising can be used for extremely focused events or trends, such as site launches, seasonal information/sales, sudden changes in consumer behavior, breaking news.

→ **Control**—Not only do you control the wording of your paid ads but you also control exactly which page the person is taken to. You also control how much you'll be charged per day.

> **?** Search engine ads may appear on other sites as well. Google AdWords, for example, can display on a variety of partner sites as well as websites running the AdSense program.

However, there are things to consider before rushing out and starting a search advertising campaign:

+ **Cost**—Depending on the keywords you're pursuing, the competition for paid ads can drive up the cost per click. For companies with low cost, low margin products, or for noncommercial sites, it just might not be worth getting those clicks.

+ **Complexity**—It might be easy to set up paid search advertising, but it requires a fair bit of work and understanding to make it pay off. You constantly need to be testing results, trying new wording and new keywords.

The good thing is that you can set up paid search very easily and monitor your costs, so it can be worth trying.

In addition to buying ads on search engines there are several options for paid advertising on the Web. This part of the answer provides a very brief overview of the principal choices you have with these other paid ads.

Outside of search engines there are four key places to buy online advertising:

+ Ads on websites

+ Ads in or sponsorships of newsletters, podcasts, and so on

+ Paid classified listings

+ Paid directory listings

The two most common ways for small- to medium-sized advertisers to purchase ads are:

+ Directly contacting a website

+ Joining an ad network

Rule of Thumb   Any ads you buy should come with detailed reports about how they perform.

Some of the formats for online ads:

+ Graphical banners in varying sizes

+ Text ads

Carefully consider whether to use ad formats and delivery that can be annoying to visitors, such as animated ads which can't be controlled by the visitor, or popup ads of any type.

- Animated or multimedia banners in varying sizes
- Video ads

Some of the ways online ads can be delivered:

- Simple display
- Popups
- Interstitial or between pages.
- Contextual (based on page content)

There are four ways in which online advertising charges are calculated:

- **Cost per click**—When someone clicks your ad and visits your site, you pay an amount per click. If no one clicks, you pay nothing.
- **Cost per view**—You pay based on the number of views or impressions—how many times your ad is seen by visitors.
- **Cost per action**—You pay based on the actions taken by visitors. One version of this is affiliate marketing, which is covered later in this chapter.
- **Cost per period**—You pay for an ad space or sponsorship for a certain period of time or a particular newsletter, and the number of clicks or views is not measured and does not affect the price.

The most widely used form of advertising is pay per click, for the obvious advantage that you pay nothing unless someone clicks through to your site, and visiting your site is the principal goal of advertising.

As far as the cost of advertising, there's no way to give general rates for any types of ads. You'll want to research costs of similar ads on similar sites. Tools offered by pay per click services will tell you how much you need to bid in order to reach a certain spot.

Related Questions

- 67. Will you be selling online? **Page 185**
- 84. What are your search engine expectations? **Page 238**
- 85. How do you plan to research useful keywords for your site? **Page 240**

Action Items

➡ Do searches for keywords on your site and note if any paid search ads come up, how many there are, and what they're saying in their ads.

➡ Keep notes of where competitors are advertising and what they're advertising.

➡ Educate yourself about how to use online advertising. Search for 🔍 how does Internet advertising work? and narrow the search to results within the last year.

80. Is Affiliate Marketing Something You Could Use?

Importance

Affiliate marketing is a method of driving traffic to your site by having other sites advertise your products in return for a percentage of any sales made by visitors coming from their sites.

One of the advantages of affiliate marketing is that the affiliates sometimes do much more than display banners. They write reviews or link to your site from many different areas of their content. In that sense, affiliates are often like salespeople rather than a medium in which you advertise. They'll give personal testimonials or detailed descriptions or relate your product to their audience, all of which can help increase the chance of a sale.

To track sales for each affiliate, you need an affiliate manager system, of which there are two types, described in Table 8-4.

> Affiliate programs require a fair bit of time and energy to start and maintain. They, in effect, become another product that you need to market, support, and improve. You need to do some number-crunching to see whether it's worth starting.

TABLE 8-4: Affiliate Manager Systems

SYSTEM	PROS	CONS
Self-hosted affiliate software	No monthly fees if hosted as part of your website's account (the software itself might cost money). Can be fully customized to your needs.	You're responsible for all maintenance and software errors. No promotional help.
Affiliate network	A quality service can give you credibility. Promotes your program to members of the network. Usually very user-friendly. Often has extensive reporting tools. No maintenance issues Usually great support, training.	Typically a monthly fee based on a percentage of what your affiliates earn. Fairly heavy startup fees.

> You can use affiliate marketing for more than selling products. You can pay affiliates for getting leads, signing up members, selling services, and so on.

Figure 8-12 shows an example of the reports you can get from affiliate tracking programs.

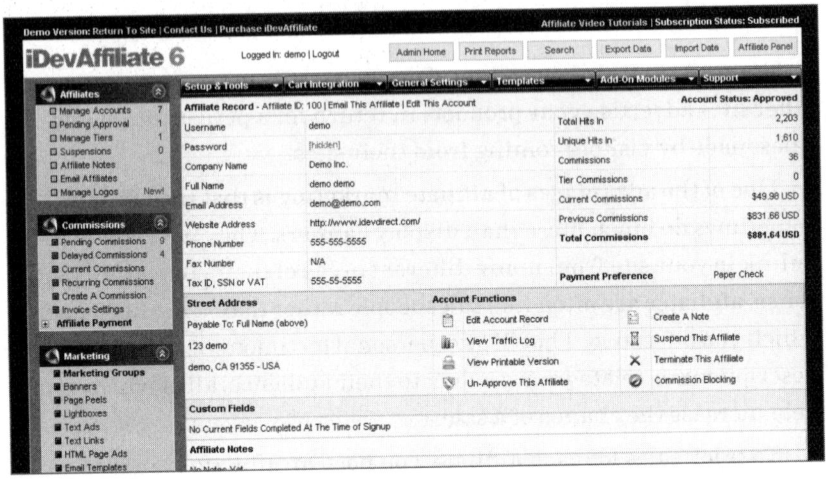

FIGURE 8-12

Here are some basic guidelines for running an affiliate program:

→ **Be selective**—It might seem like a good idea to let everyone and anyone become an affiliate, but you increase your chances of fraud and bad advertising practices, Plus you have a lot more people to support with advice, and so on.

→ **Pay generously**—You can check what other similar programs are offering, but a common percentage is 50 percent of the sale. This will vary with the product, the pricing, your margins, and so on, of course. But if you can't match what your competitors offer, you stand little chance of getting affiliates.

→ **Pay on time.**

→ **Make sure that your affiliates have a powerful, easy-to-use reporting system.**

→ **Provide lots of educational help and support to your affiliates (graphics, content, ideas).**

→ **Have clear guidelines about how you want to be promoted.**

Related Questions

➡ 67. Will you be selling online? **Page 185**

➡ 83. How do you plan to track website visitors and marketing results? **Page 233**

Action Items

➡ Think about what you have that would make a good affiliate marketing product or what you could create specifically for affiliate marketing.

➡ See whether competitors use affiliate programs and also check some affiliate networks such as ClickBank to see what affiliate programs they offer in your field.

Importance

81. What Free Forms of Advertising and Promotion Will You Use Online?

There are three free online marketing tools that can be useful to the average website:

> Even if you don't advertise your business, free classifieds sites are great places to advertise offline activities such as workshops or talks.

- ◆ Free classified advertising sites
- ◆ Free directory sites
- ◆ Free press release distribution sites

The best known of the classified sites is Craigslist, which is a good example of how they work. The scope of these sites tends to be highly local; some sites prohibit ads from outside the region or that do not have a local phone number.

If a classified site has multiple locations, you might be prohibited from posting an ad across different locations—even ads that are roughly the same.

> Don't get taken in by ads offering to place your listing in hundreds or even thousands of directories. Very few of them will be relevant to your site, which means a) not much traffic, and b) little value for search engine rankings.

It's also important to think about your image and who your audience is. Many classified sites, including popular ones, can be filled with poor-quality ads and you might not want your name found among them. Is your audience reading classified ads? It will depend on your market and who you're trying to reach.

There are literally tens of thousands of free directory sites on the Web, but that does not mean you want to get listed in them all. Aside from the fact that they are often very specialized (with particular topics or locations), they're not all worth being listed in.

Low traffic is one reason for not wanting to be listed—aside from the fact that you wouldn't get much in the way of results, it's also likely the site is not well ranked. Having it link to you can be a negative for your search engine ranking.

> One directory you want be in is called The Open Directory Project, or DMOZ for short. Pay close attention to their rules for submitting your site, and be patient—they can take some time to get back to you because it's all hand selected by volunteer editors.

However, low traffic is a relative factor. A highly focused directory in a small market will have low traffic compared with a big consumer directory, but within its own market, it could be the premier directory. If you know your market well, you'll be aware of (or can easily find) the most-used directories. Figure 8-13 shows a ranking of the most valuable directories (top) and a list of directories in a specialized field (bottom):

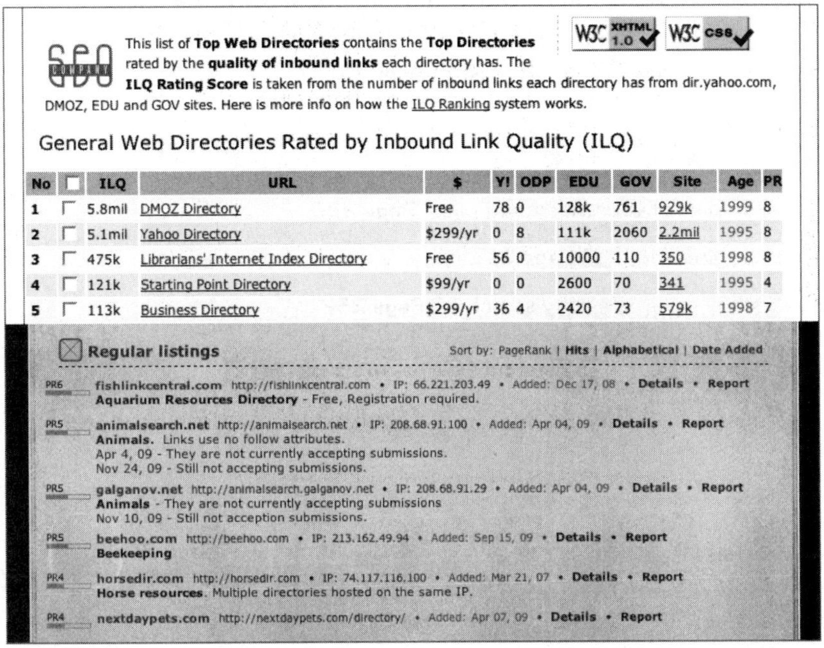
This list of **Top Web Directories** contains the **Top Directories** rated by the **quality of inbound links** each directory has. The **ILQ Rating Score** is taken from the number of inbound links each directory has from dir.yahoo.com, DMOZ, EDU and GOV sites. Here is more info on how the ILQ Ranking system works.

General Web Directories Rated by Inbound Link Quality (ILQ)

No		ILQ	URL	$	Y!	ODP	EDU	GOV	Site	Age	PR
1		5.8mil	DMOZ Directory	Free	78	0	128k	761	929k	1999	8
2		5.1mil	Yahoo Directory	$299/yr	0	8	111k	2060	2.2mil	1995	8
3		475k	Librarians' Internet Index Directory	Free	56	0	10000	110	350	1998	8
4		121k	Starting Point Directory	$99/yr	0	0	2600	70	341	1995	4
5		113k	Business Directory	$299/yr	36	4	2420	73	579k	1998	7

Regular listings Sort by: PageRank | **Hits** | **Alphabetical** | **Date Added**

PR6 **fishlinkcentral.com** http://fishlinkcentral.com • IP: 66.221.203.49 • Added: Dec 17, 08 • **Details** • **Report**
Aquarium Resources Directory - Free, Registration required.

PR5 **animalsearch.net** http://animalsearch.net • IP: 208.68.91.100 • Added: Apr 04, 09 • **Details** • **Report**
Animals. Links use no follow attributes.
Apr 4, 09 - They are not currently accepting submissions.
Nov 24, 09 - Still not accepting submissions.

PR5 **galganov.net** http://animalsearch.galganov.net • IP: 208.68.91.29 • Added: Apr 04, 09 • **Details** • **Report**
Animals - They are not currently accepting submissions
Nov 10, 09 - Still not acception submissions.

PR5 **beehoo.com** http://beehoo.com • IP: 213.162.49.94 • Added: Sep 15, 09 • **Details** • **Report**
Beekeeping

PR4 **horsedir.com** http://horsedir.com • IP: 74.117.116.100 • Added: Mar 21, 07 • **Details** • **Report**
Horse resources. Multiple directories hosted on the same IP.

PR4 **nextdaypets.com** http://nextdaypets.com/directory/ • Added: Apr 07, 09 • **Details** • **Report**

FIGURE 8-13

Press releases are a traditional method of getting the word out to the media, and the online process is made extremely easy by several free press release services. But the value of press releases has changed over time.

Although reaching media outlets is one goal of posting on press release sites, the other is search engine optimization. Instead of going into a media person's file (or garbage pail), your press release gets archived by the press release site. If you carefully write the press release to be search-engine friendly, and include a link back to your site, you can get useful search engine linking.

What does "search-engine friendly" mean? Like any content you'd put on your site, the press release needs a clear, powerful, keyword-rich title; the content itself must be useful to readers; and there should be a natural mix of keywords toward the beginning of the press release (don't repeat the keywords over and over).

On Video

Watch how you can find which press release services are well indexed by the search engines.

You need to **carefully choose** which press release site you're going to use. Some are **more popular than others;** some get used by particular sectors more **than others.** Check how they post the press releases (do they have the **proper meta and title tags** and do they give each article its own page?) to **make sure it's SEO-friendly.**

Related Questions

➜ 79. Will paid online advertising be part of your marketing plan? **Page 220**

➜ 87. Will your content be search engine-friendly? **Page 247**

➜ 88. Will your search engine strategy cover specialty searches? **Page 252**

Action Items

➜ In Google News, enter some relevant keywords for your site and see what press release sites are indexed, and then check them out.

➜ Find some directories in your field and see who is listed in them; then, check how many links Google has to their directories.

82. How Will You Be Promoting Your Site Offline?

Importance

Driving traffic to your website using offline marketing and promotion serves two purposes: It reaches potential visitors who are not very active online or not online at all, and it reinforces your message to an active online audience. The goal of this answer is to provide some ideas for promoting or advertising your site.

Some offline ways to promote your site using marketing tactics you have probably already implemented include the following:

➔ **Put your website and e-mail address on business cards and other business-related materials**—Put contact information on material such as invoices, envelopes, mailing labels, vehicle signage, and (of course) packaging.

➔ **Use printed promotional material such as brochures, bookmarks, frisbees, T-shirts, and so on**—At the very least, make sure that your domain name is on these products, but don't stop there: Have a short description in your brochure about what can be found on your site or put a challenging question on a T-shirt to get people thinking.

➔ **Include your website on answering machine messages or voice-mail systems**.

➔ **Mention your site in conversation**—We get so caught up in developing online conversations that it's easy to forget about normal everyday chats with people.

➔ **Take advantage of public speaking**—When you're speaking to groups, be sure to mention your website and have it on any printed material you give out. (There's more about public speaking in Question 78 in this chapter.)

➔ **Take part in tweet-ups or other offline gatherings**—More and more online communities actively pursue offline meetings of their members, so make sure that you're active in some of those events.

Ideas for paid offline advertising opportunities include the following:

For direct mailings, always do postcards or other printed material that's not in an envelope. Even if people are putting it immediately into the recycling bin, they'll see your name.

➜ **Use print advertising (newspaper, magazine, classified ads)**— To give a helpful tip or a provocative headline and your web address, use print advertising. Smaller, more frequent ads are possible when you're driving traffic to a website, not making the full pitch in the ad.

➜ **Create promotional items**—Design promotional items specifically to promote your website.

➜ **Take advantage of sponsorships**—If you have an online business, building community offline is important because you're not reaching people through bricks and mortar.

In print or TV advertising, be sure to use a unique URL that can help you track where people have come from (for instance: mydomain.com/tv1).

➜ **Use direct mail**—This can be particularly effective for small businesses and organizations that need to reach a very specific geographical audience. Also, there's much less advertising in the mail these days, so you're more likely to stand out.

➜ **Use the radio**—Although getting across domain names can be tricky, radio can be a powerful and affordable solution for some sites.

➜ **Reach consumers through television**—Local television can often be within reach of consumer-oriented sites, whereas Google TV has made mass market television advertising a possibility for many businesses and organizations.

Related Questions

➜ 67. Will you be selling online? **Page 185**
➜ 68. Do you have a web marketing plan? **Page 192**
➜ 83. How do you plan to track website visitors and marketing results? **Page 233**

Action Items

➜ Go through your current offline marketing activities and see which can most cost-effectively be updated to include your website. Create a timeline for updating costlier materials (such as brochures).

➜ Revisit offline marketing avenues you're not using, but which may be cost-effective now for driving traffic to your website (for example, newspaper ads or TV).

83. How Do You Plan to Track Website Visitors and Marketing Results?

No marketing plan is complete without some way to measure the results of your efforts. Fortunately, detailed information about how you're doing on your website, and across social media and the Web as a whole, is not only readily available but a lot of it is free.

For data about visitors to your site, there are two options: server statistics and page-tracking statistics.

Viewing a web page involves downloading files from a server (text, images, multimedia, and so on), and every single download is recorded on a log file. Virtually all hosts provide statistics programs that analyze these logs and produce reports about what visitors have been doing on your site. Figure 8-14 shows part of one of these reports.

> If you can't find a server statistics program in your hosting control panel, ask your hosting company how to access those statistics.

Daily Statistics for May 1999													
Day				Files		Pages		Visits		Sites			
1	3484	1.76%	3133	1.81%	528	1.89%	279	1.98%	292	2.79%	15511	1.75%
2	3446	1.74%	3040	1.76%	535	1.91%	269	1.91%	249	2.38%	14557	1.65%
3	7313	3.70%	6348	3.68%	1017	3.63%	504	3.57%	515	4.91%	31611	3.57%
4	8570	4.33%	7501	4.34%	1175	4.20%	608	4.31%	574	5.48%	37573	4.25%
5	8079	4.09%	7093	4.11%	1120	4.00%	531	3.76%	545	5.20%	37584	4.25%
6	8086	4.09%	7144	4.14%	1110	3.96%	583	4.13%	579	5.52%	35427	4.01%
7	6441	3.26%	5736	3.32%	900	3.21%	445	3.15%	443	4.23%	29932	3.38%
8	3929	1.99%	3372	1.95%	601	2.15%	295	2.09%	319	3.04%	17701	2.00%
9	3939	1.99%	3500	2.03%	549	1.96%	276	1.95%	309	2.95%	17107	1.93%
10	7005	3.54%	6109	3.54%	1009	3.60%	490	3.47%	491	4.68%	32480	3.67%
11	8225	4.16%	7237	4.19%	1115	3.98%	583	4.13%	579	5.52%	35653	4.03%

FIGURE 8-14

I highlighted the hits and the visits for a single hour. Notice how much larger the hits value is. That's because one person looking at a web page generates dozens of hits (every image, text file, and so on). So when someone says your ad could get over a million hits a month, take your money and run. These are the kinds of issues you'll need to learn in order to understand web statistics. Search for 🔍 understanding web analytics and then narrow the search to results from the last year or two.

The other way to monitor visitor activity on your site is to use page tracking, which involves placing a piece of code on each of your pages.

> Your web designer or developer can help you place this code (usually at the very end of the web page); if you use a CMS, it might allow you to paste the code into a text box in the admin area.

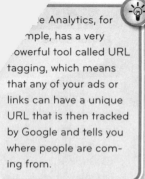

...e Analytics, for ...mple, has a very ...owerful tool called URL tagging, which means that any of your ads or links can have a unique URL that is then tracked by Google and tells you where people are coming from.

This code is tracked by statistics software that produces the reports. The easiest way to do this is to subscribe to free services such as Google Analytics. They automatically generate the code for you to place on each page of your site. Figure 8-15 shows an example of a Google Analytics page.

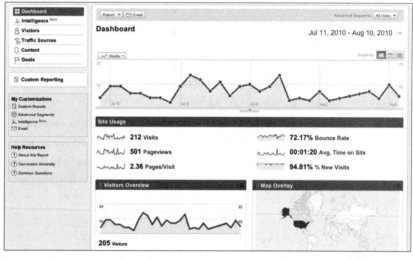

FIGURE 8-15

One of the most important tools for making marketing decisions is A-B testing, and the Internet makes this quite easy to do. In e-mail marketing, for example, most mailing list managers have the ability to send out different versions of a newsletter so you can see which one gets the better response. Ad managers offer the ability to track the effectiveness of different versions of an ad. Or you can even test different versions of pages on your website.

Many page-tracking statistics packages offer you the ability to measure return on investment by tracking progress from one page to another. This can help you measure the success of marketing campaigns, special offers, online purchasing habits, and much more.

Whatever statistics package you choose, make sure that you can easily understand what it's telling you. Some of that involves educating yourself about page views, unique visitors, and other terms, but you also want a statistics package that's easy to use.

Offsite data about you is available from a number of sources:

➤ **Advertising statistics**—data generated from people viewing and clicking ads.

➤ **Social media monitoring services**—These check mentions of your name on Twitter, Facebook, and so on.

➤ **Webmaster tools**—Google and Yahoo!, for example, provide tools for tracking who is linking to your website.

On Video

Watch more details of using server statistics and page-tracking statistics packages.

There are also many tools available for free to find out general statistical information about the Web. Google Trends, for example, will help you understand what people are searching for. Microsoft Advertising offers tools for knowing demographics: Who is searching for what.

Related Questions

➔ 10. Does the web hosting provider have a good hosting control panel? **Page 23**

➔ 68. Do you have a web marketing plan? **Page 192**

Action Items

➔ Find out how to access the statistics package(s) on your hosting account.

➔ To sign up for Google Analytics, you'll need to have a Google Account—both are free.

Chapter

Search Engine Optimization

Importance

84. What Are Your Search Engine Expectations?

Search engines are the number one way people find websites. If your site can't easily be found through the search engines, you're at a serious disadvantage. Unfortunately, the importance of search engines can lead people to throw money at the problem or fall victim to false promises, when what is required is a bit of understanding and the willingness to take the many small steps necessary for good search engine ranking.

Don't expect overnight successes in search engine rankings. Getting to the top 10 for a particular search word or phrase (known as a keyword) takes time. Not a lot of time in traditional marketing terms, but a few months in the world of the Internet can seem like a long time.

> **Rule of Thumb**   With a new website, expect a minimum of three months for the effects of SEO to start to show.

Then there are expectations about how high your site will rank. If you think you're going to be number one for every keyword you want, expect to be disappointed. Even when your site does rank well, don't expect to remain there without continual work. And don't expect that a good ranking for a keyword will always bring traffic because people's use of that keyword might change.

Bringing your search engine expectations in line with reality requires understanding the goals and methods of search engines. Once you know what search engines want and how to give it to them, you can move beyond promises of easy money and quick fixes.

Understanding Search Engines

By this point in the book, you know its primary message: great content, regularly updated, is the key to a successful website. It should also be enough for search engine success because search engines want to provide the most relevant content for their users. If search engines were human, that might be true, but being computer programs, they need some help determining relevance. Search engine optimization (SEO) is all about helping search engines analyze and rank your content.

Although searching on both is similar, search engines are very different from directories. A search engine uses automated programs (robots) to index every website it can find. Directories rely on submissions from the public and manual additions by staff.

Search engines use literally hundreds of factors to determine the ranking of pages. Some of them might have very little weight, but they're still part of the equation. As more knowledge is gained, these weights can change, as can the factors themselves.

The techniques of SEO are based on understanding how search engines try to mimic what human beings do when they judge whether content is relevant to their needs. Search engines begin by analyzing data about a website that has been gathered by robots—computer programs that read the HTML code. From this analysis, search engines know how many times a word appears on a page, whether a word appears in the title of the page, who is linking to the page, how old the page is, how old the content is, and much more. Now the real work begins.

All the facts about a website are run through complex mathematical formulas that give different weight to each fact as well as to relationships between facts, after which the results are compared to results for other sites, and in the end a ranking is determined for each site. Add to this the fact that the data being collected and the way these formulas process it are always changing, and you see why SEO can be a bit daunting.

Thankfully, this constant change has one purpose only: to more accurately represent and rate the content of websites. Search engines will only get better and better at analyzing content, so keep writing great content and you'll be on the right track.

In the meantime, your SEO efforts need to match the current knowledge of the factors that search engines look at and what weight they give to them. The rest of this chapter is about the basics of that current knowledge.

> Although you can submit new sites to search engines, it's not necessary. They'll find you very quickly.

Related Questions

→ Introduction—Why do you want to build a website? **Page 00**

→ 68. Do you have a web marketing plan? **Page 192**

→ 79. Will paid online advertising be part of your marketing plan? **Page 220**

→ 83. How do you plan to track website visitors and marketing results? **Page 233**

Action Item

→ Visit some websites that talk about SEO in realistic terms (see the links in Appendix A.

Importance

85. How Do You Plan to Research Useful Keywords for Your Site?

People use words and phrases to search the Internet. SEO is all about making sure search engines recognize that your content is relevant to particular keywords. Before you can do SEO, then, you'll need to know what keywords to optimize for. This is not as simple as it sounds because the keywords you need are the ones people actually use, not the ones you would use. That means doing some research.

Keyword Research

Start with your customers. Create a list of keywords you think they would use to search for what's on your site. Then listen to how they talk on the phone, observe how they write e-mail, and note how they ask for something in the shop. You might talk about *commercial properties*, but potential customers say they're looking for *office space*. Add this new information to your list.

Monitor the competition. Find the keywords your competitors are using. It's best to choose the sites of competitors who rank highly in the search engines. Add to your list.

Next, run your list through keyword tools, such as Google AdWords, Wordtracker, or Keyword Discovery. You're looking for three pieces of information in particular:

+ Additional keyword ideas

+ How many people are searching for a keyword

+ How many websites are competing for a keyword

Figure 9-1 shows keyword results from Google AdWords.

As you can see just from this portion of the results, you've got even more keywords to sort through. At some point the research has to stop, and you have to decide which keywords you will use for SEO.

> Keep an eye out for topical keywords that can fit with your site: hot topics in magazines, new trends in the news, or the latest buzz on social media. If you can tap into the cache of those terms, it can produce some good short-term traffic.

> Use several keyword tools because they differ in what search engine data they use, how they analyze it, and the kinds of information they report. You'll find a list of tools in Appendix A.

Keyword		Competition	Global Monthly Searches	Local Monthly Searches	Local Search Trends
steel roofing			60,500	33,100	
fiberglass roofing			14,800	9,900	
roll roofing			22,200	18,100	
roofing supplies			90,500	33,100	
roofing materials cost			590	-	-
asphalt roofing materials			1,600	1,300	
estimate roofing materials			140	-	-
roll roofing materials			140	-	-
copper roofing materials			320	260	
shed roofing materials			480	-	-
fiberglass roofing materials			480	390	
composite roofing materials			320	210	
shake roofing materials			170	-	-
rubber roofing materials			1,000	880	
roofing materials shingles			1,000	880	
cement roofing materials			210	-	-

FIGURE 9-1

Finalizing Your Keywords

Here are a few ways to narrow the list of keywords to something manageable:

- **Reexamine relevance**—Does the word "craft" really fit your particular hobby shop? If you're still not sure, enter the keyword into a search engine and see whether sites like yours show up.

- **Focus on simpler words and phrases**—Optimizing for the keyword "model trains" will likely get traffic from searches for "toy model trains" or "scale model trains." These longer versions of the same basic phrase are referred to as *long tail* search terms.

- **Low search volume isn't always bad**—The few people searching for that keyword might be exactly the visitors you want. Plus you won't have much competition.

- **Heavy competition isn't always bad**—A keyword might be so important to your site that even with millions of competitors, it can be worth trying to get a small slice of that pie.

➡ **Set aside keywords with bad grammar or spelling**—You'll come across highly relevant, high-volume keywords that don't make much sense grammatically (such as "model trains buildings") or are even misspelled, but there's no way to use them in your content.

➡ **Set aside valuable keywords for which you don't currently have content**—Highlight them for ideas on creating new content.

Armed with your short list of keywords, you're ready to optimize your site. Remember, this is your starting list and it will keep getting revised over time, as will your SEO efforts as a whole.

On Video

Watch examples of doing keyword research using free online tools.

Related Questions

➡ 56. Will your content serve your site's purpose? **Page 146**

➡ 79. Will paid online advertising be part of your marketing plan? **Page 220**

➡ 92. Will you need to hire anyone to help optimize your site for search engines? **Page 266**

Action Items

➡ Set yourself a fixed period—at least a week—to consciously listen for the words used by your clients or customers, in relevant articles or news stories, on blogs and their comments, in social media, and in broadcast media and books.

➡ Keep your keyword list in a spreadsheet and don't remove anything, even if it turns out to be a word you no longer need. You want to keep track of everything you try. It can also be interesting to highlight the words you thought of to compare them with the words people really use.

86. Will Your Pages Have the Hidden HTML Tags Necessary for Search Engines?

For website owners, one of the most mysterious aspects of SEO is a set of HTML tags that don't produce any actual content on the web page. The mystery is due in part to the fact that they're hidden in the source code, but perhaps more because of rumors about exactly what they do and how important they can be to search engines. This answer should help to clear up some of those mysteries.

Title Tag

The title tag `<title>` is arguably the most important of the hidden HTML tags because search engines use it:

➜ To help determine the relevance of your content

➜ To create a title for the page's search engine results

Technically, the title tag isn't hidden because it does show up at the very top of the browser window, as shown in Figure 9-2.

FIGURE 9-2

Figure 9-2 shows how the title tag is placed in the HTML. You can also see how this tag forms the title of the page's listing in the search engine results. In other words, you control one of the key parts of search engine results.

> If you're considering a content management system (CMS), make sure it allows you to write a custom title tag for each page.

> Of course, you need to remember to write a title tag. A common mistake is to not change the default titles assigned by some site-builder programs. You can see the results if you search for 🔍 Page title.

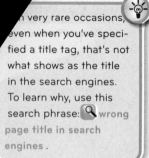

n very rare occasions, even when you've specified a title tag, that's not what shows as the title in the search engines. To learn why, use this search phrase: 🔍 wrong page title in search engines.

A title tag should clearly describe the content on the page and should be unique for each page. Ideally, the keyword for the page should appear as close to the beginning of the title as possible. Title tags should also include information such as a company name or a location. But don't put your company name first:

Use `<title>In-home Chef Service - Cleveland | Karla's Kitchen</title>`

Don't Use `<title>Karla's Kitchen | In-home Chef Service - Cleveland</title>`

People are searching for in-home chef services or Cleveland in-home chef services, but not for Karla's Kitchen. Putting the same information at the start of all your title tags can make search engines think your pages all deal with the same topic.

> **Rule of Thumb**   Title tags should be fewer than 60 characters (about 12 words), which is the maximum displayed by most search engines.

Meta Tags

Meta tags are visible only in the source code of web pages and, like the title tag, are placed at the beginning of an HTML document. Two of these tags in particular—the description and keywords tags—developed a kind of a cult status within SEO because long-ago search engines not only used meta tags to help determine ranking but they also used virtually no other factors, such as links to the site.

Virtually no search engines take the keywords meta tag into account for indexing or ranking sites. However, if you do use the tag, be sure not to overuse your keywords (keyword stuffing) or use popular keywords that aren't relevant to your site (names of celebrities, and so on), and be sure words and phrases are separated with a comma. Even though the tags are not used by search engines to rank sites, the mystique continues and you'll still hear people breathlessly ask if you've optimized your meta tags. However, meta tags can still provide a bit of control over search engines.

DESCRIPTION META TAG

Just as the title tag controls the title used in search engine results, the description meta tag can sometimes control the description in results. Look at the highlighted sentences for the search engine listing shown in Figure 9-3; they're generated by the description tag shown below that.

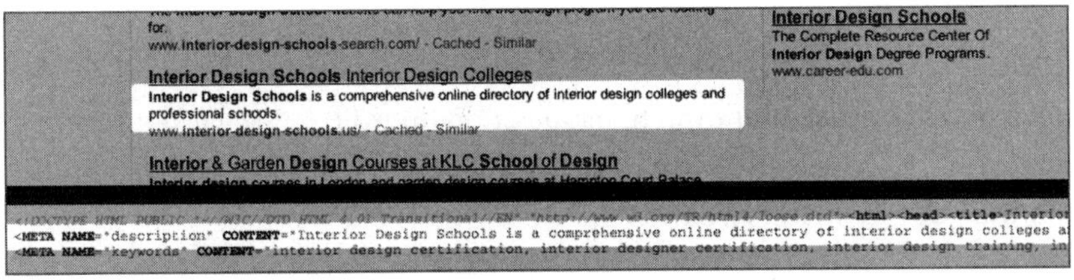

FIGURE 9-3

However, many search engines use the description tag only if it contains the keyword being searched. Figure 9-4 shows the search engine result for the same page but using keywords that don't appear in the description. The words that do show in the results are taken from within the body of the page at the point where the keyword appears.

> If a keyword appears in the description tag but not in the page content, Google won't use the description tag.

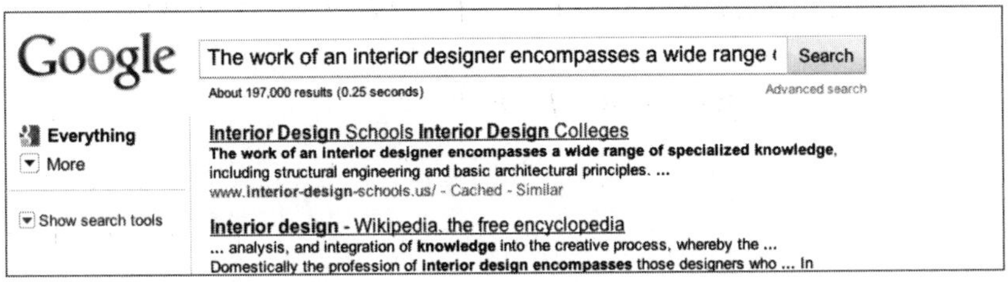

FIGURE 9-4

> An efficient way to control the actions of search engines is with a single `robots.txt` file for the whole site. To learn how to use these files, search for 🔍 robots.txt .

Rule of Thumb   Descriptions should be fewer than 160 characters in length. That's the maximum size of descriptions shown by Google. Other search engines show more, but it makes sense to stick to the smallest length.

ROBOTS META TAG

This tag can be used to control the actions of search engine robots that crawl through your site indexing pages, and it looks like this:

```
<meta name="robots" content="noindex, nofollow">
```

There are two primary functions controlled by the robots tag: indexing the page contents and following the links on the page. By default, search engines will index and follow, so the robots tag is used only to tell them not to index a page, not to follow the links, or both.

> Before launching your site, check that there are no robots tags or a robots file preventing pages from being indexed or links followed (unless they're supposed to).

On Video

Watch some examples of good and not-so-good title tags at work, and how they help or hurt what people see in search engine results.

Why would you not want the search engines to index a page or follow the links on it? During site construction, you wouldn't want search engines indexing incomplete pages and you might not want a links page indexed because it has no real content, but you still want the links on the page to be followed.

Related Questions

➤ 58. Will the content of each page have a single focus? **Page 151**

➤ 91. Will the HTML code for your site be search engine-friendly? **Page 264**

Action Items

➤ Make sure you'll be able to easily manage the title and description tags for pages on your site. If your site is custom-built, have that ability included. If you're considering an existing CMS, check that it has this ability or that it can be added.

➤ Without thinking about keywords or exact length, write title tags for all your pages. Later, go through them and look for keyword opportunities; and edit for clarity, length, and uniqueness. Do the same for page descriptions.

87. Will Your Content Be Search Engine-Friendly?

Importance

Whether you do any SEO or not, search engines will index and rank your site according to the rules they follow. Without SEO you're leaving it to chance that your content will get ranked the way you want. But if you optimize the structure and the writing of your content to follow the rules, you vastly increase the odds of a good useful ranking.

Structuring Content

Search engines work on the assumption that first in line means more important. It's not a bad assumption; the trick is to realize that they really mean it. Not mentioning a keyword until the first sentence of the second paragraph has meaning to a search engine: This page is not primarily about this keyword (there are other factors, of course). The structure of your site and of each page needs to take into account assumptions like this.

SITE STRUCTURE

Search engines use a site's home page as the starting point of site structure. Then they look at what gets linked directly from the home page—the second level of the site structure. Pages that link directly from the second level form the third level, and so on. The higher a page is within this structure, the more important it becomes to the search engine.

The beauty of websites is that you can create multiple "structures" at the same time—you are not tied to one set of connections in the way a physical file folder system would be. You have the ability to create different pathways for different purposes, and therefore different keyword optimization.

Suppose you're building a website for your wool shop. You sell products such as yarns, patterns, and accessories (needles); plus you have classes on knitting, crocheting, and cross-stitching. Add some basic pages such as About and Contact and you have your second- and third-level structures, as shown in Figure 9-5.

Displaying these levels visually on a site map is more than just a way of making it easier to understand; you're laying out a blueprint for search engines. That's why it's also vital to indicate on the map all the links between pages so you can see how search engines will interpret the relationships.

On sites with fewer than five or six pages, site structure probably won't be much of an issue, and the focus would be on page structure alone.

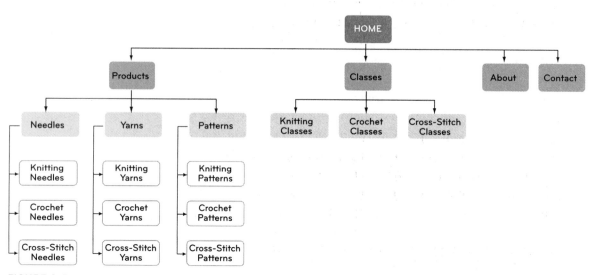

FIGURE 9-5

> Don't move the physical files for your content once you've launched your site because that means they'll have a different URL, and all your hard work to get it ranked under the old URL will be lost.

However, if you've done your keyword research and thought about what potential customers are looking for, you realize that this structure reflects your own thinking about your business. You carry products and hold classes, but customers don't search for "products"; they search for knitting yarn or crochet needles. As it stands, your site structure plays down pages that would have keywords like that.

The problem is easily solved without moving a single file on your server—simply link the pages differently so keyword-rich pages appear on the second level instead of the third or fourth. Figure 9-6 shows the new customer and search engine–friendly structure.

What's exciting from an SEO standpoint is that related pages that were unconnected are now clearly linked together. Knitting Yarn was under Yarns, Knitting Patterns was under Patterns, and so on. Now they're all linked directly to a Knitting page. That means searches for the term "knitting" have a focal point, confirmed for the search engines by all those knitting pages on the site linking to it.

Notice, too, that the Classes page still gathers all the class pages into one place so it remains useful for optimizing the keyword "classes." Always keep an eye open for opportunities to gather related pages on your site into a kind of index page that makes disparate pages available all in one place and can be used to optimize for the keyword(s) they share.

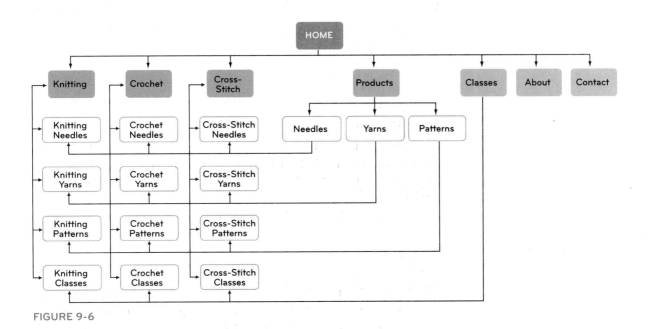

FIGURE 9-6

PAGE STRUCTURE

Just as search engines see your site according to the structures you create through linking, they see your pages according to the structures you create using placement and headings.

Placement means that your most important point on a page is made in the first paragraph, your next most important in the second, and so on. If you have more than two or three paragraphs, you'll probably want to break things up using sections, and this provides an additional opportunity to make your structure clear to search engines.

You can break up sections by having a heading that's been styled bold. To humans this has significance, but it means nothing special to search engines: They see it as a one-sentence paragraph.

HTML heading tags, on the other hand, do provide a kind of meaning for the search engine robots. Using H1 (highest) to H7 (lowest), you can tell search engines how sections relate to one another. If H1 is used for the page/content title, then H2 will be the first main section. Perhaps this section has a subthought worthy of separation, so it gets an H3 heading. Then the next main section gets an H2, and so on.

> Be sure the filenames of pages reflect the specific content: `heat-pump-service.html`, not `heat-pumps.html` (which could be a product sales page); or something cryptic such as `hp-service.html` or `page5.html`. Specific naming can help search engines understand what a page is about.

> There should be only one H1 heading on a page.

Writing Content

When done properly, writing with search engines in mind should not only sound natural, it should actually be clearer for visitors. Here are two of the most important elements of writing for search engines.

KEYWORDS IN CONTENT

Having emphasized the importance of keywords in SEO, the risk is that people let this color their writing. They think the more a keyword is used, the better the ranking. Writing and editing becomes an exercise of hitting so-called magic numbers on a keyword density analyzer (it measures the percentage of keyword mentions to all other words on the page).

Rule of Thumb   Write for your audience, not for keyword density analyzers.

Common sense will tell you if you're overusing keywords, but if you really need a number to work with, 3–5 percent is generally a good range. That's 3 to 5 keywords per 100 words of content.

Forget magic numbers and write your pages so that they clearly communicate a message that will benefit visitors in some way. SEO is best left to the editing stage, when you can stand back and look for opportunities to use your keyword more, but without overusing it.

One way to avoid repeating keywords too much, but still keep your page focused, is to use variants of the keyword—remember those longer keywords you left off your final list? In fact, these closely related keywords are an important part of long tail optimization.

If the keyword for one of your pages is "patio tables," use the longer keywords you found, such as "outdoor patio tables," "garden patio tables," or "patio dining tables." Fewer people might search for them, but because they're searching for something more specific, they might be better prospects. And you won't drive your visitors "patio table" crazy.

Section headings are also useful places to work in your keywords. Not only will the keywords be in HTML that's been flagged as important for the search engines but your visitors will also see them easily as they scan the page.

DESCRIPTIVE LINK TEXT

The wording of text for links within your content—the anchor text—is important to SEO in two ways:

- To help decide if the link is relevant to the focus of the page

- To explain what content will be found when the link is clicked

If the anchor text for a link just says "click here," it isn't helpful. Make sure the text clearly describes what the link is about: "snowshoeing article in National Geographic." Notice the keyword at the start of this description. If the link is on a page about snowshoeing, that's great, but even on a page about winter sports it will be clear that the link is relevant (and not trying to sell a time-share).

Notice that both of these criteria need to be in agreement. A well-described link that goes to the wrong sort of site is bad for visitors; a poorly described link that goes to a good site, although marginally better for visitors, is still not optimal. Any disconnect between the anchor text and the linked site is a negative to the search engines because it means the visitor isn't getting the best experience possible.

Related Questions

- 42. How user-friendly will your links be? **Page 109**
- 58. Will the content of each page have a single focus? **Page 151**
- 59. Will your written content be correct, clear, and well structured? **Page 153**
- 60. How effectively will your content use links? **Page 158**

Action Items

- Review your site map for its effectiveness based on your keyword list. Add all links between pages so you can clearly see the relationships. Look for alternative or additional site structures.

- Review the text of each page of your site. First, if a visitor read only the first paragraph, would they get the main message of that page? Second, does your keyword for that page appear at least near the start of that first paragraph.

Importance

88. Will Your Search Engine Strategy Cover Specialty Searches?

Search engines have long offered specialized searches, such as for books or images, but too few people took advantage of them. So they began integrating results from these specialty searches with regular web page results, to create what's called universal or blended searches. Search pages now display blocks of results, such as Image, Video, Book, or Local results, as illustrated in Figure 9-7.

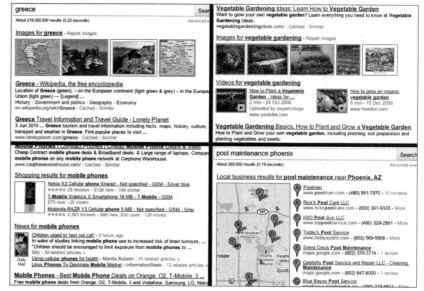

FIGURE 9-7

Although specialty indexing is growing fast, there are still opportunities to get good rankings for specialty content, such as a video, when the page it's on is not having luck in the regular page results because of greater competition there.

Which blocks you get will depend on what you're searching for and what's indexed by the specialty searches, but, when they're displayed, people are paying attention. Studies have shown, for instance, that image results often get more clicks than regular web page results. This means you need to optimize the content these specialty searches are looking for.

Images

Search engines can't see images so you need to help them understand what an image is about. This kind of optimization is important not just for image searches, but for regular search rankings as well. The basics of image optimization start with the image's HTML tag. Figure 9-8 shows an image tag that has not been optimized, and each part of the tag has been labeled.

File Name	alt Attribute	title Attribute
`<img src="my-dog-playing-frisbee.jpg" alt="My Dog Playing Frisbee" title="The Big Catch"`		

FIGURE 9-8

Starting with the filename for the image—img839287.tif—it tells you nothing except what number it was in someone's camera. If this is a picture of your new car, name the file something like "honda-civic-2010-blue-4-door.jpg". If you're reviewing the car, the filename matches the content of the page. The bonus is that if someone searches for "honda civic 2010," not only could your web page come up but your image could also come up as its own listing.

The next piece of the image's HTML that needs optimizing is the `alt` attribute. (It stands for "alternative" and it's the text that shows on the web page if the image is broken or if images are turned off.) It's also indexed by the search engines.

If the `alt` attribute says something like "Honda Civic 2010 blue 4-door," it matches the filename, fits with the page content, and gives you another little check box on the search engine's relevance checklist. If it has the keyword for the page in it, the `alt` attribute becomes even more useful—but make sure it's part of the image's description, not just thrown in to get more keywords.

The final element of the image tag is the `title` attribute. Text placed in it will be displayed by the browser as a small popup box when visitors mouse over the image. Although it's more a benefit to users than to search engines specifically, the `title` attribute does add additional text to the description of the image.

The location of an image on the page also affects how it is ranked by search engines. First, make sure the image is surrounded by the text it is related to, such as the Honda photo in the car review, not on

> **?** Don't confuse optimization of images for reduced size with SEO. Images need to be specially saved for the Web in order to keep their file size small; that's known as optimization.

> **💡** Putting a hyphen between words in a filename allows search engines to read the individual words. Spaces or underscores won't do the trick.

> **?** For more details about image optimization, search for 🔍 images seo.

> **💡** Don't confuse the `alt` and `title` attributes of an image. If you put text only in the `title` attribute, it does not get picked up by the search engines in the same way.

the opposite end of the page. Second, try to keep images as close to the top of the page as possible. You might even consider creating a separate page for the image, perhaps showing a larger version of it, along with more descriptive text.

Finally, creating a page that displays a large version of an image can also help to boost visibility in a specialty search. The page title would basically be the text in the `alt` attribute (don't forget to make the page's filename descriptive as you did for the image filename).

Video

Video is a powerful draw on websites, and searches for videos continue to grow at a fast pace, so make sure video search optimization is part of your SEO strategy.

For a lot of people, the simplest way to handle videos is to upload them to a video-sharing service such as YouTube and then use the embed feature (a piece of HTML to copy and paste) to display the video on their website. Here are the main points for video SEO when you're taking this route:

> Every video-sharing service will have its own particular way of optimizing video for search results within its site.

- When you're producing your video, make sure to use keywords in the script; if you have captioning or a transcript, make sure keywords appear in them as well.

- Use your keywords in the title, description, and tag boxes when you're uploading the video.

- Make sure you include the URL of your site in the information accompanying the video.

- Give your video a descriptive filename.

- Heavily promote new videos on your site to your mailing list, through social networks, and so forth. Videos that get a lot of views in a short time often get pushed to the front page of sharing sites.

If you host your video on your own server, these are some key points for SEO:

> Making videos has become a lot easier, but deciding which format to use is not so simple (MOV vs. AVI vs. MPG, and so on). For the latest on what formats are most common, search for 🔍 most compatible web video format

- Give your video its own page with good descriptive text to accompany it, and optimize the usual elements of the page to match the keyword(s) for the video.

➤ Name your video file descriptively and if possible place it in a directory with other videos.

➤ Make sure the video player you use has the ability for people to easily embed the video on their site, automatically providing a link back to you.

> For more details about optimizing video for search engines, use the search term
> 🔍 video seo

Local Content

More and more people are using the Internet to find local information, so local search is taking off. With search engines such as Google you can improve the "local status" of your site by listing yourself in their local directories or even creating a business page on their site that links directly to your website.

For the optimization of your site, these are some ways to get better ranking in a local search:

➤ Putting your location in the title tag of pages

➤ A detailed contact page with location names near the top of the page

➤ Displaying contact information, including location on every page of the site

➤ Using your location name regularly in your content, without overdoing it, of course

➤ Get relevant local sites to link to you.

➤ Get listed in popular local directories. Search engines index these directories and give them prominence in the results as the highlighted listings in Figure 9-9 show.

There are many other specialty searches—Books, News, Blogs—and no doubt more will emerge. So watch for ways you can optimize specific content to take advantage of these focused searches, in which the competition can be significantly less.

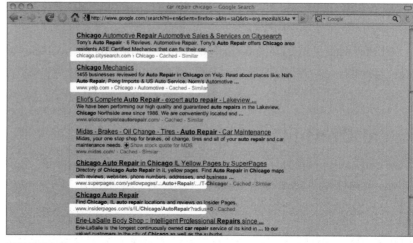

FIGURE 9-9

 Related Questions

➧ 54. Will your nontext files use the proper file types? **Page 140**

➧ 61. Will you effectively use images in your content? **Page 160**

➧ 62. How will you use video or audio in your content? **Page 164**

Action Items

➧ Go through the images on your site and check the optimization criteria for each. CMSs typically make it very simple to add details such as `alt` attributes.

➧ If you're using a CMS, check to see whether it's automatically creating individual pages for images; if it's not, how you would go about doing that. Do the same for video.

89. Will Your Links to and from Other Sites Be Search Engine-Friendly?

Importance

If optimized content is the most important factor for search engine ranking, links to and from other sites must come a close second. Some argue that they're even more important than content. It really depends on the search engine—some put slightly more weight on one or the other. The bottom line is this: Pay as much attention to links as you do to optimizing content and you can't go wrong.

When it comes to links, search engines place the most weight on which sites are linking to yours. These are known as inbound links and they're an indicator of your site's relevance and importance. Search engines also take some account of which sites you link to in your content, known as outbound links. In each case, the better the link, the more it counts in your favor.

Inbound Links

Having other sites linking to yours is very important to search engines, but thankfully it's not just a high school popularity contest. Large numbers of inbound links won't necessarily win you a lot of points in the eyes of the search engines—it's the quality of the links that matters, and quality is based on several factors.

RELEVANCE

Suppose you get 50 friends to link their site to your bake shop site. It sounds like a good idea, but unless their site is closely related to baking, a simple link won't do much good. If they have a review of your bake shop that includes a link, it might be somewhat useful, although a review on a car repair site will carry less weight than on a blog about family outings. Sites that would make a bigger impact with a link would be restaurant review sites or shopping sites or directory sites.

Use one of the many free online link analyzers, such as Yahoo! Explorer, to find out who's linking to the sites of highly ranked competitors. This can provide you with leads or at least ideas for getting your own inbound links. See Question 76 for more details.

It's possible to tell search engines not to follow any links on a page (with the robots meta tag) or to follow just a particular link `<a rel="nofollow" href="http://...`. If the site linking to you has a nofollow directive for your link, you won't receive any search ranking benefit from that site because the search engine won't go to your site.

Much has been made of avoiding "nofollow sites" (sites that block search engines from indexing sites they link to) when looking for inbound links, but remember that getting traffic to your site is the goal, and if a nofollow site has good potential for sending you traffic, the link is still worthwhile.

AUTHORITY

Even when a link is from a relevant site, however, it's better to have a link from what's sometimes called an authoritative site. Authority or trust are terms that have emerged over the last few years as search engines looked for better ways to rank sites. Google's PageRank system, which initially focused mostly on inbound links, is an example of one type of ranking method (PageRank was then used as a factor in determining placement on Google's results pages).

Just as you come to trust other people over time by observing their actions, for example, search engines look at a huge number of factors to determine the trust level of sites, such as the age of the site, how many other authoritative sites link to it, how helpful the site is to visitors (linking to other useful sites), how often content is updated, and even how secure the site is.

Something to keep in mind when looking for sites you want to have linking to you: Authority gets passed from one site to another. A leading website in your field (X) might have no reason yet to link to your new site (Z), but you know someone whose site (Y) has an inbound link from X. Because of that link, search engines give Y a bit of the authority developed by X. If Y links to Z, the search engines grant Z a bit of the authority given to Y. It's not a lot, but until you can gain the trust of X, you're gaining a measure of authority.

INBOUND LINK CODE

The marketing chapter in this book has some answers for getting other sites to link to you. Here the discussion will be confined to the technical issues concerning the links on those other sites.

If possible, make sure that inbound links have your correct name, and that the URL is the one you consistently use for that page. In the case of CMSs, that means using what are called permanent links. These are URLs over which you have varying degrees of control, but that masks the actual URL generated by the CMS, such as `http://mydomain.com/?page=387`.

However, because the page with this URL is listed in category 34, another link to the same page could be `http://mydomain.com/?page=387&cat=34`. If one inbound link goes to one address, and another inbound link goes to the other, the search engines see two links to two

---

Authority is not a zero-sum quality. In other words, by linking to another site, you don't lose any portion of your authority, the other site simply picks up a bit of authority for itself.

You should be linking only to sites that are useful to your visitors, but authority is another reason for not linking to just any site—you're granting them some authority and you need to ask yourself if they deserve it.

separate pages. What could have been two votes for a single URL becomes one vote each for two URLs. The solution is to have a permanent link such as http://mydomain.com/knitting/winter-patterns/.

If you can control the alt attribute text for the link, along with the anchor text for the link, it would be ideal. One way to do this is to provide the full HTML of the link to your site, which people can then copy and paste onto their site. A couple of examples are shown in Figure 9-10.

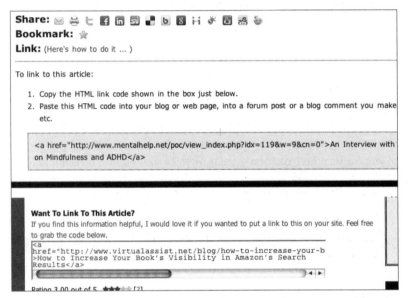

FIGURE 9-10

Unfortunately many copy and paste links fail to take advantage of the alt attribute, such as the ones in these examples.

If you're contacting a site about linking to you, have a fully formatted link ready to send them. They might not use what you send them, but they'll probably appreciate that you've made it easy for them to set up the link.

Outbound Links

Although outbound links—links to other sites—do not play nearly as important an SEO role as inbound links, you still need to pay attention to them.

It's possible to have too many outbound links on a page. If you're in the range of 100 or more links, search engines could flag it as a link farm (a large group of usually unrelated links designed to try and boost the search ranking of the sites participating in the farm).

There are lots of free link checkers online. Just enter a URL and you get a report on all links and which ones are broken. For a list of some link checkers, see this chapter's section in Appendix A.

Unlike inbound links, you have full control over the writing of outbound links, so you can follow the points made earlier in this chapter about writing descriptive text for links.

It's important for your visitors and for search engines that your outbound links be relevant to your content. A link might not be relevant to your site in general, but it needs to be relevant to the content in which it appears.

Make sure the sites you link to are not just relevant but also have great content. If you're writing about wood carving, a link to a wood carving site that has poor-quality tutorials is not only a disservice to your readers but it's also unlikely that the site has a good search engine ranking.

It's easy to create an outbound link and then forget about it, but if the page you linked to disappears, you're left with a broken link, and that can have serious consequences for SEO. Broken links can lower page relevance or, worse still, cause robots to give up indexing your page. Checking for broken links is an ongoing task that should be done primarily to prevent your visitors from being frustrated, but also as part of your SEO strategy.

Related Questions

▶ 42. How user-friendly will your links be? **Page 109**

▶ 60. How effectively will your content use links? **Page 158**

▶ 76. Do you have a plan for getting important sites to link to you? **Page 213**

Action Items

▶ Make a list of sites you think would be beneficial to have as inbound links. Then check their authority level using one of the online tools listed in Appendix A. Keep in mind that a site can still be a good inbound link for bringing traffic, even if it doesn't have a lot of authority.

▶ Review your outbound links to make sure you're linking to sites that will provide good value to your visitors.

90. Do You Know What Your Site Will Look Like to Search Engines?

Importance

Earlier in this chapter I gave a bit of background on how search engines work because it will help you understand what you need to do to get indexed accurately and ranked higher. Another part of that education is to see your site in ways the search engines see it.

The number of times a keyword is used on a page is a factor in search engine ranking. A quick way to get an overview of the relationships between words on a page is to use what's called a keyword density tool. Enter the URL of your page, and the tool tells you how much a word is used on the page, as a percentage of all the words. Figure 9-11 shows the output of a keyword analyzer.

A new and accurate tool: Keyword Density Analyzer

http://tool.motoricerca.info/keyword-density.phtml   Google

Analysis of page: http://www.veggiegardeningtips.com/

Words: 349, Count: 1745

Word	Count	Density
garden	125	7.16%
gardening	62	3.55%
growing	47	2.69%
greens	28	1.6%
vegetable	25	1.43%
summer	23	1.32%
seed	21	1.2%
plants	21	1.2%
heirloom	19	1.09%

Phrases: 146, Count: 466

2 Words	Count	Density
gardening tips	14	3%
gardening secrets	10	2.15%
leafy greens	10	2.15%
garden faire	9	1.93%
vegetable gardening	9	1.93%
article rarr	8	1.72%
secrets newsletter	8	1.72%
read full	8	1.72%
vegetable garden	8	1.72%

Phrases: 56, Count: 178

3 Words	Count	Density
gardening secrets newsletter	8	4.49%
herb garden faire	8	4.49%
full article rarr	8	4.49%
read full article	8	4.49%
veggie gardening tips	5	2.81%
leafy greens summer	5	2.81%
museum herb garden	4	2.25%
greens summer gardens	4	2.25%
valley museum herb	4	2.25%

FIGURE 9-11

There is no magic number for correct keyword density, nor is density in and of itself much of an issue for search engine ranking. Rather these tools can help in other ways:

➜ Are you using the keyword too little or way too much?

➜ Are there other words that might overshadow your keyword?

➜ What keywords are your competitors using? (Just enter their URLs.)

Another way of seeing your site through the eyes of a search engine is with a text-only web browser such as Lynx. It doesn't do any formatting, ignores JavaScript, and simply shows text along with links.

There are also keyword density tools that allow you to paste in text you're working on without having it published on the website. But if you're constantly using these keyword density tools, you're probably thinking about keywords too much. Close the tool and go back to writing for your audience.

Figure 9-12 shows a page in a regular browser and the same page in a Lynx simulator plug-in for Firefox.

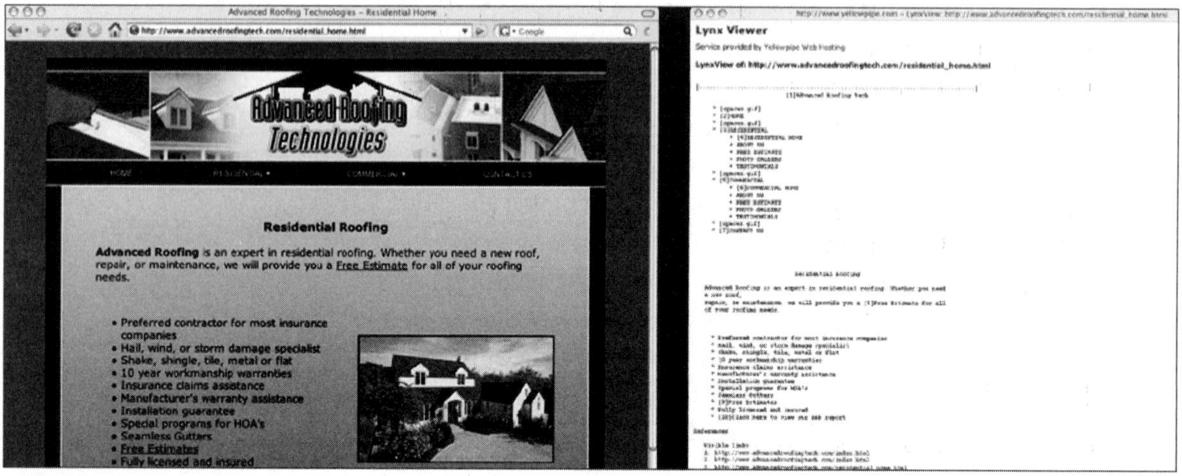

FIGURE 9-12

The resources section for this chapter in Appendix A has information on where to get text-based browsers or any of the other tools discussed here.

Things to watch for when viewing your site in a text browser:

→ Does the page stop loading at some point? This could indicate that a script is interfering with the search engines seeing your site properly.

→ Are all links displaying properly? This is also a fast way of getting an overview of link usage on your site. Are you using internal links to full advantage?

→ What text is displaying first? Is your content high up the page?

Another way to understand how a search engine is seeing your site is to subscribe to the free webmaster tools offered by search engines such as Google, Bing, and Yahoo!. They provide reports and notifications on the status of your site as crawled by their robots—who is linking to you, errors encountered, and much more.

One final source of information on how search engines see your site is to follow what's being said on company blogs by the search engine people. They offer lots of tips, and you can keep up with the latest trends.

On Video

Watch some ways to use keyword analyzers and see how sites look through the eyes of a Lynx browser simulator.

Related Questions

➜ 52. Will your HTML be bloated? **Page 134**

➜ 53. Will your site files be clearly organized? **Page 137**

➜ 86. Will your pages have the hidden HTML tags necessary for search engines? **Page 243**

Action Items

➜ Run several competitors' sites through a keyword analyzer to see how often they're using keywords. Do the same with a text browser and look at their content structure.

➜ As soon as possible in the development stage, run your site through the tools covered here to catch any issues early on.

Importance

91. Will the HTML Code for Your Site Be Search Engine–Friendly?

HTML code does not directly affect your search engine rankings, but it can present some barriers to the programs (robots) used to gather website data.

In Appendix A, you'll find the link for this and the other tools mentioned in this chapter.

Search engine robots are not like web browsers. Browsers want to give their users the best possible experience viewing sites, so they tend to be very forgiving of HTML that breaks rules. Robots, on the other hand, are interested in indexing content and they simply work their way through every character in the HTML. Many of the errors they encounter won't cause a problem, but sometimes they're enough to cause the robot to miss content or stop indexing.

You can quickly spot major errors in your HTML without having to be an HTML expert. There's a free validation service provided by the organization for HTML standards, known as the W3C consortium. All you have to do is enter a page's URL into the validator, and it will provide a report on errors it finds, as shown in Figure 9-13.

FIGURE 9-13

Don't be too shocked at the errors you'll see for your pages. If you enter the URLs of several major websites, including Google, you'll discover that they don't validate, either. In fact, the vast majority of sites don't validate, so don't get hung up on trying to eliminate every little error on your pages. You do want to catch serious errors, and the validations give you some guidance about what's important and what's not.

From an SEO perspective, what you want to look for in particular are unclosed tags. In the vast majority of cases, HTML uses an opening tag and a closing tag: `<title>This is my title</title>`. Sometimes the closing tag is missing and that can cause serious problems, such as preventing the rest of the page from loading. Some unclosed tags are clearly visible in your browser (why is this page bold starting halfway down?), but many aren't or they'll produce a problem that isn't directly related to the tag.

However, putting your site through a validator does not tell the whole story of whether your HTML is search engine–friendly. For instance, a validator does not tell you that you should be using a heading tag instead of a bold tag to highlight sections of your content. Both tags will validate, but only the heading tag is useful to search engines in terms of telling it something about the importance of the text. Similarly, validators won't tell you that it's a mistake to use the `<h1>` heading tag more than once on a page.

Semantic errors in your code—errors that make meaning unclear—need to be checked by looking at the source code of a page. That's how you can make sure sections of text are designated with the correct heading tags; or you can tell whether the page is being laid out with tables or easier-for-robots-to-read, more efficient style sheets. As well, you can check to make sure robots don't have to sift through JavaScript or style sheet rules that belong in separate files, not in the HTML itself.

> Use HTML entities instead of characters. Search engine robots can be stopped in their tracks by characters such as # or |, but they read the HTML equivalents (entities) &023 or &pipe just fine. You can check the code of your site to see whether the designer has used these properly.

Related Questions

→ 49. Will you use tables or style sheets to lay out your site? **Page 126**

→ 50. How effectively will style sheets be used on your website? **Page 129**

→ 52. Will your HTML be bloated? **Page 134**

→ 59. Will your written content be correct, clear, and well structured? **Page 153**

Action Items

→ Check your site in the HTML validator and look for serious errors.

→ Look at the HTML code of your pages to make sure that headings are being used and used correctly.

Importance

92. Will You Need to Hire Anyone to Help Optimize Your Site for Search Engines?

> Do not pay anyone to submit your site to search engines. The robots come around automatically, so you'll be indexed without anyone doing anything.

> Paying to have your site listed with large numbers of directories is not a good idea. You can easily find useful directories in your area of interest, and if you don't have the time, hire an SEO consultant to research it for you. A reputable company will find you relevant useful directories, and not just submit to hundreds of them.

SEO is big business. There are tens of thousands of SEO specialists who offer to get better rankings for your site. Most of them can provide useful help and advice, and I'll get to them in a moment. First, I need to say something about the minority of SEO practitioners who distract from the good work of the others.

The distraction comes in the form of misleading claims such as: "Guaranteed Top Placement" or "Be #1 In Google." To website owners who know SEO is vital but are overwhelmed by the details, or who are lazy and want a quick fix, these promises can be attractive. But if you can put your wallets away for a moment, the next couple of pages can save you some time and money.

First, much of what is good for search engine ranking has to do with content—and content is completely in your control. This means that a lot of SEO needs to be done by you or whoever is writing your web page content.

Rule of Thumb   When it comes to SEO services, run when you see words such as "guaranteed."

Although it's not as directly within your control, getting links from good websites is something that you can pursue yourself. It takes time and energy, but you probably have more of that than cash.

Besides saving money, avoiding the lure of big promises can also keep you from getting involved in questionable or downright dangerous SEO practices. Good search engine rankings can sometimes be achieved by finding loopholes in or new ways of using the rules that search engines follow. There are lots of clever people out there looking for ways to work on the margin of good practices, but the equally clever people at the search engines usually spot this and close loopholes or bring in new rules.

Then there are the SEO experts who achieve results by using practices that are banned by the search engines. The strategy might work

92. WILL YOU NEED TO HIRE ANYONE TO HELP OPTIMIZE YOUR SITE FOR SEARCH ENGINES?

267

for a short time—perhaps enough even to make good on their promise—but you'll end up wasting your money or, even worse, having your site banned.

When to Hire an SEO Consultant

Keyword research is one area in which an SEO consultant can be of great benefit. A company with plenty of experience can save you a lot of time and effort, not to mention coming up with a better keyword list than you could have on your own. Besides experience, a consultant will have more powerful analytical tools than the free ones on the Web.

Although there is a lot you and your web developer can do to implement SEO, hiring a consultant is often a good way of drawing up a plan for what needs doing. Their insights will make the plan more comprehensive and they can speed up the process.

Hiring an SEO consultant to help research which sites are best to approach for inbound links can save you time and energy, which are better spent personally contacting those sites.

If you have the money to do it and the need for high rankings on a lot of keywords, hiring someone to conduct your search campaign over a period of several months can be worthwhile. Campaign experts have the tools for monitoring the progress of the efforts and the experience to know when it's time to make adjustments or take new directions.

Related Questions

➧ 76. Do you have a plan for getting important sites to link to you? **Page 213**

➧ 85. How do you plan to research useful keywords for your site? **Page 240**

Action Items

➧ Ask other people if they've used any SEO consultants and what the process and results were like.

➧ Visit the sites of some SEO companies and get a feel for how they approach SEO. Are they all about promises or all about the hard work of an optimization campaign? Look for case studies you can verify using the search engines.

Chapter 10

Housekeeping and Security

Importance

93. How Will You Back Up Your Site?

At some point, your website will crash: The hard drive on the server will die, someone will accidentally erase some files, or a database will get corrupted. These are rare occurrences, but when they happen they become catastrophes only if you haven't properly backed up your website. If you have, problems like these should be only minor nuisances.

There are three basic steps to any backup routine:

➤ Making a copy of all necessary site files

➤ Storing the copied files

➤ Backing up the copied files

This process can be as simple as downloading copies of all your site files to your home computer and then making another backup on an external hard drive. But with more and more sites using content management systems (CMSs) or e-commerce programs, there are databases to consider as well as additional options for backing up.

For most people, the easiest way to handle backups is to keep one of the copies on a home or office computer. Here's one way to organize them:

➤ Navigate to the folder on your computer where you keep all your website-related materials and create a folder called something like Site Backups (this needs to be done only the first time you're backing up your site).

➤ When you're doing a backup or if you're downloading an automated backup, create a folder inside of Site Backups whose name includes the current date.

> To name the folder of a particular backup, try this convention: YYYYMMDD (for example, 20100408 for April 8, 2010). That way, the folders will line up in chronological order.

Backing Up Site Files

All websites hosted on their own server have files that need to be backed up, even with a database-driven site. There are several options for accessing the site files on your server:

➤ **FTP programs**—A File Transfer Protocol (FTP) program is useful if you are accessing several different sites (names of good programs are in Appendix A). With most FTP programs, you can view your computer on the left side, whereas the server is visible on the right. Make sure the backup folder you created is open on the left side of the window. Then on the server, navigate to the home directory of your site, and select all files and folders. Press the download button, and they'll all begin to appear on the left side of the window, as shown in Figure 10-1.

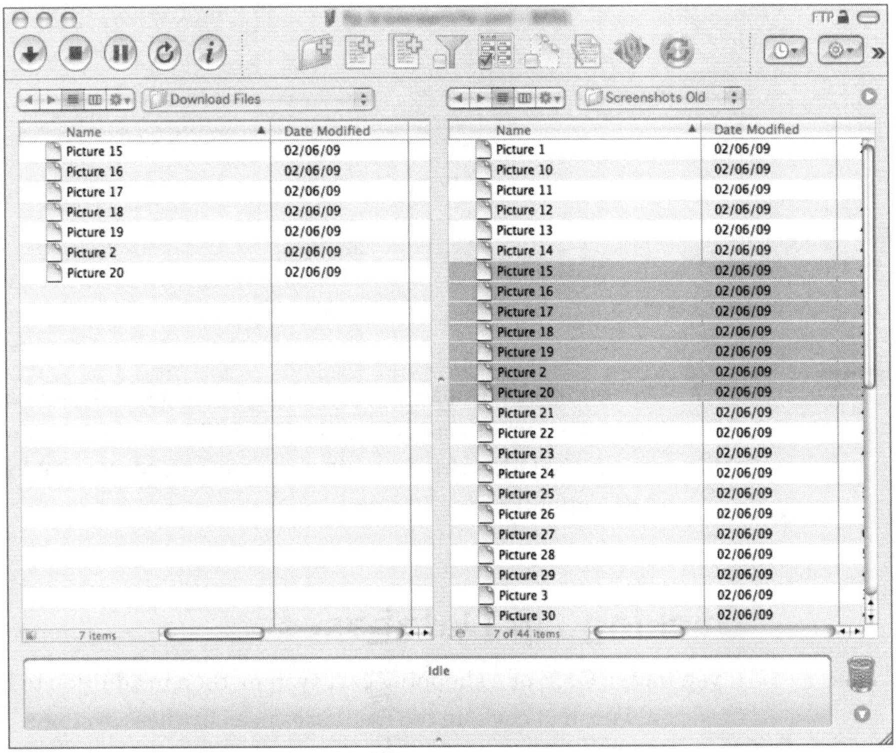

FIGURE 10-1

→ **File managers**—Most hosting control panels provide an interface similar to an FTP program for uploading and downloading files to the server—an example is shown in Figure 10-2. You simply select all the files and folders in the home directory for your site and click the download button. When prompted to save, navigate to, and select the backup folder on your computer.

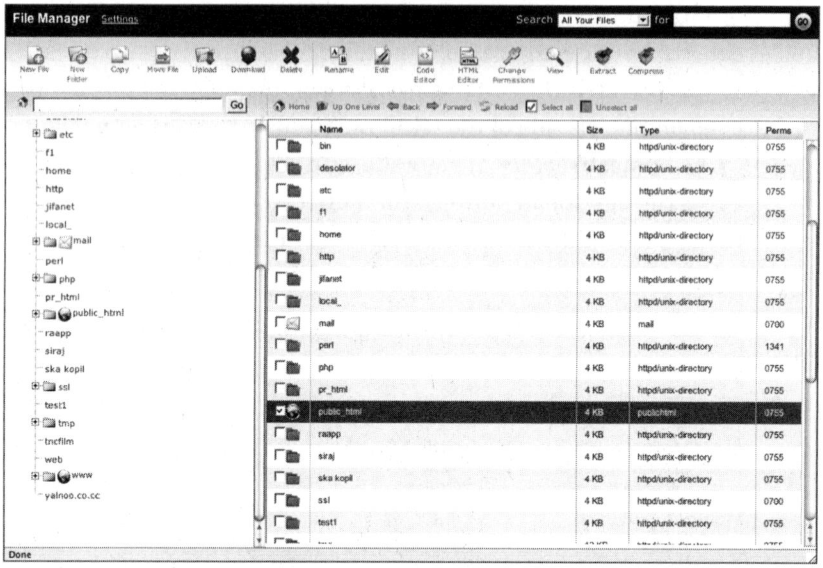

FIGURE 10-2

→ **One-button backups**—Some hosting control panels offer a one-button backup of your home directory. This produces a single compressed file, which you then save to your backup folder on your computer.

Backing Up Databases

If you have a CMS or a shopping cart system, then in addition to the site files, you'll need to back up the databases used by these systems. Again, there are several options, depending on your software and on your hosting control panel:

→ **Built-in backup**—Many CMSs and shopping carts have a backup function that makes a copy of your database and provides options for downloading that copy. You can have the copy e-mailed to you (this is handy if you're not at your computer or for automated backups) or you can download it directly to the backup folder you created. If you use the e-mail option, remember to save the copy to your backup folder when it arrives.

➤ **One-button control panel backup**—Some hosting control panels have a one-click backup of your database, and you simply choose to save the copy in your backup folder.

➤ **Manual database backup**—Most hosting control panels have an interface for working with databases (phpMyAdmin is the most common for Linux servers), and this interface will have a backup or export tool. Usually there's a default setting for these tools, but your hosting provider should have tutorials to walk you through the particular steps you need. You need to be careful when working with a database manager or you can cause real damage. This is an option for experienced users only.

You might be wondering where your hosting company is in all of this. Doesn't it keep backups of everything on its server? Many hosting companies do make a complete backup of a server, say once a week, but only the most recent copy is available. This backup is meant for general system recovery, though hosts often do their best to help recover a particular site.

Rule of Thumb   Backups are your responsibility, not that of your hosting provider.

In the end, though, the responsibility for backups rests with the site owner, as shown in the sample hosting agreement in Figure 10-3. In other words, hosting companies are not legally responsible for getting your content back to where it was.

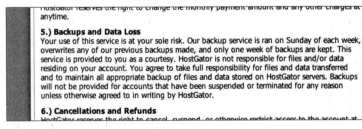

FIGURE 10-3

Many hosting companies offer full backup services as a separate package, and the price is usually quite low. You might even find one that offers it for free.

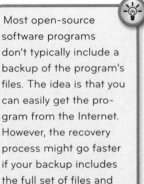

Most open-source software programs don't typically include a backup of the program's files. The idea is that you can easily get the program from the Internet. However, the recovery process might go faster if your backup includes the full set of files and databases.

Check your ISP's limit on e-mail size (these days, it's typically 5MB to 10MB) to make sure your backup files can be e-mailed to you.

Regularly check that your automated backups are working. When a crash happens, you don't want to find out that the backups stopped seven months ago.

Automated Backups

There are several options for automating the process of backing up both files and databases:

- **Built-in software backups**—The backup features or modules of CMSs and shopping carts often allow for regularly scheduled backups of content files, databases, or both. These can be set to run daily, weekly, and so on, and you have the option to store the backups on the server or have them e-mailed to you. Some modules also offer the ability to send backups to an online storage provider such as Amazon S3.

- **Dedicated backup programs**—There are free or paid programs you install on your server to automatically provide backups of both site files and databases. You set the frequency and whether the backups will be stored on the server, e-mailed, or sent to another server.

- **Online backup services**—Instead of installing software on your server, these backup services operate from a web-based panel and perform regularly scheduled backups to their servers. The cost is usually pretty small (a few dollars per month), and it saves you having to find an offsite location to store the backups.

- **Custom server programming**—You can hire your hosting company or a third party to create a backup routine on your server using what are called "cron jobs." Keep in mind that the backed-up files are still on the server, so you'll need to offload them yourself onto your computer or some other source.

Storing Your Backups

The point of backing up your website is that if anything happens to it or to the server, you can quickly upload everything to a new location and get running again as quickly as possible. If your backups are stored with your site, you might well lose them, too, if your server goes down. At the very least, you wouldn't be able to access the backups until the server is restored, so you couldn't set up a temporary site or move to a new hosting company.

Rule of Thumb   Never store copies of your site files and databases on the server where your site is hosted.

Offsite storage of backups clearly is a must, and you have lots of options for storing them:

➡ Your own computer, as I've mentioned, is the simplest choice for most people.

➡ At-home storage, but not on your computer, includes external hard drives, tape back ups, or DVDs.

➡ Your hosting company might offer backup storage in a different location than the server hosting your site.

➡ There are backup services that provide storage.

➡ There are online storage services such as Amazon S3.

➡ For small sites, you can even use something as simple as having backups e-mailed to a free e-mail account that has lots of storage space, such as Gmail or Yahoo! Mail.

> USB drives are large enough these days that they can easily handle the files and database of small to medium-sized sites.

Storing a Copy of Your Backup

Wherever your store your backups offsite, the key is to keep a second copy in yet another location. It's good to spread your risk. For example, if you're storing backups on your home computer, have another copy on an external hard drive. If you're using an online storage company, regularly download a copy of the backup to your computer. It doesn't take a lot of time, and the cost of storage is negligible, but when your server goes down and your computer crashes at the same time, you'll be glad for the second backup.

> **On Video**
> Watch demonstrations of manual backups as well as setting up automated backups.

Rule of Thumb   Always have a backup of your backup stored in a separate location.

Related Questions

➤ 9. What kind of support does the web hosting provider offer? **Page 21**

➤ 10. Does the web hosting provider have a good hosting control panel? **Page 23**

Action Items

➤ Make a list of everything that needs backing up. Talk to your hosting company or web developer if you're not sure.

➤ Research what options you have for doing backups: What does your CMS offer? What are the options with your host? Then research options for storing two different copies of the backup.

➤ Set a schedule for backing up your site (whether manual or automatic), based on the frequency of the content changing.

94. Will You Be Regularly Checking Your Site's Functionality?

Importance

Websites are becoming increasingly complex, which means you need to regularly ensure that the site is working properly. You might hear about problems from visitors, but most will just go to another site. If you consistently monitor your site, you can catch these issues before they turn away visitors.

The trouble is that site owners typically don't visit their own sites on a regular basis, so even obvious problems such as missing images or videos go unnoticed. They treat sites like printed matter—they'll always look the way they did when first published. But even a basic web page with unchanging content relies on several systems to keep it functioning—browsers, server software, code such as JavaScript, and content management software—and they can break or change.

Rule of Thumb   Go through every page of your website at least once a month.

A regular inspection means much more than glancing through your site. Here are some examples of what needs to be checked:

+ **Images**—Visually check for broken images—re-upload if necessary or correct the HTML if the image has been moved.
+ **Links**—Use a link validator service to catch broken links (see Appendix A).
+ **Forms**—Test that they send and that they arrive at the correct e-mail address. Deliberately make errors to test the form-validation process. Do the same for third-party forms such as mailing list signups.
+ **Photo galleries**—Test that they're working and images are displaying correctly.
+ **Third-party widgets**—Check that feeds from social media or syndicated content are still working.
+ **Video**—Check that videos you've embedded from sharing sites are still working (owners might have removed the video or blocked embedding).
+ **Shopping**—Check that Buy Now buttons or shopping carts are working.

Use a spreadsheet to create a checklist of all the elements on your site that need to be tested, including the URL where they're located. This will make it easier for you, plus if you need someone else to do it, everything's laid out clearly.

Changes in software are another cause of website problems. Whether it is database software (such as MySQL), scripting languages (such as PHP) or even the software running your server (such as Apache), they're all constantly being improved for features and security. Programmers work hard to take these changes into account, but the interactions are complex, and things get missed.

Your best protection is to follow the update instructions for any software you're using, such as a CMS, a shopping cart, or JavaScripted features such as slideshows. It's also important to subscribe to the notification list of your hosting company. These notices will advise of upcoming changes, such as upgrading to a new version of database software, or known conflicts that have been reported. If updating your site's software doesn't help, you'll probably need to hire your hosting company or a developer to sort things out.

Because different web browsers can display a website differently, it's important to check your site's functionality when a major change is introduced for a popular browser—the introduction of Internet Explorer 9, for example.

The ultimate functionality of a site, of course, is whether it's running or not, and regular check ups won't help with that. The simplest answer is to establish a routine of looking at your site at least once a day. If it's important that you know at any moment whether the site is running, consider a site-monitoring service. It can e-mail or text you instantly if the site goes down. You can find free and paid services with the search term 🔍 site monitoring tools.

Related Questions

➡ 31. Will your site design display well in different browsers? **Page 76**

➡ 43. Will your site have special requirements for certain features to work? **Page 111**

➡ 100. How will you protect your site from attacks? **Page 295**

Action Items

➡ If you use a CMS, check to see whether there's an updated version available.

➡ Go through each page of your site and use a spreadsheet to list the technical functions that need checking. Put the URL of the page on the list so someone can go into a specific page easily.

95. Do You Have a Plan for Updating Site Content?

Importance

Regularly updating the content on your site is vital to developing a relationship with visitors and to attracting the search engines. Typically, site owners put in a lot of time and energy for the first few weeks after the site is launched, and then activity trails off and soon the site remains static, sometimes for years.

Establishing a routine is the best way to approach content updates, but it's very important to be realistic about that routine. How much time will you truly have? How much material will you be able to come up with? Start slowly—it's always better to be increasing content updates than to have them drop off.

There are three main types of content updating for sites, and each requires its own routine:

- Fresh blogging-style content
- New pages with content
- Adding to or changing existing content

If you can establish an overall routine with a mix of these, you're well on your way to an active site. And an active site is a healthy site.

Fresh Blogging Content

In the chapter on content, I distinguished between having a blog and the act of blogging. Blogging content is anything short and usually fairly timely. Here are some examples:

- Company news—staff changes, new equipment
- Sector news—anything from the sector you serve that has an impact on you or your visitors
- Testimonials or reviews
- Personal observations
- Quotations
- Tip of the day/week

> If you have friends or staff who can help with adding content, all the better. But again, start slowly and see how the plan works. Circumstances change and you don't want to be left trying to maintain a routine of 30 updates per week.

> Real simple syndication (RSS) feeds from other sites (short snippets of frequently updated information that appear on your site) are sometimes hailed as a way to easily fill your site with fresh content. Although these feeds can be useful to your visitors, they aren't a substitute for creating your own content.

For short, very time-sensitive material, consider setting up your mobile device to allow posting entries to your CMS. You can also set up a folder for your mobile device's recording function, so you can make notes to yourself quickly and then write the piece later in the day or week.

Setting aside a couple of hours each week is a good routine for this type of content. It's frequent enough to be timely and it keeps you from building up so much material that it becomes onerous. And because most CMSs allow you to schedule material, you do the writing all at once and then publish pieces over the seven days.

How much you write will depend on your topic and your writing ability, but if you aim for two or three pieces per week, that's a good amount to keep visitors coming back and for search engines to know you're active.

Make sure your CMS allows you to input these items as individual pieces of content, not just adding them to the same page. The individual items might appear in headline form on a single page (as with a blog), but it's important for search engine purposes, as well as for organizing your content in the future, that each entry be separate.

Keep your eyes open for videos other people have done or ones you can do yourself—this kind of content is particularly popular. Same with images—always ask if there's an image to go with what you've written.

New Pages

Always be on the lookout to add new pages to your site. Some will be obvious, such as the addition of a new staff member or expansion into a new area of business. But don't miss other opportunities.

For instance, if you notice increased interest in an aspect of family counseling that's currently just a part of your family counseling page, create a separate page focused primarily on that aspect. Or if there is a hot trend in fashion, you can pull together a page that talks about the trend while providing images and links to all your related products.

Be on the lookout for new pages that can feed one of your key pages. In the chapter on search engines I talked about keyword-focused pages that have several related pages all linking to it: the knitting page that has links from a knitting needle page, a knitting pattern page, and a knitting classes page. By brainstorming ways to add links to the knitting page, you might think of doing a series of knitting videos, each with its own page linking to that central page.

Always check your statistics to see which pages or areas of your site are most popular. Is there new material you can add that deals with the same topic?

Although new pages are great, make sure they're justified. Don't create a new page if it essentially repeats what's on another page or if you can simply update an existing page. It's a matter of volume and logic—do you have enough material to warrant an addition, and is it separate enough in some way from the existing content?

Be sure to highlight new pages for a time on your home page.

Update Existing Content

Making revisions to or adding new material to an existing page is an often overlooked part of a content management plan. Make it part of your routine to look through your site every couple of weeks or so to see if anything new can be added.

Be careful not to change the primary topic of a page when you're adding new material. You've hopefully optimized the page for search engines based on it being focused a particular way. Adding too much content (or the wrong sort) can change that focus in the eyes of the search engine (and probably for visitors, too).

It might be that the content has changed sufficiently that you need to reoptimize the page, but that will be a fair bit of work. Always see if you can add the material with different wording perhaps or maybe it's worth filling out the new content more and creating a new page.

On Video

See examples of blogging content and demonstrations of the scheduling function in a CMS.

If you're adding a note to part of your content, it can be useful to highlight the new material with an update notice and the date. If you're changing large portions of the text, put an update notice at the very beginning of the content.

Related Questions

→ 48. Will your site be built with a content management system (CMS)? **Page 124**

→ 64. What content will be on your home page? **Page 170**

→ 66. Will you be blogging on your site? **Page 183**

→ 96. Will you routinely check your contact information? **Page 282**

Action Items

→ Make a list of content that you know will need or likely will need updating—separate them into weekly, monthly, and annual categories.

→ Think about what a realistic updating schedule might be. Try it for one month and then reevaluate.

Importance

96. Will You Routinely Check Your Contact Information?

E-mail, phone numbers, and addresses—they're constantly changing, and you don't want visitors frustrated by incorrect contact information. Worse still, you don't want administration of your site being hampered by not keeping your information current. Routinely checking for up-to-date contact information saves everyone time and energy.

The most important contact information you need to keep up-to-date is the one people are most likely to forget: the contact records for your domain name. Registrars use your e-mail address for all critical correspondence: notification of expiring domains, recovering lost passwords, and domain transfers. Don't risk losing control of your domain name—your whole website would be in jeopardy.

> **Rule of Thumb** The e-mail address for your domain manager and your hosting account should *not* use your domain name. If your domain expires or your server is down, an e-mail with your domain name will not be working.

It's possible to gain access to your domain without a working e-mail address, but the process involves providing a physical ID and can be time-consuming (as it should be, for your own protection). Even if your contact information hasn't changed, it's worth making sure at least twice a year that your registrar has all the correct information.

The next record to keep updated is your hosting account. Your current e-mail address once again is the primary means of contact. With the wrong address on file:

- ✦ The host can't contact you about your billing, and if you're overdue, you risk having the account terminated.
- ✦ You won't receive notification if there's problem on the site (hackers, storage limits being exceeded).
- ✦ You won't be able to receive lost password information, which is automatically e-mailed to the address on file.

Another piece of contact information to check is in the user profile for your CMS or e-commerce software. If you lose your password, and

For certain domain extensions such as .com, regulators require registrars to e-mail regular reminders about keeping contact information up-to-date. Of course, it goes to the e-mail address on record.

You might find when you check your domain registration information that you're not even listed as the registrant—it might be a hosting company you were with three years ago or the web designer you hired. Get the registration changed to your name and contact info as soon as possible.

Carefully check the spelling of e-mail addresses. They might look fine at a glance, but if even a single character is wrong, the address is useless.

the system tries to e-mail it to a nonworking address, you might have to pay someone to go into your database and make the change manually.

On your website, up-to-date contact information is obviously important. You might notice incorrect information in the large address box at the top right of your website, but you need to think about the less obvious places, too:

> Have you mentioned a phone number or address within the body of text?

> Do you have any old pages archived on your site with out-of-date contact information?

> Check the scripts that run your forms to make sure they're sending to the correct address.

> If you have multiple people working on the site, ask them to check their work—they'll hopefully remember where they used the information.

The larger and the older the site, the easier it is for incorrect information to get buried. So starting off your site with a routine to catch these changes is very important. You'll save yourself a lot of time and headaches down the road, not to mention ensuring the good will of your visitors.

> On larger sites, it can be helpful to have special codes for your company name and contact information. If you need to update them, you just change the code once and all instances on the site are updated. Talk to your web developer about whether this is possible.

Related Questions

> 5. Who will register your domain and in whose name? **Page 11**

> 10. Does the web hosting provider have a good hosting control panel? **Page 23**

> 37. Will visitors easily know how to stay in touch with you? **Page 95**

Action Items

> Keep a list of all pages or areas of the site that contain contact information. As your site grows, add to the list. When it comes time for changes, you'll be sure you've covered everything.

> Gather all your contact information into a single document and print it out with the passwords. Then erase the passwords and save the file, keeping the printed copy in a safe place.

Importance

97. Will You Have Content You Can't Afford to Have Stolen?

How do you prevent people from stealing your website content and passing it off as their own? The fact is, you can't. Anything you put on a website can be saved by visitors—text, images, documents, videos—and that's a good thing for the most part. Problems arise when people use content without giving credit or steal it to make money.

All you can do by way of prevention is clearly label your content as copywritten and provide guidelines for how people might use your content. After that, it's a matter of monitoring the Web for improper use of content.

Rule of Thumb   Don't put anything on a website that you're worried about other people stealing.

This answer is not meant to scare you—the amount of theft from the average website is negligible—but simply to make you aware. If you know what the risks are, you can make an informed decision.

The simplest step is to have a copyright notice on all your material. If you live in a country that's party to a copyright agreement known as the Berne Convention—such as the United States, the United Kingdom, or Canada—you don't technically need to put up this notice. According to that agreement, simply publishing a work (in the wide sense of making something public) gives it copyright status.

The purpose of putting a notice on your site is to remind people of this fact, and in some countries that notice can help strengthen your case because you made potential thieves aware that they shouldn't copy your work.

The best way to format a basic copyright notice is like this:

Copyright 2010 George Plumley or © *2010 George Plumley*

On websites, this notice typically is displayed in the footer area and covers the site as a whole. If you want to draw attention to a copyright on a particular piece of content, you might want to put it at the end of the article or even near the top.

Because websites are always changing, it can be useful to have the date of your copyright show the first year you were online followed by the current year (2006–2010). Most content management sites have code that displays the current year automatically—just have your web developer put the first year next to that code.

Beyond these basics, a copyright notice might include wording to tell visitors under what circumstances they can use your material. For example, you might say that material can be used without permission for noncommercial sites as long as credit is given and a link is provided back to the original page. Or you might want to specify that only excerpts might be used, or images can't be used but text can.

If you're not sure how to specify terms of usage—the circumstances under which people are allowed to make use of your material—you might consider a Creative Commons license. This organization—which is not part of any governmental copyright agency—provides creators of works with standardized terms of usage in the form of free licenses with varying levels of restriction.

You might want to take copyright protection a step further and officially register your website with your country's copyright agency. For websites, the process typically involves sending copies of site files along with a registration fee.

Copyright law is complex and varies greatly between countries. Nothing here is intended as legal advice and you should research the issue more using the search phrase 🔍 copyright law [name of country].

> If you use a Creative Commons license, keep in mind that once you place it on your site or a particular piece of content, it is irrevocable. You can stop using the license, but anyone who made use of your material while the license was in place can continue to do so.

Tracking Down Thieves

Fortunately, the same openness that makes it easy to steal from websites also makes it fairly easy to know if something has been stolen and used online.

Search engines are one of the best tools for checking to see if anyone is stealing your content and using it online—enter a long, unique phrase in quotation marks. Tools such as Google Alerts will automatically notify you if particular phrases show up and give you the relevant link. Search engines also help the cause by blacklisting sites that take content without citing the source or linking back to the original site.

There are free online services that can streamline the search process for you—use the term 🔍 plagiarism checker. Then, there are paid services, such as Copyscape, which will monitor the Web for you and produce reports on what they think is legitimate and illegitimate usage.

Preventing people from grabbing images for use online is virtually impossible. Tricks such as disabling right mouse clicks or laying a transparent image over the real image don't help in the end because it's still easy to find the URL for the image. Putting images in Flash galleries or chopping them into pieces that display as whole might be a bit more effective, but remember that anyone can take a screenshot of your page.

Of course, online searches don't address offline use of content. In the case of text, your best hope is that plagiarism is caught by editors during the publishing process.

In the case of images, there are at least two simple ways to minimize illegal use offline:

+ Make images as low in quality and physical size as possible while keeping them visually attractive (this will also make pages load faster).

+ Put a watermark (a digital image) on enough of the image to make it unusable, while still looking good.

Passworded Content

Passwording content does not mean securing content. If your site allows anyone to sign up as a member, passwording certainly won't prevent theft. Even when you give out passwords only to selected people, a determined hacker will try various methods, such as stealing passwords or using brute force (trying billions of combinations).

Sometimes the best content on a site is hidden behind passwords, which means search engines won't be able to index it. The desire for higher search engine rankings sometimes gets the better of people and they hire a programmer to allow search engines to index, but not allow anyone else in without a password. Trouble is, search engines cache (keep copies of) pages and your password-protected content is suddenly accessible through a search (there are ways to stop the caching).

Again it comes down to this: Either you want material on the Web for the public to see, or it's too sensitive and should either be inside an intranet or virtual private network, or it shouldn't be online at all.

Protecting E-Mail Addresses

Forms are also helpful for cases in which the visitor doesn't have access to an e-mail program.

Spammers have robots that do nothing but scour the Web to find e-mail addresses on websites and add them to lists that are sold to marketers. The simplest way to beat these robots is to use well-written content forms instead of putting e-mail addresses on your site.

Rule of Thumb   Avoid putting e-mail addresses on your website. Use forms instead.

You hear about tricks to hide addresses from the spammers—such as writing an address as *myname[at]mydomain.com*—but these either don't work (robots just look for [at] instead of @), or they can make life difficult for the user (making e-mail addresses as images).

With a form, the e-mail address to which it is sent is never shown in the browser or in the HTML source code. Most web hosts offer easy to use and effective e-mail form software, and contact forms are built-in to most CMSs. You can keep an e-mail form very simple so that users have pretty much the same experience as using their e-mail program.

On Video

See how to do a search for possible plagiarism. See how easily the URL for an image can be found, even from a JavaScript. .

Related Questions

➤   39. Will your forms be easy to use? **Page 101**

➤   77. Do you have content you can offer to other sites? **Page 216**

Action Items

➤   Decide how and where you want your copyright notice to appear. Use only a name that's legally entitled to hold a copyright—either an individual or a registered company/organization.

➤   Double-check that images have been sufficiently reduced in size for the Web.

Importance

98. Will Your Site Administration Be Securely Accessed?

In the age of CMSs and hosting control panels, and when the administration of your site can be conducted from anywhere in the world, issues of secure access are greatly magnified. Safely accessing sites is not complicated, but forming the necessary habits takes effort.

First and foremost, you need a secure username and password for any interface that provides access to your site or the tools necessary to run the site. These include the following:

- Domain name manager
- Hosting control panel
- FTP access
- CMS
- E-mail accounts

Even if you have an extremely secure password—like, hk3#N9e5W%—do not use the same one for all these systems.

One of the problems with usernames is that often you don't get to choose what they'll be. Hosting companies, for example, often automatically assign a username that's either the same as the domain or some shortened version of it. All the more reason to make sure you have a good strong password.

If you're able to choose your username, make it a combination of letters and numbers, and at least seven characters long. Although a memorable name is okay, try to make it very unrelated to the domain name or any obvious personal information (such as your middle name or the city you live in). The numbers can also be memorable, but don't use personal numbers such as your birthday.

Armed with a secure username and password, the challenge is to make it difficult for people to steal them. This includes the obvious points such as not keeping them on your hard drive in a text file or writing them on a sticky note pasted to the wall. Less obvious but equally dangerous are the ways people use computers and access sensitive material over the Internet.

> For added security, change your passwords every few months or more.

Home and Office Security

Unless you disconnect your modem at night or unplug your computer from a network when not in use, your machine is a potential target 24 hours a day. If hackers can get into your computer, they can either look for passwords in files or set up monitoring tools that capture your keystrokes as you enter usernames and passwords (including when you change passwords to try and be more secure).

The most important step you can take to secure your computer(s) is to have a router or some other type of physical firewall between your modem and your computer/network. What these hardware firewalls do essentially is present the rest of the Internet with a fake computer. Instead of getting to your machine, intruders make it only as far as the firewall.

Don't confuse this with a software firewall, which tries to do something similar but from inside your computer. This is a physical box that would look the same to hackers whether you had any computers hooked up at the other end or not.

Of course, this hardware firewall isn't much help in your immediate vicinity if you leave your wireless network unguarded. Especially in larger cities, there could be hundreds of people close enough to get into your network if you let them, and once on the network a person potentially has access to your computer. You need to implement wi-fi security through your router, as shown in Figure 10-4.

You can open up hardware firewalls in ways that would allow intruders in, but you'd have to do that deliberately in your settings. Other than setting your wireless network security, you shouldn't need to touch anything—if you do, make sure you know what you're doing.

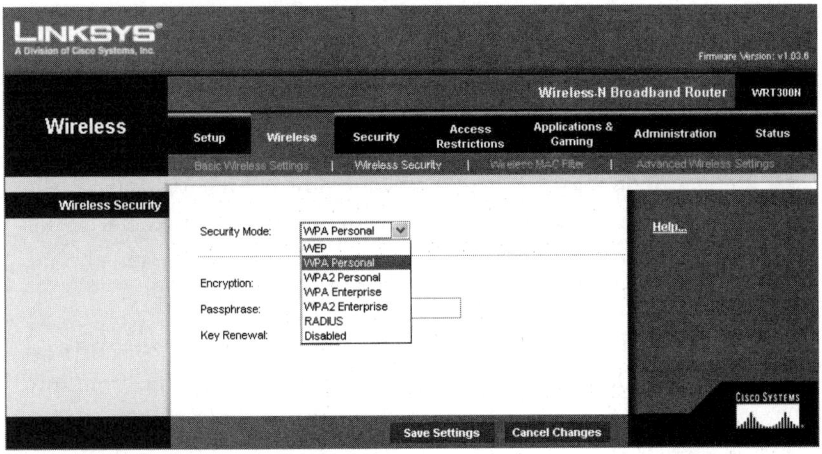

FIGURE 10-4

? Wi-fi Protected Access (WPA) is the minimum level of security you should use. You'll see a setting on your router called WEP or Wired Equivalent Privacy, but it's far less secure—among other things, it allows secret keys to be reused plus it has a far smaller number of possible keys.

A hardware firewall and secure wi-fi are your best defenses against someone getting into your computer directly and stealing passwords or monitoring your web activities. The rest is up to you: You need to decide if you're going to let in harmful programs that can do similar damage by downloading everything and anything off the Web or clicking on links that ask you for sensitive information. No firewall will protect you from these methods of spreading viruses and programs that can steal your passwords.

Aside from using your common sense, you would do well to regularly scan your computer with antivirus programs to catch any malware you let in.

Everything said so far applies to a small office environment, but the big difference is that you can have several people all on the same network, some using less common sense than others. Truth is, some people like to click on "you're the millionth visitor" or give out banking information whenever they're asked for it—despite knowing the dangers. Others like to leave passwords lying around. You just need to be that much more vigilant in an office.

Accessing Your Site on the Road

One of the advantages of web-based CMSs is that you can access them from any browser anywhere in the world. However, there are steps you should take to protect yourself away from home so your passwords can't be stolen:

- ➜ Make sure you're joining a legitimate open wi-fi network. The idea of these networks is that anyone can join—there's no password (just as if you didn't use any security on your home wi-fi). These open wi-fi spots are common now in airports and other public areas. However, hackers can easily set up fake networks that show on your list of available networks. Double-check that you have the correct name of the legitimate network.

- ➜ Whether it's an open or secure network, remember that it's a network. Other people on the network could potentially get into your machine, so use internal firewalls, turn off file sharing, and use only login pages that are secure (they'll have https in the URL).

→ If you absolutely must use a public machine or someone else's machine, make sure you erase your session. To learn how, and for more suggestions, use this search phrase: 🔍 **tips for using public computers.**

→ If you must leave your machine, even for a few moments, put it into password-protected mode.

→ Do not stay logged on to an administrative area while surfing the net. Log off and then log in again when you need to.

Related Questions

→ 5. Who will register your domain and in whose name? **Page 11**

→ 15. Do you have a strong hosting username and password? **Page 35**

→ 19. Can you access your domain e-mail through a web browser? **Page 48**

Action Items

→ Check to make sure you have a router between your modem and your computer/network. Some routers and modems are combined into a single unit—check with your ISP.

→ Put travel security tips on an index card that you can keep in your computer case so they're always available on the road.

Importance

99. Will You Be Collecting Sensitive Visitor Information on Your Site?

More and more detailed information is being gathered from website visitors, not simply because of e-commerce but also because any data about visitors is vital to establishing relationships and providing more relevant content. It's up to site owners to ensure that this information is protected in every way possible.

> **Rule of Thumb**   Do not store any type of important information online.

To understand how easily unprotected information can be found online, look at the spreadsheet in Figure 10-5, which contains passwords and credit card numbers. This was found in less than a minute with a simple search.

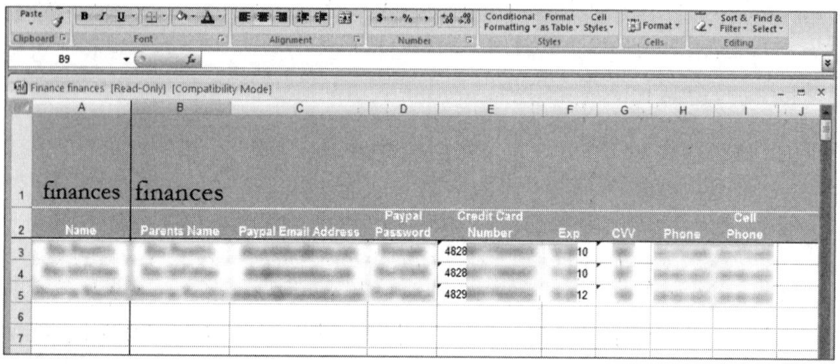

FIGURE 10-5

This spreadsheet was actually uploaded to a server, but it could just as easily have been the text file generated by a form on a website. The bottom line is this: You can't have sensitive information stored online, however temporary it might be.

That's why it's simplest to leave data collection to third parties. For example, by using a third-party shopping cart system, the collection of

99. WILL YOU BE COLLECTING SENSITIVE VISITOR INFORMATION ON YOUR SITE?

293

credit card information can be taken care of on their servers. Mailing list services handle the collection and storage of your data, instead of you having to install your own mailing list program and dealing with the protection of the list data once it's collected.

If you do plan to collect any sort of vital information from visitors (without storing it), keep in mind that the transmission of information poses almost as much risk as the storage of it.

When you send any information through your browser—submitting a form is one example—it's as public as the website data you download through that browser. That's why browser encryption (the little lock you see at the bottom of your window when viewing pages starting with https://) is so important. It encrypts the data being transmitted through the browser so that anyone who grabs it can't read it.

To activate this encryption, you need an SSL certificate for your website. There are various levels of certificates, each costing progressively more but offering stronger security. For a basic site, you can get certificates for as little as $70 per year, but carefully research what level of certificate you need and how reliable the vendor is. Some certificates do a very cursory check of the domain and therefore don't provide a lot of trust.

The next security issue is this: How will you transmit the information collected through your form? A contact form, for example, would normally send its information to you by e-mail, but that's not at all secure for sensitive information. You have to secure e-mail by using an encryption system such as OpenPGP. It creates a key that you use with your form processing script and another key that you use on your e-mail client. The e-mail is encrypted when it's sent and decoded when it arrives in your e-mail program.

> Even if you leave collection of sensitive data to a third-party site, you need to have a privacy policy that makes this clear to visitors.

> If possible, use a secure URL for any login pages to protect passwords.

Related Questions

→ 39. Will your forms be easy to use? **Page 101**

→ 67. Will you be selling online? **Page 185**

→ 69. How Will You Build Your E-mail List? **Page 194**

Action Items

➤ Before considering collecting sensitive data on your site, compare the costs with those of using a third-party service.

➤ Verify with your developer that form data is being securely sent where necessary.

100. How Will You Protect Your Site from Attacks?

Importance

Hackers are constantly looking for ways into servers, and they succeed in part by finding holes in the programs and scripts that run websites. Although site owners often don't have direct control over keeping these holes plugged, there are some steps they can take to help, including knowing some questions to ask of hosting providers and developers.

There is one important way that hackers get into servers over which site owners have a great deal of control: detecting passwords. By having weak passwords or not protecting passwords from being stolen, site owners provide hackers with their most useful way of getting into the back end of websites.

Another important source of information for hackers is the files you forget to remove from your website. Aside from files that might contain passwords, they include programs you loaded on your server in the past, aren't currently using, and are now out-of-date and vulnerable to security breaches.

Here are more steps you can take to help ensure your site is less vulnerable to attacks:

➤ **Keep software updated**—Programs such as CMSs or shopping carts will notify you when they need updating. Often these updates are to fix security issues, and the longer you wait to do it, the longer you're leaving potential holes unplugged.

➤ **Don't use unknown software**—If you come across a script for a feature you want on your website, check it out carefully. If it's poorly written, it could leave your site insecure. Stick to software that has a wide user base, or ask your web developer or host if it's trustworthy.

➤ **Check that your directories are secure**—Using the name of one of the directories on your server, try entering that address in your web browser (for example, `http://mydomain.com/images/`) and see what you get. If there's a blank screen or an access forbidden notice, you're good. If you see a list of folders and files, you need to ask your host to turn off directory listing.

➤ **Have error messaging turned off**—If your site runs on a scripting language such as PHP, ask your hosting provider or web developer if error messaging is turned on. If it is, ask them to turn it off because these messages can provide hackers with valuable information.

➤ **Make sure your forms are secure**—Submitting a form sends information to your server. If the contents of the form aren't cleansed before getting to the server, they could be sending dangerous programs placed in the form by hackers. This is not simple form validation, which tests things such as the formatting of postal codes, but a thorough examination of every bit of data to make sure nothing bad is getting through. Most hosts offer good quality form-processing programs or check with your web developer to make sure secure form processing is being used.

➤ **If you have any custom programming done, ask the developer about the security of the coding**—If it's a complex program, you might want to have a third party check it over for vulnerabilities.

These are some of the main ways you can help keep your website secure. By choosing a reliable host and using reliable software, you know that the programmers are doing their best to keep up with many other issues of web security.

Related Questions

➤ 8. How reliable is the web hosting provider? **Page 19**

➤ 15. Do you have a strong hosting username and password? **Page 35**

➤ 98. Will your site administration be securely accessed? **Page 288**

Action Items

➤ Talk about security with your web developer as soon as possible (before software is chosen, for example) and follow the checklist of items mentioned previously. In particular, make sure form data is being cleansed.

➤ Before launch, talk to your developer about running one of many programs for analyzing website security as a final check. This could made part of your regular site checkup too.

Resources

The resources for building, maintaining, and marketing a website are not only overwhelming in quantity, but they're growing by leaps and bounds every day. This appendix provides some good basics to develop your own set of resources.

For more links and suggested reading, visit the website for this book: www.ahundredquestionstoask.com. The resources at the website are continually updated.

Site Map Creation Tools

http://creately.com/

http://cacoo.com/

Chapter 1: Domain Names

Online Tools

www.bustaname.com/   A powerful domain name search that allows you to choose two or more words and see what's available for various combinations. You can also register the name directly through a choice of registrars.

www.domaintools.com/   A wide range of tools relating to domain names, including Whois information about existing domains, a domain names suggestion tool, and much more. Most tools are free or inexpensive.

http://domai.nr/   Suggests domain names using the extension as part of the name, as in wis.dm.

Chapter 2: Hosting

Reviews of Web Hosting Providers

www.hostdiscussion.com/

http://reviews.cnet.com/web-hosting/

www.webhostingreviews.com/

www.webhostingtalk.com/

webhostinggeeks.com/

Websites about Web Hosting

http://webdesign.about.com/od/webhosting/Web_Hosting.htm

www.webhosting.info/

www.w3schools.com/hosting/default.asp

Chapter 3: E-mail

www.yousendit.com/   When the file you want to send is too big for your e-mail, send files up to 100MB in size for free.

http://email.about.com/od/freeemailreviews/tp/free_email.htm   Reviews of free e-mail services.

To learn how to check your e-mail account on your computer, use this search term: 🔍 **how to set up e-mail for** [enter the name of your e-mail program here: **Outlook**, **Thunderbird**, and so on].

Chapter 4: Design and Layout

Background Generators

www.bgpatterns.com/   Backgrounds with small images.

www.pixelknete.de/dotter/   Dotted backgrounds.

www.stripemania.com/   Striped backgrounds.

http://tools.dynamicdrive.com/gradient/   Gradient backgrounds.

Miscellaneous Design Tools

www.emailtheweb.com/   E-mail a snapshot of any web page to anyone. This is handy for sending out site samples to friends for their opinions.

www.usereffect.com/topic/users-dont-read-the-ride   Enter a URL, and all letters and numbers on the website are replaced with Xs and Os. This is an interesting way to see where your eye is drawn if you're not reading the text.

www.conceptfeedback.com/   You can get free feedback on design, usability, and marketing from an online community if you post five reviews of other people's sites.

http://fivesecondtest.com/   Users have five seconds to view whatever image you upload (your home page design, for example) and then answer the questions you set. Reasonably priced, but you can get a free test if you do some testing for them.

www.cymbolism.com/   People vote on which color they feel matches words such as *authoritative*, *hygienic*, and so on.

Color Scheme Tools

http://colorschemedesigner.com/

http://colorschemegenerator.com/

http://kuler.adobe.com

www.colorsontheweb.com/colorwizard.asp

Find Colors for a Site or Image

www.colorhunter.com/

http://redalt.com/Tools/I+Like+Your+Colors

Screen Resolution

http://viewlike.us/   View your site in various screen resolutions (size of the screen area), including the iPhone.

http://marketshare.hitslink.com/report.aspx?qprid=17

www.screenresolution.org/

Browser Compatibility Checks

http://browsershots.org/   Free.

http://crossbrowsertesting.com   Free trial; screenshots plus live testing.

http://ipinfo.info/netrenderer/   Free; shows sites in Internet Explorer only.

https://browserlab.adobe.com   Free; requires an Adobe ID.

Websites for the Design Portion of Web Design

www.alistapart.com/articles/

http://designm.ag/

www.noupe.com/

http://sixrevisions.com/

www.smashingmagazine.com/

http://speckyboy.com/

http://vandelaydesign.com/blog

http://webdesign.about.com/

www.webdesignfromscratch.com/articles-and-tutorials/

www.webtypography.net/

www.webpagesthatsuck.com/

Lists of More Web Design Sites

www.delicious.com/popular/webdesign

http://designbump.com/WebDesign

www.graphic-design-links.com/category/WebDesign

Books about Web Design and Design in General

Beaird, Jason. *The Principles of Beautiful Web Design.* Collingwood, NJ: Sitepoint, 2008.

Bringhurst, Robert. *The Elements of Typographic Style.* Point Roberts, WA: Hartley & Marks, 2005.

Lopuck, Lisa. *Web Design For Dummies*, Second Edition. Hoboken, NJ: John Wiley & Sons, 2006.

McNeil, Patrick. *The Web Designer's Idea Book: The Ultimate Guide to Themes, Trends & Styles in Website Design.* Cincinnati, OH: HOW Design, 2008.

Meyer, Eric A. *Eric Meyer on CSS: Mastering the Language of Web Design.* Indianapolis, IN: New Riders Publishing, 2003.

Niederst, Jennifer. *Learning Web Design: A Beginner's Guide to HTML, Graphics, and Beyond*, Third Edition. Sebastopol, CA: O'Reilly Press, 2007.

Warner, Janine and David LaFontaine. *Mobile Web Design For Dummies.* Hoboken, NJ: John Wiley & Sons, 2010.

Zeldman, Jeffrey and Ethan Marcotte. *Designing with Web Standards, Third Edition.* Berkeley, CA: New Riders Publishing, 2010.

Chapter 5: User Experience

Sites for Testing Users' Experience

www.userplus.com/   Has a free version that allows you one screenshot that's matched against various standards.

http://usabilla.com/   Test a page of your site with 50 real users for free.

http://uitest.com/   A list of tools for analyzing your site, including user experience.

www.deyalexander.com.au/resources/uxd/accessibility-evaluation-tools.html A list of tools for assessing your website's accessibility for visitors with physical impairments.

Online Site Loading Tests

www.iwebtool.com/speed_test

http://loadimpact.com/   Simulates a lot of concurrent users.

http://tools.pingdom.com/

www.websiteoptimization.com/services/analyze/

Websites about User Experience

www.adaptivepath.com/ideas/

www.useit.com/alertbox/

www.usereffect.com/blog

www.uxbooth.com

www.uxmatters.com/

www.webcredible.co.uk/user-friendly-resources/

User Experience Books

Buxton, William. *Sketching User Experiences: Getting the Design Right and the Right Design*. Amsterdam, Netherlands: Elsevier/Morgan Kaufmann, 2007.

Garrett, Jesse James. *The Elements of User Experience: User-Centered Design for the Web*. Berkeley, CA: New Riders Publishing, 2006.

Krug, Steve. *Don't Make Me Think! A Common Sense Approach to Web Usability*, Second Edition. Berkeley, CA: New Riders Pub., 2006.

Maier, Andrew and Matthew Kammerer. Norman, Don. *The Design of Everyday Things*. New York: Basic, 2002.

Chapter 6: Construction

Online Tools

http://validator.w3.org/   HTML validation.

http://validator.w3.org/checklink/   Link checker.

www.picnik.com/   Edit photos online for free.

Software to Help Maintain Sites

The software listed here can help with tasks you'll perform while building and maintaining your site. For example, if you need to take some text from a Word document and work with it in a web-friendly way (clean code), then you'll want a basic text editor. If you need to reduce the size of images coming out of your camera, an image editor is handy. Or, if you need to create a small ad to place on your site, there are simple graphics programs.

All programs are free for commercial and noncommercial use, except where noted.

If you're trying to build your site or an HTML page using software, you need programs like Dreamweaver. Use the search term 🔍 website creation software.

WINDOWS SOFTWARE

GRAPHICS CREATION

Paint.net   www.getpaint.net/

VCW VicMan's Photo Editor   www.vicman.net/vcwphoto/index.htm

IMAGE EDITORS

FastStone   www.faststone.org/ $34.95 in 2010 for commercial users.

Irfanview   www.irfanview $12 in 2010 for commercial users.

TEXT EDITORS

Notepad2   www.flos-freeware.ch/notepad2.html

Notetab Light   www.notetab.com/

Total Edit   www.codertools.com/TotalEdit.aspx

MAC SOFTWARE

GRAPHICS CREATION

ImageWell   www.xtralean.com/IWOverview.html
No free mode, but only $19.95 in 2010.

IMAGE EDITORS

Acorn   http://flyingmeat.com/acorn/acornfree.html
Limited, but still useful functions after a free trial.

GraphicConverter   www.lemkesoft.com
Slight limitations if used in unregistered mode.

TEXT EDITORS

Bluefish   http://bluefish.openoffice.nl/

TextWrangler   www.barebones.com/products/textwrangler/

Form Creation

These sites allow free creation of a limited number of forms.

www.formsite.com/

www.formstack.com

http://wufoo.com/

Browser Tools for Web Development

These browser add-ons allow you to analyze the construction of any website in various ways, such as playing with the CSS, viewing the site without JavaScript, or testing the loading speed.

https://addons.mozilla.org/en-US/firefox/addon/1843/   Firebug (Firefox).

https://addons.mozilla.org/en-US/firefox/addon/60/   Web developer (Firefox).

www.microsoft.com/downloads   Internet Explorer developer toolbar.

https://chrome.google.com/extensions/featured/web_dev   Chrome web development extensions.

Sites about Building Websites

http://devcheatsheet.com/   Cheat sheets for HTML, CSS, PHP, and much more.

www.hypergurl.com/

www.sitepoint.com/

www.thesitewizard.com/

http://thinkvitamin.com/

www.webdeveloper.com/

www.webmonkey.com/

www.webstyleguide.com/index.html

Sites about CMSes

www.cmscritic.com/

www.cmswire.com/

http://php.opensourcecms.com/

Books about Building Websites

Crowder, David A. *Building a Web Site For Dummies,* 4th Edition. Hoboken, NJ: John Wiley & Sons, 2010.

Freeman, Elisabeth and Eric Freeman. *Head First HTML: with CSS & XHTML*. Sebastopol, CA: O'Reilly Press, 2005.

Lloyd, Ian. *Build Your Own Web Site the Right Way Using HTML & CSS,* 2nd Edition. Collingwood, Vic., Australia: Sitepoint, 2008.

MacDonald, Matthew. *Creating a Web Site: The Missing Manual*. Sebastopol, CA: O'Reilly Media, 2009.

W3Schools. *Learn HTML and CSS with w3Schools*. Hoboken, NJ: John Wiley & Sons, 2010.

Chapter 7: Content

Sites about Writing for the Web

http://confidentwriting.com/blog/

www.contentstrategyweblog.com/

www.copyblogger.com/category/1/

http://crofsblogs.typepad.com/ckbetas/

http://grammar.quickanddirtytips.com/

www.shayhowe.com/notebook/

http://styleguide.yahoo.com/writing

Although there aren't a lot of sites devoted entirely to content for websites, you can find lots of articles. Try this search term: 🔍 **creating great web content.**

Downloadable Books

`www.conversationmarketing.com/2008/11/seo-copywriting-ebook.htm`   An excellent guide to writing copy for your site with search engines in mind.

`www.problogger.net/scorecard/`   Scorecard for Bloggers is not just for bloggers; it's for anyone writing copy for websites.

Simple Online Stores

`www.wazala.com/`   Free version available.

Books about Web Content

Barr, Chris. The Yahoo! Style Guide: *The Ultimate Sourcebook for Writing, Editing, and Creating Content for the Digital World*. New York: Yahoo!/St. Martin's Griffin, 2010.

Fogarty, Mignon. *Grammar Girl's Quick and Dirty Tips for Better Writing*. New York: Henry Holt, 2008.

Halvorson, Kristin. *Content Strategy for the Web*. Berkeley, CA: New Riders Publishing, 2010.

Handley, Ann and C.C. Chapman. Content Rules: *How to Create Killer Blogs, Podcasts, Videos, Ebooks, Webinars (and More)*. Hoboken, NJ: John Wiley & Sons, 2010.

Kilian, Crawford. *Writing for the Web*. 4th ed. North Vancouver, B.C.: Self-Counsel, 2009.

McGovern, Gerry. Killer Web Content. London: A. & C. Black, 2006.

Redish, Janice (Ginny). *Letting Go of the Words: Writing Web Content that Works*. Amsterdam, Netherlands: Elsevier/Morgan Kaufmann, 2007.

Sheffield, Richard. *The Web Content Strategist's Bible*. Atlanta, GA: ClueFox Publishing, 2009.

Veloso, Maria. *Web Copy that Sells*. New York: American Management Association, 2009.

Books about Online Stores

Holden, Greg. *Starting an Online Business For Dummies*. 6th ed. Hoboken, NJ: John Wiley & Sons, 2010.

Loveday, Lance and Sandra Niehaus. *Web Design for ROI: Turning Browsers into Buyers & Prospects into Leads*. Berkeley, CA: New Riders Publishing, 2008.

Miller, Michael. *Selling Online 2.0: Migrating from eBay to Amazon, craigslist, and Your Own E-Commerce Website*. Indianapolis, IN: Que Publishing, 2009.

Chapter 8: Marketing and Promotion

Free Website Statistics

www.google.com/analytics/

http://web.analytics.yahoo.com/

Free Social Media Monitoring

http://addictomatic.com/

www.blogpulse.com/

http://boardreader.com/   Forums only.

www.boardtracker.com/   Forums only.

www.google.com/alerts

www.oneriot.com/

www.socialmention.com/

http://trendistic.com   Twitter only.

www.twazzup.com/   Twitter only.

Sites about Web Marketing

http://adage.com/power150/   Daily ranking of marketing blogs.

www.conversationmarketing.com/

www.copyblogger.com/

www.marketingprofs.com/

www.micropersuasion.com/

http://sethgodin.typepad.com/

www.toprankblog.com/

Sites about Social Media

www.chrisbrogan.com/

http://kikolani.com

http://mashable.com/social-media/

www.problogger.net/

www.socialmediaexaminer.com

www.socialmediaexplorer.com/

Sites about E-mail Marketing

www.mailchimp.com/blog/

www.aweber.com/blog/

http://blogs.constantcontact.com/commentary/

http://email.about.com/od/emailmarketing/Email_Marketing.htm

Sites about Web Analytics

www.kaushik.net/avinash/

www.michaelwhitaker.com/blog/

www.webmetricsguru.com/

Books about Web Marketing

Arnold, John, Ian Lurie, Marty Dickinson, Elizabeth Marsten, and Michael
  Becker. *Web Marketing All-in-One Desk Reference For
  Dummies*. Hoboken, NJ: John Wiley & Sons, 2009.

Brogan, Chris and Julien Smith. *Trust Agents*. Revised and Updated ed. Hoboken,
  NJ: John Wiley & Sons, 2010.

Eley, Brandon and Shayne Tilley. *Online Marketing Inside Out*. Collingwood,
  Vic., Australia: SitePoint, 2009.

Halligan, Brian and Dharmesh Shah. *Inbound Marketing: Get Found Using Google,
  Social Media, and Blogs*. Hoboken, NJ: John Wiley & Sons, 2010.

Hughes, Mark. *Buzzmarketing: Get People to Talk About Your Stuff*. New York:
  Portfolio, 2005.

Kaushik, Avinash. *Web Analytics 2.0: The Art of Online Accountability and Science
  of Customer Centricity*. Indianapolis, IN: John Wiley & Sons, 2010.

Lurie, Ian. *Conversation Marketing: Internet Marketing Strategies*. Victoria, B.C.:
  Trafford, 2006.

Qualman, Erik. *Socialnomics: How Social Media Transforms the Way We Live and
  Do Business*. Hoboken, NJ: John Wiley & Sons, 2009.

Scott, David M. *The New Rules of Marketing and PR: How to Use Social Media, Blogs,
  News Releases, Online Video, and Viral Marketing to Reach Buyers Directly*, 2nd
  Edition. Hoboken, NJ: John Wiley & Sons, 2010.

Sernovitz, Andy. *Word of Mouth Marketing: How Smart Companies Get People
  Talking*. New York: Kaplan Pub., 2009.

Tobin, Jim. *Social Media Is a Cocktail Party: Why You Already Know the Rules of
  Social Media Marketing*. Cary, North Carolina: Ignite Social Media, 2008.

Chapter 9: Search Engine Optimization

Sites for Keyword Research

```
https://adwords.google.com/select/KeywordToolExternal?defaultView=2
```

www.google.com/trends

www.google.com/insights/search/#

www.seomoz.org/term-extractor

www.wordstream.com/

www.wordtracker.com/

Link-Checking Tools

www.opensiteexplorer.org/

http://validator.w3.org/checklink/

Sitemap Generators

www.xml-sitemaps.com/

Free Tools from Search Engines

www.google.com/webmasters/tools/

www.bing.com/toolbox/webmasters/

help.yahoo.com/l/us/yahoo/search/indexing/webmaster-01.html

Browser Add-On Tools

www.seoquake.com/

http://tools.seobook.com/seo-toolbar/   Firefox only

Free Search Engine Optimization (SEO) Guides in PDF Format

www.google.com/webmasters/docs/search-engine-optimization-starter-guide.pdf

http://download.microsoft.com/download/0/D/9/0D94EECB-C767-445E-B708-9C829275995F/Bing—NewFeaturesForWebmasters.pdf

Sites about SEO

www.conversationmarketing.com/

www.searchenginejournal.com/

http://searchengineland.com/

http://searchenginewatch.com/

www.seobook.com/blog

http://sphinn.com/

www.wolf-howl.com/

Books about SEO

Clay, Bruce and Susan Esparza. *Search Engine Optimization All-in-One For Dummies*. Hoboken, NJ: John Wiley & Sons, 2009.

Enge, Eric, Stephan Spencer, Rand Fishkin, and Jessie Stricchiola. *The Art of SEO*. Sebastopol, CA: O'Reilly Press, 2010.

Fleischner, Michael H. *SEO Made Simple: Strategies for Dominating the World's Largest Search Engine*. Trenton, NJ: MarketingScoop, LLC, 2009.

Grappone, Jennifer and Gradiva Couzin. *Search Engine Optimization: An Hour a Day*, Second Edition. Indianapolis, IN: John Wiley & Sons, 2008.

Jones, Kristopher B. *Search Engine Optimization: Your Visual Blueprint for Effective Internet Marketing*, Second Edition. Indianapolis, IN: John Wiley & Sons, 2010.

Lieb, Rebecca. *The Truth About Search Engine Optimization*. Upper Saddle River, NJ: FT, 2009.

Lutze, Heather F. *The Findability Formula: The Easy, Non-Technical Approach to Search Engine Marketing*. Hoboken, NJ: John Wiley & Sons, 2009.

Walter, Aarron. *Building Findable Websites: Web Standards SEO and Beyond*. Berkeley, CA: New Riders Publishing, 2008.

Chapter 10: Housekeeping and Security

Online Backup Services

These sites are free up to 2GB.

www.backupify.com

www.dropbox.com/

http://mozy.com

Free Online Reminder Services

These sites are great for backup reminders, updating your content, and other maintenance tasks.

www.hassleme.co.uk/   Sends e-mail at semipredictable intervals.

www.task.fm/   You can enter items in natural language.

www.rememberthemilk.com/   A full-blown task manager, too.

Free Website Security Checks

www.zerodayscan.com/

Password Generators

www.xorbin.com/tools/password-generator

www.onlinepasswordgenerator.com/

www.techzoom.net/tools/password-generator.en

Sites about Website Security

www.clerkendweller.com/

There aren't a lot of sites devoted entirely to security for websites, but there are lots of articles. Try this search term: 🔍 how to keep your website secure.

Website Monitoring Services

These sites include free versions.

www.pingdom.com/

http://site24x7.com

www.siteuptime.com/

www.serviceuptime.com/

Glossary

This book covers a lot of subjects, each of which has its own unique terminology. I've tried throughout the book to briefly explain terms as they're introduced. Those terms, along with many others, are gathered here. You can also find additional terms in the glossary on the book's website at www.ahundredquestionstoask.com.

404 error The error message or page displayed when an address for a nonexistent web page is entered in a browser.

above the fold When a web page is first loaded and without scrolling, this is the visible content above the bottom edge of the visitor's browser window.

Active Server Pages (ASP) A server-side scripting language developed by Microsoft.

ad tracking The statistics gathered about advertisements on the Web, including how many times viewed and how many times clicked.

add-ons Small scripts that add functionality to web browsers, content management systems (CMS), or other software.

affiliate A website that advertises for a merchant in return for a share of any sales or other actions resulting from visitors clicking through from that site.

affiliate link A specially coded link on an affiliate website that allows the merchant to track visitors from that site and credit the affiliate.

anchor text Text that has been hyperlinked to another page or site.

anonymous FTP A file transfer account that allows anyone to access a web hosting account without a username or password.

Apache An open source web server software package that is the most common web server software in the world. Primarily used on Linux platforms.

attribute Additional elements of tags in HTML. For example, the image tag `<img>` can have attributes such as location `<img src="http://mydomain.com">` or alternative text `<img alt="Picture of my cat">`.

authentication On the Web, this refers to verifying the identity of a user in a secure area of a website.

autoresponder In e-mail marketing, this is used to send out prewritten messages at specific times (for example, one week after a person signs up to an e-mail list).

back up For websites, the process of making a copy of all files necessary to run the site and storing them safely elsewhere in case of server problems.

bandwidth In common usage, the total size of all files uploaded to and downloaded from a website in one month. Technically refers to the amount of file uploads and downloads a server can handle at any specific moment.

banner ad In web marketing, a graphical advertisement that links to another website.

below the fold When a web page is first loaded, this is the unseen content below the bottom edge of the visitor's browser window.

blacklist To block a website, an IP address, or an e-mail address for bad practices such as spamming or stealing content.

bookmark On a web browser, storing a link for future reference. In social media, storing a link online to share with others.

breadcrumb navigation A short text-based navigation menu (usually horizontal) that shows the links connecting the current page to the home page.

browser compatibility How uniformly a website is displayed in different browsers and different versions of the same browser.

cache Web browsers store copies of web pages on your hard drive to make it faster to load when you return to the site. With heavy traffic sites, servers will sometimes store the most recent copies of pages to better handle all the requests.

callout A loose term for boxes of additional text or images that sit outside the flow of text on a page.

cascading style sheet (CSS) A set of rules created to define the layout and style of web pages (such as position, spacing, backgrounds, fonts, sizing, color, and so on).

chat A program that allows live text messaging between two or more users on the Internet. Often used as support tools to get help online. Also called Live Chat.

clickthrough rate or click rate The percentage of clicks on a link (usually an advertisement) compared with the number of times the page has been displayed.

client/server A client is a computer program that requests a service from a program on another computer. On the Web, a browser is a client because it requests pages from a web server program sitting on a host's computer. E-mail programs are another example of a client.

client-side Refers to languages that operate on your computer instead of a web server. JavaScript is client-side because it runs in your browser.

color scheme A set of colors that goes well with the parent color. There are many different color schemes for any one parent color.

compression Reduction in size of images, documents, or multimedia for faster delivery on the Web.

contextual advertising The delivery of ads over the Web, based on the content of the page in which the ad is to appear. The process of choosing the ad occurs at the moment the page is accessed.

content management system (CMS) Software that allows users with little or no technical knowledge to be able to change or add content on a website. A CMS provides simple interfaces for entering and formatting text, uploading and manipulating images, creating new pages, and so on.

contrast In graphic design, the grey scale difference between two colors. Too low a contrast (such as blue on red) is difficult to read.

conversion rate The number of visitors to a site who take a specific action (buying something or signing up for something, for example).

cookie User-specific information stored on your computer as a text file or on a server that is used during the current or subsequent visits (for example, your name or membership status). Although there can be malicious cookies, 99 percent of them are perfectly harmless and are used on virtually all *dynamic websites*.

copyright The exclusive rights granted to the creator of an original work governing the copying, distribution, or adaptation of the work.

Cost per Action (CPA) How much is charged every time a visitor takes a particular action (buys, joins, and so on),

Cost per Click (CPC) How much is charged every time a visitor clicks a website advertisement.

Cost per Impression (CPM) How much is charged for a certain number of views of a website ad. Usually given in terms of cost per thousand (*M* stands for the French *mille*).

crawl The act of automated programs (robots) reading every file on a website. Often used to refer to the action of search engine robots.

database A computer application for storing and retrieving data. Databases are used by web software such as *content management systems* and *shopping carts*.

dedicated server A server that is not shared with any other hosting accounts and over which the owner has complete control.

deep link A link to a page within a website below the level of the home page (for example, `http://mydomain.com/company-history.html`).

domain extension The letters following the last period in a domain name (for example, .com, .us, .info, .uk, .net, and so on). See also *top-level domain (TLD)*.

domain name The name that identifies a website, such as wiley.com, instead of having to use IP addresses such as 192.168.1.1.

domain name service or domain name server (DNS) Translates domain names (mydomain.com) into IP addresses (192.168.1.1).

domain registrant The person, company, or organization who controls a domain name for the period of time it is registered (no one owns domain names).

domain registrar A provider who can register domain names on your behalf.

double opt-in In e-mail marketing, the process of verifying that a person has filled out the initial signup form (usually through a link in a welcome e-mail).

download On the Web, the transfer of files from a server to a user's computer (see also *upload*). Viewing a website involves downloading the site files to your computer.

downtime The period of time when a web server or a particular website is not available to visitors.

duplicate content In search engine terms, when large or entire portions of content on one site are duplicated on another site (with or without permission).

dynamic website A website whose pages are assembled from numerous files before being displayed in a browser. (Opposite of *static website*.)

e-mail account Space on a web server in which mail is stored for a particular e-mail address.

e-mail alias An e-mail address that does not store e-mail for downloading, but simply passes the e-mail on to another address.

e-mail forwarding On web servers, the process of sending a copy of an e-mail to one or more other addresses.

e-mail marketing Sending information and offers in the form of e-mail to subscribers who have requested that their address be placed on a mailing list.

e-mail server A web server whose sole function is to deal with e-mail.

encryption The conversion of data into a form that can be read only by someone who has the decryption software. Used on the Web to secure information passed between browsers and servers.

Extensible Hypertext Markup Language (XHTML) XHTML is the latest version of HTML.

external link A link from one website to another. (Also known as an outbound link.)

ezine The name given to e-mail written in the style of a magazine. Sometimes used as a synonym for e-mail newsletters.

feed On the web, a method of enabling content on one website to simultaneously be published on other websites or read by users through feed readers. See also Really Simple Syndication (RSS).

File Transfer Protocol (FTP) On the Web, a method of uploading or downloading files from a computer to a server.

firewall Hardware or software that protects a network or individual computer from unauthorized access.

fixed-width layout A website layout that does not change its width as the user changes the width of their browser window.

Flash A multimedia format developed by Adobe for use on the Web.

fluid layout A website layout in which the width of the site changes to match the width of the user's browser.

footer The bottom area of a website after all the content.

form validation The process of checking the data being submitted through a form.

forum Website software that allows members to post messages and reply to existing messages.

Frequently Asked Questions (FAQ) The name typically used for pages on websites that feature common questions along with (usually) short answers.

gigabyte (GB) One billion bytes or one thousand megabytes (MB).

Google AdSense A service that places contextual ads from the Google Adwords system on a website on a pay per click (PPC) basis.

Google AdWords A service that enables advertisers to bid for ads on Google and participating search providers, as well as on sites in the AdSense program. The ads are targeted at specific keywords and charged on a pay per click (PPC) basis.

Google PageRank Google's rating of a website based on the quality of the inbound links to that site. Known simply as PR, the rating is a crucial component in Google's positioning of a site in its search results.

Google Sitemap A special kind of sitemap registered with Google that helps its robots find all your content properly.

Graphics Interchange Format (GIF) A compression format for storing images that is best used for images with large areas of a single color.

hacking The act of getting into other computers and servers, with or without having to crack any codes to do so.

header The top portion of a website before the content begins. Typically contains the site's name and navigation menu.

hit A website statistic of how many times a file (page, image, document, and so on) has physically been downloaded. Do not confuse with PageViews or Unique Visitors.

host or web hosting provider In the context of websites, any provider that stores files and makes them available for others to view on the Web.

hosting control panel A user-friendly interface that allows the average person to perform server-related tasks, such as creating e-mail accounts, passwording directories, uploading files, creating databases, and much more.

HTML 5 A major upgrade of HTML that, among other things, will make it possible to play video and audio without having a browser plug-in.

HTML tables HTML tags used to display data in rows and columns. Until cascading style sheets (CSS), tables were used to lay out web pages as well.

hyperlink A pointer to another document, most commonly another web page and most commonly referred to as a link.

hypertext Text that is linked to other pages, documents, or sites.

Hypertext Markup Language (HTML) A set of tags used to define the layout, links, and formatting of web pages.

Hypertext Preprocessor (PHP) The most widely used server-side scripting language.

Hypertext Transfer Protocol (HTTP) The standard set of rules for sending text files across the Internet.

Hypertext Transfer Protocol Secure (HTTPS) Like HTTP, but also provides secure Internet communication using Secure Socket Layer (SSL) technology. When using HTTPS you'll see a small lock symbol at the bottom of your browser. See also *Secure Socket Layer (SSL)*.

icons Small symbolic graphics used to indicate specific kinds of content on a website (such as list items, e-mail, headings, and so on).

image editor Software that enables the user to crop, resize, and adjust image files.

image resolution The number of dots per inch (dpi) in an image (72 dpi is the standard for the Web).

image size The physical size of the image as it would display on a screen (expressed in pixels for use on the Web) or the amount of storage space the file takes up (2MB, 50K, and so on).

inbound links Links from another website to your site.

indexing The process of search engines gathering data about a website and then storing that information for retrieval when people are doing searches.

inline styles Cascading Style Sheet (CSS) rules that are placed directly in HTML tags rather than in style sheets.

Internet A worldwide network connecting millions of computers. The Web is a portion of the Internet.

Internet Information Server (IIS) Web server software for Windows operating systems.

Internet Message Access Protocol (IMAP) A communication protocol for managing e-mail without having to download it to a server. (See also POP).

Internet Protocol (IP) address A unique number identifying every computer on the Internet (for example, 64.143.26.342).

Internet service providers (ISPs) Cable companies, phone companies, and so on that provide people with access to the Internet.

Java A programming language developed by SUN mostly for programming web servers and web applets.

Java applet On the Web, a small program that is used by websites for highly specialized interactive purposes.

JavaServer Pages (JSP) A server-side scripting language often used by very large websites in part because of its highly efficient caching methods that can speed up the serving of web pages.

JavaScript The most popular scripting language on the Internet, developed by Netscape.

JPG and JPEG Compression formats for reducing the size of photographs in particular.

keyword With respect to search engines, a word or phrase used to search for relevant web information.

keyword analyzer A tool for quickly displaying keyword information about a web page.

keyword density The ratio of instances of a keyword to the total number of words on the page.

kilobyte (K or KB) Equal to roughly one thousand bytes of information (actually 1,024). A photo that would fill a computer screen can be as small as 50K or about 50,000 bytes.

Knowledge Base A comprehensive database of information intended to answer questions from visitors in a far more detailed way than an FAQ page.

landing page A page specifically designed to be a destination point from an advertisement or promotional link. One version is known as a squeeze page.

layout On a website, this is the placement of various parts of a site, such as the header, footer, sidebar(s), and content, as well as the placement of elements within each of those areas.

leading In typography, the amount of space between lines of text.

link A connection between an element on a web page (text or image) and another page or file, on or off the site. (See also *inbound links* and *outbound links*).

link checker or link validator A tool for checking whether links on a website are still active or not.

Linux An open-source operating system based on UNIX. A majority of websites are hosted on Linux servers.

live chat A two-way text-based messaging system commonly used by websites to provide support to visitors.

loading time The time it takes for a web page to fully appear in a user's browser.

long tail keywords In a list of related keywords, these are the ones with fewer searches and therefore less competition from marketers.

mail server The portion of a server devoted to handling e-mail or a dedicated server that only handles e-mail.

mailing list In e-mail marketing, the list of people who have signed up to received a newsletter or other information.

megabyte (MB) 1024 KB or roughly one million bytes.

membership site A site or portion of a website that requires a username and password and that might or might not require payment for access.

meta tags Tags in a document that describe the document. In HTML documents these are usually placed in the head section at the top of the document.

mockup In web design a graphic representation of what the site will look like.

modem Hardware that connects a computer to a network. For most people their ISP provides them with a modem to connect to the Internet.

Multipurpose Internet Mail Extensions (MIME) types An Internet standard for defining types of files such as .jpg, .gif, PDF, Flash, .mov, and so on.

MySQL The most widely used open-source database software for websites.

negative space See *white space*.

newsletter In e-mail marketing, e-mail sent on a regular basis to subscribers of a mailing list.

nofollow An attribute of certain HTML tags used to tell robots not to follow a link (or any link on a page).

off-page search engine optimization (SEO) Factors that affect a website's position in search engine results and are outside of the site itself (most importantly the links to the site from other sites). See also *search engine optimization (SEO)*.

on-page search engine optimization (SEO) Factors within a website that affect its position in search engine results (most importantly, the quality of the content and use of relevant keywords in various parts of the site). See also *search engine optimization (SEO)*.

opacity In web design, the level of transparency for an image; how much you can see through the image to what's behind it.

operating system (OS) The software that manages the basic operation of a computer, including web servers (for example, Windows, Linux).

opt-in In e-mail marketing, the process of verifying that a person has asked to subscribe to an e-mail list.

optimization In search engine marketing, the process of helping search engines properly index your site. In graphics, the process of reducing the size of an image by compressing it.

organic search results The various websites, videos, images, and so on that are found by a search engine—as opposed to paid search advertisements that display around them.

outbound links Links from your site to other websites.

outsourcing Hiring others on a contractual basis to do work for you instead of you or your staff doing it.

PageRank See *Google PageRank.*

pay per click (PPC) advertising Any advertisement for which the advertiser pays only if a visitor clicks the ad.

payment processor A company that processes payment transactions, in particular credit card transactions, including authorizations, refunds, and transfers of money between merchants and the bank handling the merchant account.

permalink A permanent link to a piece of content on a website. The idea is that even if the content is reorganized in other ways, this link will never break.

ping A method for testing communication between two computers on a network. In blogging, it refers to the notification of special servers that your content has been updated (these servers, in turn, broadcast notices to users of their services). It also refers to being notified that someone has linked to one of your posts.

platform A common way of referring to the operating system used by a web server, such as Linux or Windows.

plug-ins Small programs that can be added to a base program to provide additional functions. Sometimes called add-ons or extensions.

podcast An episodic set of audio or video files often produced in formats similar to offline broadcast programs.

popup Any object that appears over the top of the current browser screen, either automatically or as the result of clicking a link.

Portable Document Format (PDF) A document file format developed by Adobe that can be read by virtually any browser.

Portable Network Graphics (PNG) An image compression format intended to replace GIF, which is not as powerful and has patent restrictions on its use.

Post Office Protocol (POP) The most common communication protocol for retrieving e-mail from a server. See also *Internet Message Access Protocol (IMAP)*.

Practical Extraction and Reporting Language (Perl) A server-side scripting language most often used on Linux or UNIX servers.

public domain A technical term for a creative work not covered by copyright. When a copyrighted work goes into the public domain depends on a country's copyright laws. Being on the Internet does not make a work public domain.

Really Simple Syndication (RSS) The most common syndication format that creates what's referred to as a feed from a website. This feed can be read by RSS readers or other types of programs.

reciprocal link When two sites link to each other.

redirecting On the Web, an automated process of sending a visitor to another location. This can be done through a meta tag refresh in the HTML or on the server with a 301 redirect (permanent) or a 302 (temporary).

Return on Investment (ROI) The profit or loss resulting from an investment and often expressed in percentage terms. It can refer to the overall profit or loss of a company or of specific actions (an e-mail marketing campaign, the return generated by a particular advertisement).

robot A program that automatically goes from web page to web page gathering certain information. Used by search engines to index sites and by hackers to harvest e-mail addresses and other information.

robots file A text file that is placed in website directories to control search engine robots (to stop them from indexing certain pages, and so on).

router Hardware or software that can control access to various parts of a computer or computer network.

sans serif font A font with no edge elements at the ends of strokes. On the Web, the most common sans serif fonts are Verdana, Arial, and Helvetica.

scanning On websites, people's habit of glancing through content looking for headlines or words that catch their attention.

screen resolution This is the setting that determines how much you can see on your computer monitor. The physical size of a screen is fixed, but you can adjust the screen resolution to show more pixels. The average screen resolution today is 1024 × 768 pixels.

script A collection of statements written in a scripting language such as JavaScript or PHP.

search engine Run by programs that automatically catalog information on the Web (as opposed to directories that are compiled manually). The most popular search engines are Google and Bing.

search engine optimization (SEO) A combination of organizing, writing, and coding websites so that search engines can better understand what the site is about and how the content relates to specific keywords.

search engine results page (SERP) After you enter a search term (or terms), this page displays the results of your search.

search volume The number of people searching for a particular keyword.

Secure Socket Layer (SSL) On the Web, software to secure communication when a browser is transmitting data.

serif font A font that has flourishes of varying styles and sizes at the ends of each stroke. The most common serif fonts on the Web are Times New Roman and Georgia.

server-side Having to do with a server. Scripts that are processed by a server are called server-side scripts, and the language of the script is a server-side language.

shared server A server containing multiple hosting accounts, running into the several hundreds or even thousands.

shopping cart Software that collects purchase information; adds it up; processes any shipping, taxes, or other conditions; and then passes the totals and the information to a payment processor.

sidebar The areas of a website to the right or left (or both) of the content area, and between the header and footer.

Simple Mail Transfer Protocol (SMTP) A communication protocol for sending e-mail. For most people, their SMTP server is with their Internet service provider (ISP).

site builder software Programs of varying complexity that enable you to build a website with little or no knowledge of HTML. They can be on a server or on your computer.

sitemap On the visible portion of a website, a page containing a full list of all pages on the site. Behind the scenes, a sitemap can be coding that helps search engines navigate through your site.

social bookmarking Publicly sharing favorite web links with anyone or a select group of people, via a social media tool (for example, Delicious).

social media Web-based services that provide interaction between users through simple publishing tools. Common examples include Twitter, Facebook, and LinkedIn.

spider Another name for programs or robots that automatically search through websites gathering information.

splash page Usually a graphics-based page that acts as a gateway to a website's real home page.

spyware Software hidden in a computer with the purpose of collecting information such as passwords.

squeeze page A type of web page in which the visitors' options are very limited (they can either buy/sign up for something or leave).

static website A website whose files do not need any assembly before being displayed in a browser. In other words, the HTML you see in your browser is contained in a single file on the server. (Opposite of *dynamic website*.)

streaming A way of transmitting video and audio files over the Web so that users can see or hear part of the file while the rest is being transferred.

style sheet On the Web, a text file containing a set of rules governing the look and layout of a web page.

subdomain A domain name that depends on a parent domain name (for example, `http://myphotos.mydomain.com` is a subdomain of `http://mydomain.com`).

subscriber In e-mail marketing, someone who has signed up to be on a mailing list. For websites, someone who has registered to access password-protected material on the site.

tag line A short descriptive phrase that goes with a company or organization's title (for example, "Makers of fine contemporary furniture").

template On the Web, a file that contains all or part of the design and structure of a page, separate from the content.

text editor A program that enables you to work with text but not add any hidden characters that can interfere with how that text displays on the Web.

tiling In web design, the process of repeating an image over and over again to form what appears to be a single image. This way the entire background of a site might be nothing more than a 10 x 10 pixel image.

title tag An HTML tag that is displayed at the top of browser windows, on browser tabs, and as the title of a search engine result.

top-level domain (TLD) Refers to the set of letters following the final period in a domain name (for example, .com, .uk, .net, .tv, .info, and so on).

turnkey website service A ready-made website that is hosted by a third party and for which you don't need to do any software maintenance or updating. In simple terms, you choose a design from a series of templates and then add your content.

typography The art of making text or type easy to read.

Uniform Resource Identifier (URI) Any means of identifying a resource (website, document, a set of characters that identifies a resource) on the Internet, such as web pages, documents, images, mailboxes, services, and so on. A URI might or might not identify the location of the resource. If it does give a location, then it's usually referred to as a uniform resource locator (URL).

Uniform Resource Locator (URL) A URL identifies the location and method of accessing a resource on the Internet. For instance, `http://mydomain.com` gives the location of a website (`mydomain.com`) and it specifies how to access the files (using http protocol). If the URL is `ftp://mydomain.com`, the location is the same, but the method of accessing the files is different. Because a URL identifies a resource on the web, it is a type of uniform resource identifier.

universal search Search results that include data from specialized searches such as images or videos, not just the usual website results. Also known as blended search.

unzip To uncompress a file that has been compressed, or zipped.

upload On the Web, the transfer of files from a computer to a web server; the opposite of *download*.

uptime The period of time when a website is visible on the Internet.

validator A tool for making sure that elements of a website meet certain standards (HTML, CSS, and so on). There are online validators as well as validator software.

viral marketing Getting a small number of people interested and then letting them spread the information to others. Also known as word-of-mouth marketing.

virtual private network (VPN) A secure connection allowing users to access a private network over a public communications structure such as the Internet.

visitor On the Web, someone who views at least one page of a website. Visiting a page must be clearly distinguished from the hits generated by viewing the page.

web address See *Uniform Resource Locator (URL)* and *Internet Protocol (IP) address.*

web developer vs. web designer A web developer deals with the technical aspects of websites, in particular any scripting or database work. A web designer comes up with the look of the site and usually helps implement that look in HTML and CSS.

web hosting provider Provides server software, storage space, and bandwidth for making files and websites accessible over the Web.

web mail Online programs that allow you to access your e-mail from any device with a browser that's connected to the Internet.

webmaster tools Usually a free service offered by search engines to help site owners make their sites more search-engine friendly.

web server A server with specialized software for making websites accessible over the Internet.

webinar A seminar/workshop delivered visually through a web browser.

What You See Is What You Get (WYSIWYG) In web design, the capability of software to display a web page during editing exactly the way it will be displayed on the Web.

white space In web design, the space between elements on a page, such as the space between content and the sidebar or even between lines of text. The space need not be white, just blank. Also known as *negative space.*

WHOIS A communications protocol that is commonly used to access databases of information about domain names. A WHOIS search for a domain name can tell you to whom it is registered, how long it's been registered for, when it expires, and more. Many WHOIS search tools exist on the Web, including on any domain registrar's site.

widgets Code that connects a website to a third-party provider of various kinds of content (weather reports, clocks, news feeds, currency converters, and much more).

wi-fi Wireless Internet access that is made available to the public, with or without passwording.

wireless security The encryption of data transmitted wirelessly over a network. There are various levels of security available, but most wireless devices have no security by default.

World Wide Web (WWW) A section of the Internet intended for public use.

World Wide Web Consortium (W3C) The organization responsible for managing standards for the World Wide Web (WWW) portion of the Internet.

ZIP A compression format for computer files. Compressing files before making them available for download on the Web not only makes them load faster, but it also helps protect against viruses.

What's on the DVD?

This appendix provides you with information on the contents of the DVD that accompanies this book. For the most up-to-date information, please refer to the ReadMe file located at the root of the DVD. Here is what you will find in this appendix:

- ➡ What's on the DVD?
- ➡ System Requirements
- ➡ Using the DVD
- ➡ Troubleshooting

What's on the DVD?

There are videos to accompany more than 50 of the questions in this book. You can see demonstrations of online tools, more examples of websites, and hear additional commentary.

The DVD also contains a worksheet for your site requirements, a prelaunch checklist, and an alternative table of contents.

System Requirements

Make sure that your computer meets the minimum system requirements listed in this section. If your computer doesn't match up to most of these requirements, you might have a problem using the contents of the DVD.

Necessary requirements are the following:

→ PC running Windows XP or later, or Mac running OS X

→ DVD-ROM drive

→ Adobe Flash Player 9 or later (free download from Adobe.com)

The interface won't launch if you have auto-run disabled. In that case, click Start → Run (for Windows Vista, click Start → All Programs → Accessories → Run). In the dialog box that appears, type **D:\Start.exe**. (Replace *D* with the proper letter if your DVD drive uses a different letter. If you don't know the letter of your DVD drive, see how it is listed under My Computer.) Click OK.

Using the DVD on a PC

To access the content from the DVD, follow these steps:

1. Insert the DVD into your computer's DVD-ROM drive. The license agreement appears.

2. Read through the license agreement, and then click the Accept button if you want to use the DVD.

3. The DVD interface displays. Select the lesson video you want to view.

Using the DVD on a Mac

To install the items from the DVD to your hard drive, follow these steps:

1. Insert the DVD into your computer's DVD-ROM drive.

2. The DVD icon will display on your desktop; double-click to open it.

3. Double-click the Start button.

4. Read the license agreement, and then click the Accept button to use the DVD.

5. The DVD interface will display. Here you can install the programs and run the demos.

Troubleshooting

If you have difficulty installing or using any of the materials on the companion DVD, try the following solutions:

- **Turn off any antivirus software that might be running—** Installers sometimes mimic virus activity and can make your computer incorrectly believe that it is being infected by a virus. (Be sure to turn the antivirus software back on later.)

- **Close all running programs—**The more programs you run, the less memory is available to other programs. Installers also typically update files and programs; if you keep other programs running, installation might not work properly.

- **Reference the ReadMe file—**Please refer to the ReadMe file located at the root of the DVD-ROM for the latest product information at the time of publication.

- **Reboot if necessary—**If all else fails, rebooting your machine can often clear any conflicts in the system.

Customer Care

If you have trouble with the DVD-ROM, please call the Wiley Product Technical Support phone number at (800)762-2974. Outside the United States, call 1(317)572-3994. You can also contact Wiley Product Technical Support at http://support.wiley.com. John Wiley & Sons will provide technical support only for installation and other general quality control items. For technical support for the applications, consult the program's vendor or author.

To place additional orders or to request information about other Wiley products, please call (877) 762-2974.

Index

A

A-B testing, 234
About Us page, 171, 174–176
above the fold, 59, 316
Access (Microsoft Access), 27
accessibility
  secure access to websites, 288–291
  website content accessibility,
    148–150, 302
accounts. *See* e-mail accounts; hosting
  accounts
Active Server Pages. *See* ASP
ad tracking, 316
Add This, 212
Add to Any, 212
add-on functions (domain registrars),
  9, 10
add-ons, 125, 130, 132, 212, 305, 311,
  316, 324
Adobe, 320, 325, 332. *See also*
  Flash; PDFs
advertising, 220–224, 228–230. *See also*
  marketing
affiliates, 316
affiliate links, 316
affiliate marketing, 225–227
affiliate networks, 225
aliases. *See* e-mail aliases
anchor text, 159, 211, 251, 259, 316
animations, 84–85, 143, 167–168.
  See also Flash
anonymous FTP, 316
antivirus software, 290, 333
Apache, 28, 278, 316
Arial font, 325
ASP (Active Server Pages), 27, 94,
  143, 316
ASP.net, 27, 28
attacks, 295–296
attributes (defined), 316
audio (usage in website content),
  164–166. *See also* multimedia
authentication, 316
authoritative sites, 258
authority/trust, 258
auto lock (domain registrar service), 10

B

auto renewal (domain registrar
  service), 10
automated backups, 274
automatic popups, 99
autoresponders, 24, 42, 43, 204, 316

background generators (online
  sites), 299
backgrounds (website backgrounds),
  70–72
backups, 270–276, 313, 316
bandwidth, 31–32, 316
banner ads, 211, 316
barriers (website barriers), 111–112,
  167–168
below the fold, 316
Bing, 220, 262, 311, 326
blacklisting, 204, 285, 317
blended searches (universal searches),
  252, 328
bloated HTML, 134–136
blogging content, 183–184, 279–280
blogs, 183–184
bookmarks, 317
breadcrumb navigation, 101, 317
broken links, 158, 260, 277
browsers (web browsers)
  browser compatibility (cross-browser
    compatibility), 76–78, 317, 318
  browser compatibility checks, 300
  domain e-mail access with, 44–46
  robots v., 264
  site requirements and, 111
  spell-check feature, 153

C

cache, 123, 135, 240, 286, 317
callouts, 56, 73–75, 130, 149, 317. *See also*
  sidebars
cascading style sheets. *See* CSS
case studies, 179–180
catchall e-mail addresses, 48
chat, 21, 218, 317, 323
choosing domain names, 2–3
Chrome, 76, 77, 305

classified advertising sites, 228
clear content, 154
click rate (clickthrough rate), 220, 317
client, 317
client-side, 143, 317
client-side scripting languages, 143–144
clip art, 161
CMSs (content management systems),
  124–125
  back ups and, 270
  blogs and, 184
  defined, 317
  image resizing, 161
  mobile phone site viewing and, 80
  site promotion and, 212
  web-based, 290
CMYK, 68
color scheme tools, 69, 300
color schemes, 68–69, 89, 110, 317
colored links, 109
colors, 68–69, 300. *See also* backgrounds
"common content" issue, 122
companion DVD, 331–334
compression, 140, 141, 317
construction (website construction),
  121–144
construction tools (online), 303
contact information, 91, 95–97, 282–283
Contact page, 176–177
content (website content), 145–189
  accessibility, 148–150, 302
  audio use and, 164–166
  blogging content, 183–184, 279–280
  clear, 154
  content offerings to other sites,
    216–217
  content pages, 174–182
  correctly written, 153
  focused, 151–152
  highlighting, 149
  home pages and, 170–173. *See also*
    home pages
  images in, 149, 160–163
  keywords in, 250–251
  links in, 158–159. *See also* links
  long, 113, 155

image stealing and, 286
menus and, 83
MIME and, 323
site special requirements and, 111, 112
splash page and, 168
Flickr, 31, 205
fluid layout, 58–59, 61, 320
focused content, 151–152
fonts, 60, 61, 325, 326. *See also* typography
footer menus, 91–92
footers, 320
forms
  e-mail address protection and, 286–287
  e-mail signup forms, 195
  form validation, 102–103, 277, 296, 320
  online forms, 101–103
404 error, 104–105, 316
free advertising/promotion, 228–230
free directory sites, 228
free hosting, 33
free press release distribution sites, 229
free turnkey solutions, 14
frequently asked questions. *See* FAQs
Front Page extensions, 28
FTP (File Transfer Protocol), 35, 270, 271, 288, 316, 319

G

GB (gigabyte), 320
generic TLDs, 2, 4
Georgia font, 326
GIFs (Graphics Interchange Format), 140–141, 320
gigabyte. *See* GB
Gmail, 38, 41, 44, 275
Google, 220, 255
Google AdSense, 151, 221, 320
Google AdWords, 220, 221, 240, 320
Google Alerts, 200, 285
Google Analytics, 234
Google PageRank, 258, 320
Google Sitemap, 320
Google Trends, 235
gradients, 71
graphics, 63–64
Graphics Interchange Format. *See* GIFs

H

hackers, 20, 35, 282, 286, 289, 290, 295, 296, 320
hardware firewalls, 289–290
header, 59, 63, 72, 73, 76, 83, 84, 96, 107, 320
heading tags, 249, 265

height (website height), 59
help function (domain management interface), 9
Helvetica font, 325
hexadecimal code, 68
hidden HTML tags, 243–246
highlighting content, 149
hiring SEO consultants, 266–267
hits, 320
home pages, 52–53, 57, 170–173
home/office security, 289–290
Horde, 46
horizontal main menus, 90
horizontal placement of content, 149
hosted CMSs, 124–125
hosted e-mail list managers, 202
hosted shopping carts, 185–188
hosting (web hosting), 13–36. *See also* shared servers
  free, 33
  online information, 298
  prices for, 33–34
  shared, 26–27, 33
hosting accounts (web hosting accounts), 17, 35–36
hosting control panels, 12, 23–25, 42–43, 321
hosting providers (web hosting providers)
  backups and, 273
  defined, 320, 329
  domain registrars v., 9
  ISPs v., 17–18
  reliability of, 19–20
  reviews of, 298
  support from, 21–22
housekeeping, 270–296. *See also* backups; security
HTML (Hypertext Markup Language). *See also* scripting languages
  bloated, 134–136
  defined, 321
  entities, 265
  heading tags, 249, 265
  limitations of, 143
  search engine-friendly, 264–265
HTML 5, 321
HTML tables. *See* tables
HTML tags (hidden), 243–246
HTTP (Hypertext Transfer Protocol), 321
HTTPS (Hypertext Transfer Protocol Secure), 321
hyperlinks, 316, 321. *See also* links
hypertext, 158, 321
Hypertext Markup Language. *See* HTML
Hypertext Preprocessor. *See* PHP

Hypertext Transfer Protocol. *See* HTTP
Hypertext Transfer Protocol Secure. *See* HTTPS

I

ICANN (Internet Corporation for Assigned Names and Numbers), 2, 7
icons, 64, 82, 95, 321
IIS (Internet Information Server), 28, 322
image editors, 93, 131, 132, 141, 142, 161, 303, 304, 321
image size, 321
images, 63–64. *See also* colors; graphics; photos
  categories, 63
  in content, 149, 160–163
  effective usage of, 160–163
  elements, 63, 64
  page loading time and, 93
  specialty searches for, 253–254
IMAP (Internet Message Access Protocol), 322
inbound links, 213–215, 257–259, 321
indexing (defined), 321
inline styles, 129, 130, 135, 321
internal e-mail server, 38
Internet, 321
Internet Corporation for Assigned Names and Numbers (ICANN), 2, 7
Internet Explorer, 76, 79, 278, 300, 305
Internet Information Server (IIS), 28, 322
Internet Message Access Protocol (IMAP), 322
Internet Protocol addresses. *See* IP addresses
Internet service providers. *See* ISPs
IP (Internet Protocol) addresses, 39, 317, 318, 322
ISP hosting, 17–18
ISPs (Internet service providers), 17–18, 322

J

Java, 143, 322
Java applets, 322
JavaScript
  defined, 322
  dropdowns and, 90
  in external files, 134–135
  libraries, 135
  as scripting language, 143
  Show More solution and, 113–114
  turning off, 111, 143
JavaServer Pages (JSP), 34, 143, 322

tiling, 70, 71, 72, 328
Times New Roman font, 326
title tags, 243–244, 328
TLDs. *See* top-level domains
top-level domains (TLDs), 2, 4, 5, 7, 8, 328
tracking marketing results/visitors, 233–235
trust/authority, 258
turnkey website services, 14–16, 34, 328
tweet-ups, 231
Twitter, 93, 205, 207, 208, 209, 210, 327
typography, 60–62, 153, 301, 328

U

under construction notices, 104
Uniform Resource Identifiers (URIs), 328
Uniform Resource Locators. *See* URLs
universal searches (blended searches), 252, 328
UNIX, 27, 323, 325
unplanned downtime, 19, 20, 319
unusual domain names, 3
unzip, 328
updating website content, 184, 279–281
uploading, 328
uptime, 19, 34, 314, 328
URIs (Uniform Resource Identifiers), 328
URLs (Uniform Resource Locators)
  defined, 328
  ISP hosting and, 17
  misspelled, 105
  permanent links and, 258, 259, 324
  shortened, 93, 209
user experience, 87–119, 302, 303
user forums (web hosting provider support), 22
user-friendly links, 109–110
user-friendly sites, 118–119
usernames, 36, 40

V

validation service (W3C), 264–265
validators, 328. *See also* link checkers/validators
Verdana font, 325
vertical main menus, 90
vertical placement of content, 148
video. *See also* multimedia
  specialty searches for, 254–255
  usage in website content, 164–166
  web hosting provider support and, 21
video hosting, 33

viral marketing, 164, 310, 328
virtual private networks. *See* VPNs
viruses, 27, 290, 330, 333
visited links, 109–110
visitors (website visitors)
  contact information and, 95–97
  defined, 329
  sensitive visitor information, 292–294
  social media and, 95–96
  tracking, 233–235
visual appeal, 50. *See also* design
visual clutter, 113–115
VPNs (virtual private networks), 329

W

W3C (World Wide Web Consortium), 264, 298, 306, 330
W3C validation service, 264–265
Wal-Mart site, 88
watermarks, 286
web addresses. *See* IP addresses; URLs
web browsers. *See* browsers
web designers, 329. *See also* design
web developers, 329
web hosting. *See* hosting
web hosting accounts. *See* hosting accounts
web hosting providers. *See* hosting providers
web mail, 24, 38, 44–46, 329
web marketing. *See* marketing
web pages. *See* pages
web servers. *See* servers
web site files, 137–139, 270–272
webinars, 196, 219, 307, 329
webmaster tools, 234, 262, 311, 329
websites
  barriers, 111–112, 167–168
  domain names v., 12
  dynamic, 122–125, 318, 319, 327
  eye movements over, 55–56
  height, 59
  monitoring site functionality, 277–278
  multifocus, 170
  reasons for building. *See* site's purpose
  self promotion, 211–212
  site specific details, accessing, 116–117
  site's appearance to search engines, 261–263
  social media/website integration, 209–210
  software requirements, 28–29
  static, 122–123, 319, 327

templates. *See* templates
  value of, 88
  width, 58–59
website backgrounds. *See* backgrounds
website builder software. *See* site builder software
website construction. *See* construction
website content. *See* content
website design. *See* design
website layout. *See* layout
website maps. *See* site maps
website navigation. *See* navigation
website organization. *See* organization
website promotion. *See* promotion
website visitors. *See* visitors
well-structured content, 154–156
What You *See* Is What You Get (WYSIWYG), 132, 329
white space (negative space), 65–67, 329
WHOIS search tools, 11, 298, 329
widgets, 143, 277, 329
width (website width), 58–59
wi-fi, 289, 290, 329
Wi-fi Protected Access (WPA), 290
Wikipedia, 205
Windows (OS), 27
wireless security, 329
word of mouth marketing, 310, 328
WordPress, 14, 28, 114, 125
Wordtracker, 240
World Wide Web (WWW), 321. *See also* Internet
World Wide Web Consortium. *See* W3C
WPA (Wi-fi Protected Access), 290
www, domain names and, 3
WYSIWYG (What You *See* Is What You Get), 132, 329

X

XHTML (Extensible Hypertext Markup Language), 319

Y

Yahoo! Answers, 205, 216
Yahoo! Explorer, 213, 214, 257
Yahoo! Mail, 38, 44, 275
Yahoo! webmaster tools, 234, 262
YouSendIt, 299
YouTube, 31, 33, 93, 118, 165, 205, 207, 254

Z

zip format, 328, 330